Conflict Transformation

Conflict Transformation

Essays on Methods of Nonviolence

Edited by Rhea A. DuMont,
Tom H. Hastings and Emiko Noma

Foreword by Cynthia Boaz

McFarland & Company, Inc., Publishers
Jefferson, North Carolina, and London

ALSO OF INTEREST: *The Lessons of Nonviolence: Theory and Practice in a World of Conflict*, Tom H. Hastings (McFarland, 2006); and *Nonviolent Response to Terrorism*, Tom H. Hastings (McFarland, 2004).

LIBRARY OF CONGRESS CATALOGUING-IN-PUBLICATION DATA

Conflict transformation : essays on methods of nonviolence / edited by Rhea A. DuMont, Tom H. Hastings and Emiko Noma ; foreword by Cynthia Boaz.
    p.   cm.
   Includes bibliographical references and index.

   ISBN 978-0-7864-7251-2
   softcover : acid free paper ∞

   1. Nonviolence. 2. Conflict management. 3. Peacebuilding. I. DuMont, Rhea A., 1984– editor of compilation. II. Hastings, Tom H., editor of compilation. III. Noma, Emiko, editor of compilation.
   HM1281.C66 2013
   303.6'9—dc23   2013000003

BRITISH LIBRARY CATALOGUING DATA ARE AVAILABLE

© 2013 Rhea A. DuMont, Tom H. Hastings and Emiko Noma. All rights reserved

No part of this book may be reproduced or transmitted in any form or by any means, electronic or mechanical, including photocopying or recording, or by any information storage and retrieval system, without permission in writing from the publisher.

Cover photograph © 2013 Stockbyte/Thinkstock

Manufactured in the United States of America

McFarland & Company, Inc., Publishers
   Box 611, Jefferson, North Carolina 28640
   www.mcfarlandpub.com

For the testimony of change, the power of hope, and the possibility of a brighter future where global citizens recognize and respect each other's humanity, and peace prevails.
–Rhea A. DuMont

For my illustrious, industrious students, the seed crop for a new world of conflict transformation from the atrocities of destruction to the creative nonviolence of construction.
–Tom H. Hastings

Table of Contents

Foreword
    Cynthia Boaz   1

Preface
    Tom H. Hastings   5

Introduction
    Rhea A. DuMont and *Emiko Noma*   7

SECTION I — NONVIOLENCE IN PRACTICE

Conflict Transformation Through Nonviolent Resistance
    Véronique Dudouet   9

The Activist and the Olive Tree: Nonviolent Resistance in the Second Intifada
    Julie M. Norman   34

"If You Use Nonviolence, I Will Respond with Nonviolence": The 2007 Pattani Protest in Southern Thailand
    Janjira Sombatpoonsiri   52

"We Want Freedom!" Nonviolent Conflict to Curb Corruption
    Shaazka Beyerle   66

The Roots of Resistance: Victims' Responses to Genocide
    Laura K. Taylor   86

SECTION II — IN FROM THE MARGINS

Voices from the Diaspora: Reconciliation and Capacity Building in Refugee Communities from the Great Lakes Region of Africa
    Barbara Tint, Julie Koehler, Vincent Chirimwami, Marie Abijuru, Sa'eed Mohamed Haji, Djimet Dogo, Carmina Rinker Lass and *Mindy Johnston*   109

Mainstreaming Feminism in Conflict Resolution
  Rhea A. DuMont　126

CHamoru Values Guiding Nonviolence
  LisaLinda Natividad　134

Section III — Expanding Identity: The New Conflict Worker

A Paradoxical Identity: From Conflicted to Hybrid
  Robert J. Gould　141

The Journey to Conflict Resolver: Peace-Scapes
  Patrick T. Hiller and *Paloma Ayala Vela*　152

Listening as a Practice of Conflict Transformation: Learnings from a Death Penalty Compassionate Listening Project
  Rachel H. Cunliffe　167

Violent Worldviews and Self-Projected Use of Violence
  Meredith Michaud　180

Parenting for a Better Future
  Terri L. Shofner　199

Power in the People: Urgent Transformation Toward Integration
  Stephanie Nicole Van Hook　208

Gandhi: The Grandfather of Conflict Transformation
  Gail M. Presbey　213

About the Contributors　225

Index　229

Foreword

Cynthia Boaz

"I've never focused on answering what nonviolent action can't do. I focus on what it has done. If we can't push back that barrier of impossibility, then violence will be used, and that will be out of our control. But if we can keep pushing it back, and revealing that nonviolent action can do much more than was ever expected, pretty soon there will be almost nothing left for violence." — Gene Sharp

Upon being asked to write the foreword for this collection focusing on conflict transformation and nonviolence, I knew immediately how I intended to use the opportunity to introduce this subject to a general audience. For the first time in history, nonviolent people power movements have begun to gain traction on the public perception that they are not simply spontaneous flare-ups that occasionally achieve accidental victories. Successes in places from Serbia to Tunisia to the Maldives have demonstrated to a global audience that more often than not mass civil uprisings are systemic and organized. They are not accidents of history, but the result of carefully planned and meticulously implemented strategy and tactics. The opportunity this creates for scholars and advocates to advance our collective wisdom on this topic is enormous. And yet, there are still several stubborn assumptions about violence and power that persist, despite the real-world experiences of millions of regular people-turned-activists over the past decade.

The most insidious of these assumptions (or what I have referred to elsewhere as "meta-frames") is the notion that, at the end of the day, violence is still the most effective force for social or political change. That such a perception can hold in face of an ever-expanding set of empirical evidence to the contrary speaks volumes about the Herculean nature of the task of unlearning hardened beliefs. But if anyone can help us along in this evolution, it is the people of Egypt. And Tunisia. And Iran. And Burma. And Palestine. And

Ukraine. And West Papua. And Tibet. And every other place on the globe where, over the last decade, mass nonviolent civil resistance has challenged oppression, claimed rights, or begun the process of establishing freedom.

Indeed, the most significant consequence — and there are many — of the Egyptian people's success in forcing out President Hosni Mubarak through a stunning display of sustained nonviolent pressure is the potential it has to demonstrate to the world, and to angry, disaffected peoples in particular, that there is a realistic alternative to violence as a tool for overcoming injustice. The victory of the Egyptians, Tunisians, and others of the past decade has direct implications for terrorist organizations and other violent groups seeking to recruit to their cause. This is because as nonviolent methods succeed, they delegitimize violence as a means of pushing grievances and creating change. They offer a realistic and powerful form of struggle. If we acknowledge that violent and nonviolent movements tend to share the same recruitment bases, then with every nonviolent success, the public relations campaigns of violent organizations are directly threatened. And in that sense, the people of Egypt and Tunisia and Serbia and the Maldives and elsewhere have done all of us a great favor. By demonstrating that mass nonviolent action by the people can get better results than violence, they have made the world safer, and saner, for all of us.

But that is not all. The success of nonviolent methods also models for the global audience the notion that ends and means are inseparable and that victories won through nonviolent means carry an innate legitimacy that makes it much less likely that violent methods will be called upon to maintain the new system later. There is a growing body of empirical evidence to suggest that new democracies created through mass civil action by the people are much less likely than those created through force to see democratic backsliding down the road. This should not be surprising, given that participation in a nonviolent struggle provides most of the tools democratic citizens need to contribute to the maintenance of their democracy, starting with the understanding that power and accountability lie ultimately with the people.

Like the courageous activists around the globe who are presently risking their lives and livelihood to model what Gandhi called "satyagraha" (holding to truth), in pursuit of a more just and humane world, the editors of this collection have also done us a great service by bringing together some of the field's most respected scholars, as well as some of our newest, brightest, and committed young academics and practitioners to share with us their insights on every stage of nonviolent conflict transformation — from the mobilization of movements through the values and philosophies needed to reconcile and heal shattered societies. This work is an important contribution to an evolutionary understanding of how nonviolence in its many forms — from mass collective to compassionate individual — has shaped, is shaping, and will shape (if we are wise and courageous enough to call upon it) our collective human destiny. I'm honored to be a small part of this labor of love. To the editors, authors, activists, and all peoples fighting to push back that "barrier of impossibility," I extend my gratitude.

Cynthia Boaz is an assistant professor of political science at Sonoma State University, with interests in political development and quality of democracy, nonviolent conflict and nonviolent struggle, and media coverage of war. She is an academic advisor to the International Center on Nonviolent Conflict.

Preface

Tom H. Hastings

The field of peace and conflict studies is slowly becoming a discipline — that is, more graduate programs in conflict resolution, peace studies, and peace and conflict studies are coming into being. Still, we are working to define ourselves. The assertion of this volume is that our discipline has, at its core, the mission to examine and evaluate possible paths to the transformation of conflict from destructive to constructive. This precludes, then, the use of violence or the threat of violence, which is by definition destructive. To slightly but significantly alter the dictum of Malcolm X, "by any [nonviolent] means necessary." Whether we are examining methods of conflict resolution as they relate to child-rearing, criminal justice, the sovereignty of indigenous people, liberation from a dictator or any other conflict, the sieve is the same: are these methods transformational or do they lead to destruction?

Destructive conflict management methods are seeping into the literature that presumes to represent and instruct our discipline, and that is a pity because nothing else is truly unique about our field. For example, once we make allowances for "mediation with muscle" — that is, the mediator who can call on military might to enforce an agreement or force a party to the negotiating table — it becomes a different discipline, not peace and conflict studies and not conflict resolution.

Of course, understanding violence is key to understanding alternatives, to grasping possible remedies, just as understanding the creation of cancer cells is key to learning how to defeat cancer. Defeating violent aggression by researching methods of transforming it into nonviolent assertion, then, is at the heart of peace and conflict studies research. We've gathered some vital voices in this volume — most of them new — to contribute to this crucial exploration. There is so much more to explore. It is how we as a species will survive and thrive.

Introduction

Rhea A. DuMont and Emiko Noma

The volume before you is intentionally diverse. It is an addition to recent volumes in the field, notably *The Handbook of Conflict Resolution* (Deutsch & Coleman, 2000) and *The Sage Handbook of Conflict Resolution* (Sandole et al., 2009), which concentrate on institutionalized notions of conflict resolution, largely from a Western, nation-state-centric, and male perspective. It is our intent to look beyond these overwhelmingly top-down understandings of conflict resolution and to contribute to the conversation from different angles that have been overlooked, both in the literature in the field of conflict resolution and peace studies and in the general Western culture shaped by mainstream media. Some of these perspectives are only starting to puncture the mainstream dialogue, as is evident in coverage of the peaceful grassroots movements at the heart of the Arab Spring, the Occupy movement spreading across the world, and the "discovery" of the works of Gene Sharp — an idol in nonviolent circles for decades, but only now earning recognition in the mainstream.

As a testimony to the diversity that has been neglected in the field, this work is wide-ranging in material and voices. There are entries ranging from philosophical meditations on the nature of identity in the conflict resolver to descriptions of specific nonviolent actions and practical, grant-based projects, such as the reconciliation of diaspora communities in the Pacific Northwest; from well-respected scholars to recently graduated master's students in the field of conflict resolution; from those reminding us of our roots to indigenous voices moving in from the margins.

The reader will notice that the first essay, by Berghof Foundation researcher Véronique Dudouet, is substantially longer than the other essays in the book. This is intentional, as her contribution exhaustively defines the components of conflict transformation and the methods of nonviolent resistance (NVR) — and moreover, how only NVR can sufficiently catalyze conflict transformation and sustainable peace. It serves as the guidepost for the rest of the book, and the remainder of the essays in Section I provide further examples of the concepts Dudouet identifies. While Dudouet uses examples of NVR during the Palestinian first intifada, Julie M. Norman covers the multitude of NVR modes during the second intifada. A little known nonviolent protest — and nonviolent response by authorities — during the overwhelmingly violent conflict between the Thai state and the Malay Muslim population of the south is discussed by Janjira Sombatpoonsiri. Shaazka Beyerle, a senior advisor at the International Center on Nonviolent Conflict, looks to NVR as a potential tool in countering corruption in situations like post-accord Guatemala and protracted conflict in Afghanistan. Finally, Laura K. Taylor expands the concept of nonviolent resistance to the idea of resilience during periods of genocidal violence, using the cases of the Holocaust, Cambodia, and Rwanda. The examples she extracts from survivors' memoirs are not always what the nonviolent literature (including Dudouet's opening essay) would term "active resistance," yet Taylor challenges us to acknowledge that in the midst of situations of genocide — where death is nearly certain — maintaining one's humanity and dignity is a profound act of nonviolent resistance.

Section II highlights voices that have been marginalized — refugee communities in the U.S. (Barbara Tint et al.), feminists (Rhea A. DuMont), and indigenous peoples (LisaLinda Natividad) — and the implications of bringing them to the center of the discussion. After these practical examples are expounded in the first two sections, the final section invites readers to rethink what it means on an individual and personal level to be a conflict resolution practitioner: Robert J. Gould asks, How should we view our identity as a conflict resolver? Patrick T. Hiller and Paloma Ayala Vela inquire, How can the notion of a "peace-scape" — a journey to an integrated worldview — influence how we approach our practice? Rachel H. Cunliffe recounts her death penalty listening project, asking how, and why should we, learn to be compassionate listeners. Meredith Michaud describes her quantitative study on how our beliefs about the inevitability of violence or peace influence our actions. Terri L. Shofner explores how good parenting can help prevent future conflict, while Stephanie Nicole Van Hook asks if embracing integrative power can remake our world. Finally, Gail M. Presbey closes the volume by reminding readers of the field's Gandhian roots.

It is our sincere desire to expand the conversation on war and peace beyond the nation-state, top-down mode it has relied on and perpetuated in the past. There are many conflicts to be resolved across the globe. There are even more voices to listen to in order to transform them.

I — NONVIOLENCE IN PRACTICE

Conflict Transformation Through Nonviolent Resistance

Véronique Dudouet

> "Nonviolent action seeks to create such a crisis and establish such creative tension that a community that has constantly refused to negotiate is forced to confront the issue. It seeks so to dramatize the issue that it can no longer be ignored" [King, 1964, p. 79].

Inspired by Martin Luther King, Jr.'s, justification of his struggle for racial equality in the United States, this essay presents nonviolent resistance as an integral component of conflict transformation, particularly in highly asymmetric contexts. It stems from the observation that although nonviolent action and conflict transformation strategies share a common commitment to "social change and increased justice through peaceful means" (Lederach, 1995, p. 15), the fields seem to have grown in mutual ignorance — developing their own distinct sets of activists and practitioners, concepts and scholars, interpretative frames and techniques, research centers and education programs, organizations and forums, constituencies and institutional allies. There is thus an acute need to explore more systematically the differences as well as areas of complementarity between these distinct approaches to conflict intervention.

The vast majority of contemporary political conflicts are characterized by severe power asymmetries (e.g., minority versus majority, pro-social change versus pro-status-quo forces), where sustainable peace cannot be achieved without addressing issues of social injustice, political oppression, and economic inequity. However, the field of peacemaking is dominated by models of direct or mediated negotiations between parties which are relatively equal in terms of resources and power. In other words, these models are not sufficient for asymmetric conflict, unless accompanied by a transformation of the power balance between the contestants. For its part, nonviolent action can be employed by marginalized communities as well as international solidarity networks as an empowerment strategy to achieve sufficient leverage for an effective and sustainable negotiation process. There is therefore a strong potential for complementarity and collaboration between internal negotiators and nonviolent activists, and external mediators and nonviolent advocates, in contributing to successful and sustainable conflict transformation processes.

Empirical illustrations of these dynamics are provided through an assessment of the multiple interventions in favor of justice and/or peace in Israel-Palestine since the early 1980s, arising both from within the ranks of the conflicting parties and the international community (Dudouet, 2005; 2006; 2009).

Conflict Transformation in Power Asymmetries

This section provides a brief overview of the field of conflict transformation, examining more particularly how it addresses the challenges posed by asymmetric conflicts and their transformation into peaceful processes of social change.

Human or social relations are referred to as asymmetric or unbalanced (Curle, 1971) when the contending parties have unequal access to power, which can in turn be defined as "the ability to make or at least influence the decisions that affect one's life in the community" (Laue & Cormick, 1978, p. 220). According to Curle (1971), in "assessing balance we have to consider the extent to which, in a given setting, one party to a relationship is able to dominate another" (p. 6). While relations of symmetry are based on reciprocity (mutual influence), relations of asymmetry are based on subordination. For example, at the intra-state level, asymmetric conflicts are caused by unequal social status, unequal wealth and access to resources, and unequal power—leading to problems such as discrimination, unemployment, poverty, oppression, and crime (Fisher et al., 2000).

The concept of conflict transformation offers a pertinent approach to peacemaking in situations of power asymmetries, given its focus on addressing direct and attitudinal manifestations of conflicts, as well as their deeper structural sources (Lederach, 1995). Indeed, with the end of the Cold War and the standardization of established norms for internationally acceptable peace agreements, an international understanding of peace is developing, pushing the concept forward in the direction of "positive peace" (Galtung, 1969) and social justice, not simply the cessation of violence (Wallensteen, 2002). Laue and

Cormick (1978), who have been concerned during their academic careers with the ethics of conflict resolution in situations of inequality, defined social justice as a society in which "power is diffused, decision making is participatory, accountability for decisions is visible, and resources are adequate and equitably distributed" (p. 219).

Among many contemporary examples, the Israeli-Palestinian conflict might be described as a typical case of asymmetric conflict, taking into account the huge disparity of political, economic, and military power between the Israeli state and the Palestinian people and their representatives. When it comes to defining the conditions for conflict transformation, one can distinguish a minimalist approach to (negative) peace defined as an absence of fighting and killings from both sides, and a maximalist agenda of (positive) peace with justice. The Palestinian insistence on a just peace can be translated by a number of political, social, and economic demands, ranging from the most basic human rights (food, water, shelter, freedom from captivity, freedom of expression) to more specific demands such as the acknowledgement of the historical injustices inflicted by the other side (Said, 2002), or refugees' right of return to where they or their progenitors lived. But before any other rights, the primary element of justice in Palestinians' eyes is the political right to self-determination: regaining control over their land by ending the Israeli occupation of the West Bank and Gaza Strip and creating a separate, territorially contiguous, economically viable Palestinian state.[1] Reciprocally, for most Israeli Jews, justice means a Palestinian and Arab acceptance and security of the establishment of a Jewish State on that portion of the land on which they live (which includes, for part of the society, Israeli settlements in the West Bank and Gaza).

Shortcomings of Conflict Resolution Techniques

According to the Lebanese scholar Paul Salem (1997), "western conflict resolution through negotiation in a society of haves and have-nots may prove problematic and, at times, impossible" (p. 22). Indeed, asymmetric conflicts pose a challenge to conventional peacemaking practices such as negotiation and third-party mediation. Conflict resolution models present a wide range of peacemaking techniques, adapted to interventions at different levels of a given society, from the top-level of decision-makers (Track I), through the intermediate level of encounters between groups of influential individuals (Track II), to workshops and training at the grassroots level (Track III). Other important distinctions within the field of conflict resolution concern, for example, the divisions between official and unofficial third-party interventions, between bargaining and problem-solving styles of negotiation, or between mediation and facilitation (Fisher, 2011; Hopmann, 2001; Zartman & Rasmussen, 1997).

What all these models have in common, however, is their inability to deal with asymmetric conflict situations. For example, bargaining-style negotiation manuals and models (such as the classic prisoner's dilemma) do not consider the disparities in the power balance between the contestants as a significant variable to be taken into account. They typically underrate the relevance of power and overrate the importance of negotiating techniques (e.g., Ury et al., 1991). However, in asymmetric conflicts, the weaker party is logically forced to give up more in a negotiation process, which always tends to reflect the interests and concerns of the more powerful side (Hopmann, 2001). In this sense, conflict settlement processes can be accused of being used as an instrument of control by the dominant party to a conflict. A few pieces of research are specifically dedicated to negotiations between unequal adversaries, but they are either applied to the inter-individual level, offering strategies for unequal participants to change their "ways of being" at the negotiation table (Beck Kritek, 1994), or to the inter-state level, analyzing the avenues through which smaller states might counter-balance their power weaknesses to win international negotiations (Zartman & Rubin, 2002).

For its part, the so-called "problem-solving" socio-psychological approach to conflict resolution (e.g., Kelman, 1996) does not really provide a better framework when it comes to addressing issues of power imbalance. Although the transformation of relationships is a stated aim of such techniques, too much emphasis is put on the psychological or inter-individual meaning of relationships, and not enough on the structural causes and transformations of conflict. In fact, such conflict intervention models were founded on the premise that facilitation as a process may be extracted from the wider structural asymmetries of the conflict (Jabri, 1996). While this approach remains pertinent in many disputes, it falls short when conflict relationships are rooted in larger political or socioeconomic inequities. In those cases, such a focus on perceptual, psychological processes can be accused of creating a blind spot to substantive issues of injustice and power imbalance (Lederach, 1995); changing antagonistic feelings and hostile emotions by improving communication have to be accompanied by systemic reforms.

Finally, the requirement of impartiality or non-partisanship on the part of third-party mediators or facilitators poses a moral problem in situations of asymmetric conflict, where neutrality could be equated with indifference to oppression, and by extension, with a reinforcement of an unjust system. "Anything neutral introduced into an unequal system, in the end, supports the group in power" (Scimecca, 1987, p. 31), thus exacerbating the conflict.

In the Israeli-Palestinian conflict, similar criticisms have been directed against the various conflict resolution activities that have been taking place in the region since 1967 and up to the start of the second intifada in 2000 (Dudouet, 2005). The so-called Middle East peace process, which culminated in the Oslo agreement and the subsequent implementation negotiations, is perceived by many Palestinians as an unfair agreement because the balance of power inherent in the negotiations determined its distorted outcome. While the Palestinian side had to commit to an extensive list of engagements, the Israeli compromise comprised only one sentence, in which Prime Minister Yitzhak Rabin committed Israel to recognize the Palestinian Liberation Organization (PLO) as the representative of the Palestinian people. Inequality could only get worse in the implementation phase, allowing Israelis to further distort the original Oslo framework by "compromising on the compromise" and creating "facts on the ground" (land expropriation, settlement expansion, fragmentation of Palestinian Authority areas into non-contiguous enclaves, etc.). For Palestinians, the struggle therefore had to go on after the conflict settlement phase, to try and prevent their stronger adversaries from taking further advantage of their dominant position (Rabbani, 2001).

Many Palestinians are also critical of the various problem-solving encounter programs that were very popular from the 1980s to the start of the second intifada. Organized mostly by American conflict resolution nongovernmental organizations (NGOs) or by "internal bridge-builders" belonging to the Israeli and Palestinian societies, such programs brought together groups of Israelis and Palestinians, most often in a neutral setting overseas or in special locations like the School for Peace in the bi-national village of Neve Shalom/Wahat el Salam. These bi-national encounters were usually based on the assumption that bringing together people who belong to groups that are in conflict, and creating interaction between them on a personal basis cut off from their group affiliations, can reduce their hatred for and stereotypes about each other. However, Palestinian participants resented the fact that inter-personal dialogue did not translate to changes in their daily life under occupation, inequality, and oppression, and may have in fact strived to blur national identities and conceal the inherent inequalities of the political context in which the programs took place. They thus felt that the conflict could not be transformed without changing the social structures in which it is embedded (Abu Nimer, 1999; Kuttab, 1988; Rouhana & Korper, 1996).

The idea that dialogue is a symmetrical relationship is false, as, in a very practical sense, asymmetry starts even before such workshops take place. In order to get to the encounter session, Palestinian participants were restricted in their movement (they have to get a permit to travel, go through the humiliation of checkpoints and identity control, etc.), while Jewish Israelis were not. Another example is the use of language in bi-national encounters. Most exchanges during these workshops were in Hebrew, because Israeli Jews are often ignorant of Arabic and most Palestinians have good knowledge of spoken Hebrew. Their natural advantage of knowing the two languages ironically becomes a disadvantage, because if they speak Arabic they are accused of attempting to sabotage the dialogue, and if they decide to use Hebrew they are forced to express themselves poorly in the language of the oppressor's group and to feel both disadvantaged and humiliated (Halabi & Zak, 2004). For Palestinian participants, therefore, attempts to conceal or ignore power relationships led to the preservation of an unequal status quo, and indirectly to the promotion of the interests of the Jewish participants.

It is obvious that in these kinds of clear-cut situations of injustice, third parties' impartiality has to be balanced with a necessary partisanship for change. In particular, empowerment, the process of giving more power to the powerless, has to be supported. If the task of conflict resolution is to make conflicts more symmetrical while less violent — and to ultimately transform them — then its necessary complement is nonviolent resistance.

Nonviolent Resistance as an Effective and Constructive Conflict-Waging Strategy

Among the various conflict-waging strategies that could be used by underdogs to redress a power imbalance, nonviolent resistance (NVR) is the form of confrontation most conducive to long-term conflict transformation. Although nonviolent techniques have been used widely by single-interest groups such as trade unions and anti-nuclear, indigenous, or environmental movements, this essay refers primarily to campaigns by identity or national groups challenging internal oppression or external aggression and occupation, and seeking either self-determination or civil rights in a truly democratic and multicultural state.

Definition and features of NVR

The basic principles of NVR encompass an abstention from the use of physical force to achieve an aim, as well as a full engagement in resisting oppression, domination, and any other forms of injustice. It can thus be applied to oppose both direct (physical) violence and structural violence.[2]

Mohandas Gandhi, whose ideas and actions have most crucially influenced the development of NVR in the twentieth century, described his moral philosophy through the religious precept of *ahimsa*, which in Sanskrit refers to the complete renunciation of violence in thought and action. Nonviolence is usually defined by its opposition to physical violence, which could be described as "the use of physical force against another's body, against that person's will, and that is expected to inflict physical injury or death upon that person" (Bond, 1994, p. 62). This definition does not imply, however, that all actions without violence are therefore nonviolent. Nonviolence might be described as a direct substitute for violent behavior, but also implies deliberate restraint from expected violence, in a context of contention between two or more adversaries. One advantage of the NVR label over the more general term "nonviolence" is this emphasis on conscious and active opposition to violence.

Another advantage is that NVR is particularly suited for situations of structural violence in the absence of overt conflict, since its goals have been historically concerned with a direct engagement in resisting oppression, domination, and any other forms of injustice. NVR theory is based on a strong analysis of the socio-structural contexts that organize and institutionalize power relationships, and social patterns that explain the origins and perpetuation of injustice or authoritarianism. The nonviolent "theory of consent," first formulated by the French philosopher Etienne La Boetie (1530–1565) and further developed by early European and American NVR proponents (e.g., the Quakers, Henry David Thoreau, Leo Tolstoy), stipulates that the authority of any ruler or regime rests on the continued voluntary obedience of its subjects. Therefore, the essence of NVR rests on the withdrawal of this consent through noncooperation or civil disobedience to unjust laws so that governments can no longer operate.

NVR can also be described as a method of contending action, as it offers contentious techniques for prosecuting necessary conflicts, to the point of resolution. McCarthy (1990) describes its effect on societies as "creative disorder" (p. 110), in that it magnifies existing social and political tensions by imposing greater costs on those who want to maintain their advantages under an existing system. For this reason, some authors also prefer to use the terms "nonviolent struggle" or "nonviolent confrontation." Nonetheless, it should be stressed that the effects of NVR on its users, their adversaries, and the conflict environment are more constructive than those of armed activities. Fisher et al. (2000) establish a distinction between conflict intensification, which they define as "making a hidden conflict more visible and open for purposive, nonviolent ends," and conflict escalation, a "situation in which levels of tension and violence are increasing" (p. 5). Figure 1 summarizes the relations between various methods of conflict intervention along these different dimensions.

Finally, NVR is often described as a form of direct action due to its unconventionality and the risk of sanctions incurred by the activists (Rigby,

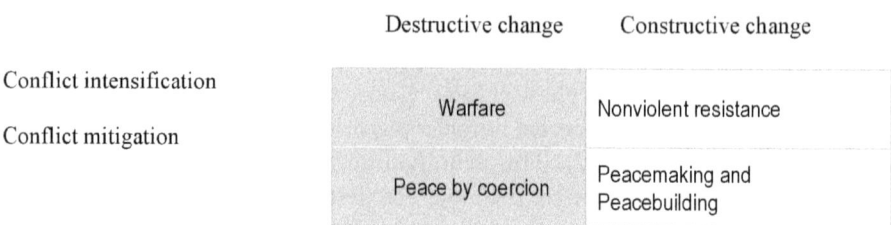

Figure 1: Dimensions and Purposes of Conflict (Dudouet, 2006).

1995). The key feature of direct action is that it is an alternative to established methods of exercising social change and settling conflicts (such as courts, legislatures, lobbying, mediation, negotiation, or elections). In this framework, conflict resolution techniques can be described as "routine actions," following regular channels provided by society for the conduct of conflict, while NVR is disruptive of public order and poses a radical threat to the status quo (Bond, 1994, p. 62).

Historically, NVR has been waged with various methods of contending and/or direct action. In his seminal 1973 manual, Gene Sharp documented 198 different forms of nonviolent action, classified along three categories according to their strategic function: symbolic protest and persuasion, non-cooperation, and intervention (confrontation without physical violence and the building of alternative institutions).

The crucial role played by NVR in the Palestinian history of resistance against Israeli occupation is underrated and largely misunderstood by many international observers[3] Palestinians, for their part, prefer to use more appealing terms, such as "civil-based jihad" or "popular resistance," that reflect more the cultural specificity of Palestinian modes of resistance than external categories which they see as imposed from outside (King, 2007; Qumsiyeh, 2011; Rigby, 2011). This section will be centered primarily on the use of NVR during the first intifada (1987–1993), through which Palestinians gained their recognition by Israel and their neighboring countries as a true nation with legitimate rights to claim (although they ultimately failed to reach) their goal of self-determination. The first intifada is not a well-recognized case of civil resistance, although it has been quantitatively assessed that at least 90 percent of its methods of insurrection were nonviolent (Sharp, 1989).

A strategy to redress structural asymmetry

If "negotiation is only possible when the needs and interests of all those involved and affected by the conflict are legitimated and articulated" (Lederach, 1995, p. 14), then NVR is its necessary complement (or precursor), because it helps marginalized communities to achieve sufficient leverage for an effective negotiation process. This section examines conceptually and empirically the power shifts which can occur through NVR, according to its effect on the resisters and the wider grievance group ("power to") as well as on the opponent group and its constituency ("power over").

NVR can firstly be described as a strategy for self-empowerment, since the very act of nonviolent action produces a change in the participants, correcting their lack of self-confidence as former subordinates and, through the development of self-reliance and courage, giving them a sense of power-over-oneself (Burrowes, 1996). The recurrent label "power of the powerless" refers to this capacity of NVR to enable oppressed and disadvantaged communities to take greater control over their lives. The first stage of self-empowerment, variously described as education (Curle, 1971), conscientization (Freire, 1972), or awakening (Francis, 2002), refers to the creation of political awareness of the nature of unequal relationships and the need for addressing and restoring equity.

It is followed by a second stage of group formation and mobilization for direct action (Francis, 2002), which usually begins with a core of activists (such as university students or trade unions), who very quickly manage to rally support from other walks of life, especially among those previously not committed to the cause (Ackerman & DuVall, 2000). Nonviolent popular initiatives indeed enable a wider participation than other forms of asymmetric conflict, providing ways for all citizens to take responsibility for changing the situation (Clark, 2005).

In practice, a number of collective forms of action are designed to reinforce the power and the will of the resistance movement. For example, "symbolic actions" (Boserup & Mack, 1974), such as large-scale demonstrations and protests, help to increase mobilization and cohesion among activists. Envisioned by Gandhi as the strongest form of nonviolent action, the "constructive program" that is part of many civil resistance movements (e.g., the setting up of alternative or parallel media, social services, tax systems, elections, institutions) is another identity-producing dynamic that supports self-transformation at the individual and collective levels (Wehr, 1979).

These empowerment dynamics could be observed in the Palestinian Territories in the years preceding the first intifada through the emergence of an organized community (charitable societies, professional and cultural associations) cultivating the values of solidarity across traditional social and class affiliations. As soon as the intifada erupted in December 1987, a multi-party central leadership (the Unified National Leadership of the Uprising) was put in place to coordinate the resistance, accompanied by decentralized structures on all levels of society. Sectorial popular committees were set up in each community to address the daily needs of the population: medical relief, food distribution, strike forces, agriculture, trade, public safety, education, information, and solidarity with families of martyrs and prisoners.

At the individual level, the very act of resistance transformed the resisters, giving them a sense of restored pride, dignity, and identity. Collectively, the use of nonviolent tactics enabled a transfer of power from the minority of militants and guerrillas to the Palestinian people themselves, allowing all sectors of society to participate in the resistance through a genuine people's struggle. Popular participation in demonstrations and civil disobedience increased the unity of the resistance, creating connections across factions, age groups, and other social and geographical divisions. However, in the wake of severe repression and an escalation in violence after 1990, some of the old social and political divisions reappeared.

When analyzing the effects of nonviolent campaigns on the targeted entity (be it an oppressive regime or an external occupier), the "mechanisms of change" (Lakey, 1968; Sharp, 1973), a crucial element of NVR theory, describe both what happens to the opponents in the course of a nonviolent struggle and the nature of their decision to give power away. Proponents of principled, Gandhian NVR favor the process of nonviolent conversion, whereby the adversaries come to embrace the point of view of the challengers. It is assumed that "the potentiality for good exists in every living person" (Gregg, 1960, p. 117), and therefore a sense of justice can be awakened in the opponent by the force of good argument. However, it seems rather unrealistic to apply this process to acute political conflicts, such as interethnic rivalries with high levels of polarization and antagonism — and violence. Conversion is more likely to occur in conflicts arising out of misperceptions (Boserup & Mack, 1974). But when human needs are involved, rulers are unlikely to yield to persuasion (Curle, 1971). Moreover, conversion is an inter-individual mechanism, which is difficult to translate to large-scale conflicts, where it would require the conversion of all the opponent's troops, supporters, and elites (Sharp, 1973).

On the contrary, the label of nonviolent coercion (Case, 1923) refers to the mechanism of change that occurs in negative conflict processes. When successful, nonviolent coercion is achieved without the consent of the defeated opponent, whose mind has not been changed on the issues and wants to continue the struggle but lacks the capability to choose a viable alternative, the demands are consequently agreed by force rather than by conviction (Burrowes, 1996).

However, in practice, the most common mechanism of change in successful nonviolent campaigns is an intermediate process of nonviolent accommodation (Lakey, 1968; Sharp, 1973). In this model, opponents resolve to grant the demands of the nonviolent activists without having changed their mind about the issues involved (nonviolent conversion), and without having lost the physical possibility to continue the conflict (nonviolent coercion). They realize instead that the balance of forces is shifting against them, and find it politically wiser to negotiate because it is cheaper or easier than holding firm.[4]

In order to understand better how these mechanisms operate, it is necessary to elucidate the power shifts which might occur through NVR. In the literature on practice, planning a nonviolent uprising is fairly similar to devising a military campaign: it starts by identifying an opponent's "pillars of support" (Helvey, 2004) and areas of vulnerability. However, whereas classical strategic studies have a tendency to equate power with military capabilities, nonviolent struggle emphasizes political and psychological factors of power, such as undermining the opponent's sources of authority and increasing division in its base of support. Different types of action are conceived to weaken the power positions of the targeted regime or occupation forces. "Denial actions," such as civil disobedience, express citizens' refusal to cooperate with the regime they oppose, while "undermining actions" aim at promoting dissent and disaffection within its ranks, and especially within key political and military groups without which it is unable to carry on its aggression (Boserup & Mack, 1974). In comparison with armed rebellion, NVR is indeed more likely to generate active sympathy in sections of the population whose support the regime had earlier enjoyed (Randle, 1994), and provoke loyalty shifts among its enforcement agents, e.g., police, army, public servants (Stephan & Chenoweth, 2008).

Furthermore, violent repression against NVR is likely to "rebound" against the attackers, by weakening their power position while internal determination of and external support for the nonviolent group become stronger (Sharp, 2005). This process has been variously described as "moral jiu-jitsu" (Gregg, 1960) or "political jiu-jitsu" (Sharp, 1973), and was recently re-examined through the theory of "backfire" (Martin, 2007).

However, these claims should be greeted with caution. For instance, the differences in the adversaries' cultures are likely to influence the outcome of NVR: if they are too far apart, the subordinate nonviolent group might be seen as foreign, sub-human, or uncivilized, and violent repression may be seen as merited or acceptable by the wider public. Therefore, nonviolence works better the shorter the social distance (Galtung, 1989). A non-democratic context can also limit the effects of a nonviolent strategy because oppressive regimes do not govern by popular consent and can repress with more impunity (McAdam & Tarrow, 2000). Some nonviolent campaigns have proven vulnerable to military and police repression (e.g., China, Kosovo, Burma), and the probability of success of NVR against brutal and "extremely ruthless opponents" has been put into question (Summy, 1996).[5] In extremely asymmetrical situations, particularly acute in ethnic conflicts, nonviolent strategies might not have sufficient leverage to bring about necessary changes.

Coming back to our example of the first intifada, although mass-based civil disobedience managed to warrant some recognition within the Israeli public that the occupation of the West Bank and Gaza Strip was no longer profitable and sustainable, Palestinians were ultimately unable to raise the costs of continued occupation to a level necessary to force their occupier to withdraw.

On the one hand, the Palestinian strategy of unlinking the West Bank and Gaza Strip from their dependency on the occupier through economic self-reliance had some negative effects on the Israeli economy.[6] Symbolically, the principle of turning the opponent's superior force to one's own advantage was embodied by the use of stones by Palestinian youth against tanks and automatic weapons. Strategically, the Israeli army was not trained for such a non-lethal form of guerrilla warfare, and its brutal retaliation upset the status quo by damaging morale in the army's troops and increasing public sympathy for the Palestinians. Some segments of the Israeli public were converted to the resisters' cause, mobilizing into an active peace movement, and the regime was enticed into adopting accommodation strategies, exemplified by the Oslo peace process and the 1993 Washington declaration recognizing the Palestinian right to statehood.

On the other hand, the Israeli government was so committed to holding on to the West Bank and Gaza Strip that it was prepared to pay an exceptionally high price to sustain its rule. An important element in understanding this equation is the fact that "Israel wants to rule the *land* of Palestine, it does not want the *people*" (Rigby, 1991, p. 196). For this reason, the regime was ready to live with the noncooperation and defiance of the intifada, hoping that increased repression would cause Palestinians to despair and emigrate, leaving more land free for Israeli settlements. Moreover, the economic costs of the intifada became less significant when the Israeli market discovered new ways of reducing its dependency upon Palestinians as a source of labor and as a captive market for its products. Finally, the high degree of inter-party polarization and social distance prevented the uprising from provoking a sufficient degree of defection within the occupation forces to make it inevitable for the government to radically alter its occupation policy. As a result, the number of army objectors ("refuseniks") and deserters remained very limited, while most soldiers became more "extremist" in their attitudes toward Palestinians (Ashmore, 1990).

A catalyst for post-war reconciliation

Many protracted conflicts do not pit a civilian population against a dictatorial elite, but rather dominant versus dominated ethnic, communal, or national groups face off, who have to learn to live together once the conflict is settled. Therefore, post-conflict reconciliation is a crucial component of sustainable peace. By using self-limiting conflict strategies which reduce inter-party polarization and encourage democratic practices, NVR can also lay the grounds for a cooperative post-conflict situation.

First, the integrative techniques of action advocated by the proponents of principled nonviolence and adopted in various degrees by contemporary NVR movements are likely to facilitate cooperative relationships between the conflict parties. Due to its deliberate rejection of violence, NVR is by its very nature a self-limiting style of struggle, which possesses built-in devices to keep the conflict within acceptable bounds and inhibit violent extremism and unbridled escalation (Wehr, 1979). It also softens feelings of humiliation, hatred, and desire for revenge — potentially the seeds of future conflicts (Randle, 1994). Therefore, it is argued that the results achieved through NVR are likely to be more permanent and satisfactory than those achieved through violence.

The emblematic leaders of principled NVR, Gandhi and Martin Luther King, Jr., held a positive view of conflict, seeing it as an opportunity to meet the opponent and transform society and the self (Weber, 2001). For instance, Gandhian theorists envisage conflict as a temporary but necessary disruption which enables deeper inter-party unity and cooperation in the future (Gregg, 1960). While winning is not rejected totally (after all, Gandhi wanted his immediate goal of freedom for India to prevail), the final aim is to reach mutual gains where there is no sacrificing of positions and no lowering of demands, but a higher level of adjustment (Weber, 2001). Likewise, for King (1957) NVR "does not seek to defeat or humiliate the opponent but to win his friendship and understanding.... The aftermath of nonviolence is reconciliation and the creation of a beloved community."

Moreover, nonviolent rules and techniques of action help to break the spiral of destructive relations and offer reassurances to the opponents about their status in the post-conflict situation, anticipating inter-group reconciliation (Miller & King, 2006; Wehr, 1979). For example, tactics such as limiting demands to initial aims in order to avoid the generalization of conflict issues, separating people and problems, being ready to make concessions on non-essentials, seeking fraternization with the opponent's troops, and maximizing inter-group contact and communication, are aimed at preventing conflict polarization and countering misperceptions. The principle of reversibility present in most nonviolent techniques also means that they inflict costs that can be withdrawn when a settlement is reached, without leaving permanent damage. "No one can take back the wounds of violence, the lost years of imprisonment, or the pain of exile — but workers can return to the factory after a strike, boycotters can begin trading at shops again, and mass meetings and marches can be called off" (McCarthy, 1990, p. 115).

How were these principles applied by activists during the first intifada? In their 1988 Declaration of Independence, Palestinians sought to make the prospect of negotiation more appealing to their opponent by unequivocally recognizing Israel's right to exist and limiting their own demands to the establishment of a Palestinian state in the West Bank and Gaza Strip. They also demonstrated this cooperative attitude through symbolic gestures during demonstrations and other nonviolent actions (e.g., by carrying the Palestinian flag in one hand and olive branches in the other), or through leaflets prepared by the Unified National Leadership of the Uprising (e.g., the declaration of a willingness to negotiate, the assertion that Palestinians did not seek the destruction of Israel). However, the indiscriminate and deliberate force used by Israeli soldiers and police created a situation of mutual hatred and distrust. There were accounts of negative Palestinian attitudes toward their adversaries, such as "verbal and physical abuses, hate-filled eyes, inscriptions everywhere making it very clear where the Palestinians want the Israelis to end up: in hell. Of fraternization, there seems to be very little" (Galtung, 1989, p. 4). Rigby (1991) also noted the counter-productivity of the (albeit limited) modes of resistance intended to inflict physical injury upon the Israelis (e.g., throwing stones and firebombs), which prevented their conversion and reinforced the "siege mentality" among the Israeli public.

This example illustrates the difficulty of applying the principles of empathy, trust, and respect for the opponents to the scale of nation-wide campaigns, since it would require an excessive amount of training and preparation (Sharp, 2005). As argued earlier, very few instances of NVR effectively resulted in the conversion of opponents and the achievement of win-win solutions. Instead, accommodation strategies were adopted, whereby NVR provided the grievance group with some bargaining power at the negotiating table, without necessarily resolving the attitudinal oppositions or leading to cooperative relationships. Therefore, process-oriented conflict transformation mechanisms remain a necessary complement to nonviolent struggles for justice and democracy.

A constructive program conducive to democratic practices

In situations of structural injustice, evicting former oppressors is not a sufficient condition to bring about positive changes. Nonviolent revolutions must also guarantee the necessary structural conditions for stable and peaceful societies. According to Sharp (2005), the choice between political violence and NVR helps determine the future capacity of that society to exercise popular control over any ruler or would-be-ruler. He describes the tendency for violent revolutions to be followed by an increase in absolute power of the state (e.g., Russia, China, Cuba). In contrast, nonviolent movements are more likely to promote democratic, decentralized, and participatory practices in the post-revolutionary phase (Randle, 1994). Being participatory rather than hierarchical, NVR is conducive to a diffusion of power within society. The constructive programs that are part of many popular resistance movements also facilitate more participative forms of democracy, since they involve embryonic parallel institutions which give expression to this tendency, such as 1989 forums in Eastern Europe, Gandhi's self-sufficiency program in India, or the "zones of peace" created by peace activists amidst violent wars in Colombia or the Philippines (Hancock & Mitchell, 2007). Quantitative analyses also demonstrate that NVR is more likely than violent rebellion to be positively related to greater freedom and democracy (Karatnycky & Ackerman, 2005).

Despite these general tendencies, campaigns which use nonviolent methods do not guarantee that a spirit of nonviolence will prevail once the cause is won, especially if the majority of activists adopt them for purely tactical reasons. In many instances, NVR has been decisive in securing a transfer of power, but has then fallen short of achieving social transformation to a more participatory society (Clark, 2005). Indeed, several successful nonviolent movements have precipitated the emergence of new versions of the old system (e.g., Iran in 1979, Philippines in 1988, Ukraine in 2005).

In Palestine, the popular empowerment resulting from the intifada was undermined during the subsequent peace process, when instead of keeping the initiative in their own hands, residents of the occupied territories let the PLO in exile negotiate on their behalf. Since its inception, the Palestinian Authority has proceeded to build centralized, bureaucratic, and often ruthless mechanisms that have fostered dependence and crushed most grassroots initiatives, resulting in a "demobilization" of the population and its deepening alienation from political action (Said, 2002). These examples illustrate the problems of political victories that are not accompanied by wider social and attitudinal change.

The limits exposed above, as well as additional strategic mistakes on the part of the Palestinian exiled leadership,[7] might help to clarify why the first intifada, despite its empowering components and ability to shift Israeli-Palestinian relations, ultimately failed to achieve a sufficient level of parity which would have enabled balanced and thus effective negotiations during the Oslo process. Another element which was certainly missing at the time, in contrast to more recent years, was the proactive role of third-party nonviolent advocates alongside internal activists, to which the next section will now turn.

Contingency Conflict Transformation and the Role of Third-Party Advocacy

Nonviolent resistance has been presented above as an effective and constructive precursor, or complement, to conflict resolution techniques in asymmetric power relationships. However, it has also been shown that in situations where the power differential or social distance between the activists (or the "oppressed" social/ethnic/national group) and the pro-status-quo forces is too big, nonviolent action by the low-power group might not provide sufficient leverage to induce social change. For instance, the Kosovo and Palestinian NVR movements during the 1980s and 1990s were not able to use strategies of noncooperation and civil disobedience vis-à-vis the Yugoslav and Israeli regimes, because these were less interested in the compliance of the oppressed population with their policies than in possessing and controlling their land. Therefore, nonviolent resisters were unable to raise the costs of continued occupation to a level necessary to cause their occupier to withdraw (Clark, 2000; Rigby, 1991).

One possible remedy for such situations consists in creating a new dependency relationship between the targeted regime and its challengers. Galtung (1989) advocates the recourse to a "great chain of nonviolence" through nonviolent action by others than the victims themselves — more precisely, by "those whose active or passive collaboration ... is needed for the oppressor to oppress" (p. 20). Indeed, a possible response to the limits posed by impartial external involvement in conflicts caused by structural imbalance is to broaden the scope of third-party conflict intervention to include intermediaries helping to "level the playing field," either by supporting local activism of the oppressed or by exerting pressure on the power-holders.

Principles of third-party nonviolent intervention

Nonviolent action has been increasingly used as a technique of cross-border intervention by third parties (most often transnational grassroots networks or NGOs) in order to prevent or halt violence, or bring about constructive social change, in acute conflict situations. This empirical trend has been accompanied by a scholarly recognition of the specificities of this mode of intervention (Clark, 2009; Hunter & Lakey, 2003; Moser-Puangsuwan & Weber, 2000).

Sharp (2005) defines third parties as "groups that are neither the nonviolent struggle group nor the opponent group. They may be parts of the overall society within which the conflict is occurring, or may be groups from outside that society" (p. 471). From this definition, two types of third parties can be identified. Internally, nonviolent activists seek allies among actors on which the opponent/regime relies, such as its domestic constituency (the white middle class during the civil rights struggles in the U.S. and South Africa, German wives of Jews in Nazi Germany, liberal Britons or Israelis in the Indian or Palestinian independence struggles), or local independent institutions (such as churches in the Philippines and South Africa, or the media in Eastern Europe). On the international level, a government also depends on the support, or at least neutrality, of external third parties such as international bodies, foreign governments, and their population. Therefore, a diplomatic battle is often engaged between nonviolent campaigners and their opponents to gain legitimacy by the outside world. For example, international pressure contributed to the general undermining of the apartheid regime in South Africa and to General Augusto Pinochet's loss of authority in Chile. This section focuses primarily on the latter (i.e., cross-border) type of intervention, but the functions and activities described below are also relevant for third-party advocacy by domestic constituencies who do not identify themselves as primary conflict parties.

A crucial distinction should be made here between third-party roles in the conflict resolution and nonviolent traditions, along their ethical stance vis-à-vis the conflict parties. Whereas the former emphasizes the need for impartiality on the part of external actors, most nonviolent advocacy interveners deliberately work on the sides of the victims or the low-power group to assist them in empowerment and the reduction of imbalance in the conflict.

Forms of intervention and relationships with internal activists

Whereas I have detailed elsewhere various forms of direct or indirect external support to local nonviolent campaigns (e.g., Dudouet & Clark, 2009), the focus here is more specifically on the use of nonviolent direct action by third parties in solidarity with, or on behalf of, low-power groups in acute asymmetric conflicts. The Israeli-Palestinian conflict offers a pertinent illustration of the power of third-party advocacy. Although there was a lack of significant international mobilization in support of Palestinian NVR during the first intifada, numerous cross-border initiatives have emerged since the outburst of the second intifada in 2000 [*Eds. note: NVR during the second intifada is expounded in the following essay*]. One of the most prominent of these initiatives, the International Solidarity Movement (ISM), fits particularly well the aforementioned description of nonviolent advocacy; it defines itself as a Palestinian-led movement committed to resisting the Israeli occupation of Palestinian land using nonviolent, direct-action methods and principles. The complementary activities carried out by the ISM or other initiatives launched by its (former) members will be used here to illustrate the principles of external advocacy of NVR.[8]

The first type of advocacy, namely *on-site nonviolent accompaniment*, refers to on-site activities carried out in conflict areas in support of local nonviolent activists, by increasing their leverage or protecting them against violent repression. Protective accompaniment is usually associated with the work of Peace Brigades International or Nonviolent Peaceforce, whose volunteers accompany threatened local human rights activists in their daily work, acting as unarmed bodyguards. However, these organizations define their role as non-interventionist and non-partisan, and deliberately refrain from taking part in direct action of their own or alongside local activists (Coy, 2008). By contrast, ISM volunteers regularly take part in nonviolent demonstrations against the separation wall or direct actions such as checkpoint removals in order to "lend support to the Palestinian [nonviolent] resistance to the occupation and their demand for freedom"[9]—while also working closely with Israeli anti-occupation activists and supporting their activities. Their effectiveness stems from the reluctance of armed forces or paramilitary groups to risk upsetting Western governments by attacking foreign volunteers during their protection missions. However, the tragic events of spring 2003, when two ISM volunteers were killed while performing protection or interposition activities,[10] have proved that this function becomes less relevant once soldiers stop being afraid of using violence against international volunteers, even at the expense of bad media publicity abroad. More generally, the combined efforts of (internal) nonviolent resistance and cross-border accompaniment have failed to induce macro-political change so far, besides a few legal successes in the nonviolent campaign against the separation wall since 2003.[11]

Therefore, ISM volunteers have also been at the forefront of international grassroots efforts to step up complementary forms of nonviolent advocacy outside of the conflict area itself, known as *off-site nonviolent campaigns*. The goal of off-site nonviolent campaigns can be either to try to halt violence or injustice directly by launching nonviolent sanctions against repressive regimes, or, indirectly, to exert pressure on Western governments to reverse policies which support these regimes. In the past few years, ISM members have been engaging forcefully in support of the Palestinian call[12] for international boycott, divestment, and sanctions (BDS) against Israeli occupation policies, inspired by the earlier international divestment campaign imposed on the South African apartheid state. There have been a number of individual and collective direct actions against products and firms associated with Israel, the settlements, and the occupation,[13] as well as an ongoing (and growing) academic, cultural, and diplomatic boycott campaign.[14]

Finally, *nonviolent invasion* represents the most disruptive and daring form of cross-border intervention. It refers to the act of entering illegally (through nonviolent direct action) a violent or potentially violent space to expedite social change. Originally conceived by Gandhi in a national context as a method to reoccupy one's land or claim ownership over one's resources (e.g., attempts to take over salt works during the 1930–31 Salt Satyagraha), it has very rarely been applied across national borders. In the Palestinian context, the Israeli closure of Gaza and the imposition of an illegal siege of Gaza and its over 1.5 million inhabitants has compelled international activists to attempt to enter the Gaza Strip through land or sea, in order to raise global attention of the plight of Palestinians and to bring support to local nonviolent activists. For instance, in December of 2009 and January 2010, the Gaza Freedom March brought 1,300 international volunteers to Cairo in an unsuccessful attempt to organize a nonviolent mass march to the Egyptian border and into Gaza. ISM volunteers and co-founders also initiated in 2008 the Free Gaza movement, which has organized 10 sea trips to Gaza (five times successfully) "as an expression of citizen nonviolent direct action, confronting Israel's ongoing abuses of Palestinian human and political rights" (www.freegaza.org). The international outrage and protests which followed the violent Israeli interception of the "Freedom Flotilla" heading for the Gaza shores in May 2010, which resulted in the death of nine activists, was unprecedented and illustrious of the power of cross-border solidarity campaigns, on several accounts. First, it led to global media attention and interest in the phenomenon of nonviolent intervention (although the nonviolent nature of the behavior and attitude of some activists aboard the *Mavi Marmara* ship should be questioned), and brought to light the legality and legitimacy of such forms of action. Perhaps more importantly, it also helped increase the appeal of NVR among Palestinian radicals, prompting for instance a Hamas parliamentarian to remark: "When we use violence, we help Israel win international support.... The Gaza flotilla has done more for Gaza than 10,000 rockets" (Levinson, 2010).

This overview reaffirms that in conflicts characterized by a huge power discrepancy between the contending parties, impartial third-party mediation or facilitation should be accompanied by complementary forms of external intervention, in the form of on-site or off-site nonviolent advocacy for justice and empowerment.

Conclusion

This essay has presented the theory and practice of NVR as a necessary component of conflict transformation in situations of power asymmetry between dominant (power-holders) and dominated groups, while the techniques of conflict resolution are better suited for relatively symmetrical power disputes (Francis, 2002). In contexts where peace cannot be reached without addressing issues of justice, occupation, and domination, the dynamics of conflict settlement (bargaining-style negotiation) and conflict resolution (dialogue of equals and reconciliation) have to be preceded by a leveling of the playing field so that both parties feel empowered and ready for a constructive dialogue.

Nonviolent resistance is particularly appropriate at the early stages of latent conflicts rooted in structural violence, as a tool in the hands of marginal or disenfranchised communities to struggle effectively for justice and democracy. This essay has indeed demonstrated the potential of NVR to encourage popular empowerment and bring pressure on the opponent, thus providing a stronger position from which to negotiate concessions. While the limits of nonviolent strategies in extremely violent situations such as mass slaughter and genocide need to be acknowledged, in many contexts of oppression and exploitation it might well be the only way to struggle for justice and democracy in a peaceful and constructive way. Indeed, the capacity of NVR simultaneously to transform power relationships and human relationships makes it unique as a method of political action, through its dual process of dialogue and resistance — dialogue with the people on the other side to persuade them, and resistance to the structures to compel change. Although it involves activism and advocacy of a particular point of view, it is deemed highly consistent with efforts at conflict resolution and consensus building, by providing the means of waging conflicts that would at once suppress direct and structural violence, and prepare the society for positive peace.

However, in practice, NVR seldom leads by itself to win-win solutions and post-settlement cooperative relationships across conflict lines; the ideal conditions that would enable such a dialectic process are too rarely present. The Palestinian example indicates that when conflicts involve highly polarized communal groups on non-negotiable issues, positive peace does not emanate automatically from the achievement of relative power balance, and NVR is not always effective at preventing inter-party misperceptions and hatred. In such situations, negotiations and process-oriented conflict resolution remain necessary to facilitate the articulation of legitimate needs and interests of all concerned into fair, practical, and mutually acceptable solutions. Therefore, NVR and conflict resolution mechanisms should be seen as complementary and mutually supportive strategies which can be employed, consecutively or simultaneously, to realize the twin goals of justice and peace.

In the Israeli-Palestinian conflict, these complementary activities were never pursued either consecutively or simultaneously. For instance, NVR during the first intifada failed to attract tangible forms of third-party support, and the subsequent mediated negotiation process failed to build on the successes of the Palestinian uprising. On the contrary, the second intifada has been characterized by numerous cross-border solidarity initiatives, but the active NVR of Palestinian villages threatened by the "security barrier" has been overshadowed by the armed strategies of the militant groups and, so far, has not led to any significant peace initiatives.

To conclude, it is hoped that this essay will encourage conflict transformation scholars, practitioners, and policymakers to think more comparatively across the spectrum of conflict intervention strategies and pay more attention to the phenomenon of nonviolent resistance. Conflicts deemed "unripe" for resolution by traditional negotiation or mediation approaches should be examined, and, conversely, at which stage of a nonviolent campaign negotiation becomes possible and desirable. Although some conflict transformation trainers have started to recognize the need to support constructive conflicts alongside trust-building and dialogue (Curle, 1971; Fisher et al., 2000; Francis, 2002; Lederach, 1995), the whole range of methods available to wage conflicts creatively has not been utilized (Clark, 2005). Finally, researchers and practitioners alike should integrate their conflict mapping exercises and intervention scenarios with the identification of structures of oppression and power asymmetry, legacies of nonviolent resistance, and local self-empowerment strategies in order to design and support more sustainable and home-grown peacemaking and peacebuilding processes.

Notes

1. It should be noted, however, that fewer and fewer Palestinians see the two-state solution as viable, given the entrenchment of Israeli settlements and bypass roads deep inside the West Bank (Shatz, 2011).

2. Galtung (1969) defines structural violence as the ongoing and institutionalized deprivation of needs of survival, well-being, identity, and freedom. In the Israeli-Palestinian context, "structural violence ... is inflicted slowly and in a chronic fashion, by keeping people in poverty ... or preventing them from pursuing their chosen life on an equal playing field. Structural violence is built into everyday life, into the economy, a political system, and into the landscape" (Bornstein, 2002, p. 6).

3. Many articles by foreign journalists or commentators in recent years have called for the emergence of a "Palestinian Gandhi," or celebrated the emergence of "new" nonviolent approaches in the occupied territories (e.g., Bronner, 2010), thus completely ignoring or misrepresenting the central role played by NVR in Palestinian history since 1936.

4. A fourth mechanism of change which is sometimes added on to this model, *non-*

violent disintegration, occurs when the government breaks down in the face of widespread nonviolent action (Sharp, 2005, p. 418).

5. Other authors are in turn questioning these claims, demonstrating that nonviolent campaigns have been successful even in the face of non-democratic and/or oppressive contexts (e.g., Ackerman & Duvall, 2000).

6. For instance, the boycott of Israeli goods resulted in a 40 percent decline in exports to the occupied territories in 1988, and a $300 million loss for Israeli businesses. Also, as a result of tax revolt of parts of the West Bank in 1988, the tax collection in the Palestinian territories was down 32 percent from the previous year (JMCC, 1989).

7. For instance, the Palestinian strategic position vis a vis Israel was further harmed by the PLO leadership and population's alignment with Saddam Hussein during the Gulf War, and the neglect of their cause at the Madrid Peace Conference in 1991.

8. The classification adopted here is partly inspired by Burrowes (2000), while the distinction between off-site and on-site intervention is drawn from Rigby (1995).

9. See http://palsolidarity.org/about/.

10. On March 16, 2003, Rachel Corrie was fatally run over by a bulldozer while attempting to protect the home of a Palestinian physician from demolition. One month later, on April 11, Tom Hurndall was shot in the back of the head by an Israeli military guard in a guard tower while escorting Palestinian children out of the line of Israeli fire. He died nine months later of his injuries. The two incidents took place in the border town of Rafah in the Gaza Strip.

11. The Israeli Supreme Court has ordered alterations to the path of the wall in some villages which took part in the so-called "third (popular) intifada," including most prominently Budrus and Bilin, but also the Beit Surik-Biddu area, Azawiya, etc.

12. This call launched in 2005 was endorsed by an extensive list of dozens of Palestinian political parties, unions, and organizations representing Palestinians under occupation, refugees, or citizens of Israel, and united under the umbrella Joint Advocacy Initiative (see http://bdsmovement.net/).

13. See for example the campaign against the Caterpillar firms in the United States and Europe, seen as a symbol of Palestinian oppression because they produce the bulldozers which destroy Palestinian houses and which killed the ISM activist Corrie (see http://stopthewall.org/worldwideactivism/903.shtml).

14. For instance, in April 2005 the British Association of University Teachers decided to cut its ties with Bar Ilan University because of its links with Ariel College, located in an illegal settlement deep inside the West Bank. Following intense opposition from universities worldwide, the decision was overturned a month later. There was also more recently a campaign to oppose Israel's admission to the Organization for Economic Cooperation and Development.

References

Abu-Nimer, M. (1999). *Dialogue, conflict resolution and change: Arab-Jewish encounters in Israel*. Albany: State University of New York Press.

Ackerman, P., and J. DuVall (2000). *A force more powerful: A century of nonviolent conflict*. New York: Palgrave.

Ashmore, R.B. (1990). Nonviolence as an intifada strategy. *American-Arab affairs* 32, 92–104.

Beck Kritek, P. (1994). *Negotiating at an uneven table: Developing moral courage in resolving our conflicts*. San Francisco: Jossey-Bass.

Bond, D. (1994). Nonviolent direct action and the diffusion of power. In P. Wehr, H. Burgess and G. Burgess (Eds.), *Justice without violence* (pp. 59–79). Boulder, CO: Lynne Rienner.

Bornstein, A.S. (2002). *Crossing the green line between the West Bank and Israel.* Philadelphia: University of Pennsylvania Press.
Boserup, A., and A. Mack (1974). *War without weapons.* London: Frances Pinter.
Bronner, E. (2010). Palestinians try a less violent path to resistance. *New York Times*, 6 April. www.nytimes.com/2010/04/07/world/middleeast/07westbank.html?ref=world.
Burrowes, R.J. (1996). *The strategy of nonviolent defense: A Gandhian approach.* Albany: State University of New York Press.
_____. (2000). Cross-border nonviolent intervention: A typology. In Y. Moser-Puangsuwan and T. Weber (Eds.), *Nonviolent intervention across borders: A recurrent vision* (pp. 45–69). Honolulu: University of Hawaii Press.
Case, C.M. (1923). *Non-violent coercion: A study in methods of social pressure.* New York: Century.
Clark, H. (2000). *Civil resistance in Kosovo.* London: Pluto.
_____. (2005). "Campaigning power and civil courage: Bringing 'people power' back into conflict transformation." London: Committee for Conflict Transformation Support.
_____. (2009, Ed.). *Unarmed resistance and global solidarity.* London: Pluto.
Coy, P.G. (2008). "Degrees and dynamics of nonpartisanship and interventionism in international nonviolent accompaniment." Paper presented at the International Peace Research Association Conference, Leuven, July 16.
Curle, A. (1971). *Making peace.* London: Tavistock.
Dudouet, V. (2005). "Peacemaking and nonviolent resistance. A study of the complementarity between conflict resolution processes and nonviolent intervention, with special reference to the case of Israel-Palestine." PhD Thesis. Bradford: Department of Peace Studies, University of Bradford.
_____. (2006). "Transitions from violence to peace: Revisiting analysis and intervention in conflict transformation." Berghof Report No. 15. Berghof Conflict Research, Berlin.
_____, and H. Clark (2009). "Nonviolent civic action in support of human rights and democracy." Directorate-general for external policies of the union, EXPO/B/DROI/2008/69. Brussels: European Parliament.
Fisher, R. (2011). Methods of third-party intervention. In B. Austin, M. Fischer, and H.J. Giessmann (Eds.), *Advancing conflict transformation: The Berghof handbook* (pp. 157–182). Opladen: Barbara Budrich.
Fisher, S., D.I. Abdi, J. Ludin, R. Williams, S. Smith and S. Williams (2000). *Working with conflict: Skills and strategies for action.* London: Zed.
Francis, D. (2002). *People, peace and power: Conflict transformation in action.* London: Pluto.
Freire, P. (1972). *Pedagogy of the oppressed.* Harmondsworth: Penguin.
Galtung, J. (1969). Violence, peace, and peace research. *Journal of Peace Research*, 6(3), 167–191.
_____. (1989). *Nonviolence and Israel/Palestine.* Honolulu: University of Hawaii Press.
Gregg, R.B. (1960). *The power of nonviolence.* Exeter: Wheaton.
Halabi, R., and M. Zak (2004). Language as a bridge and as an obstacle. In R. Halabi (Ed.) *Israeli and Palestinian identities in dialogue: The school for peace approach* (pp. 119–140). New Brunswick: Rutgers University Press.
Hancock, L., and C. Mitchell (2007). *Zones of peace.* Bloomfield: Kumarian.
Helvey, R. (2004). *On strategic nonviolent conflict: Thinking about the fundamentals.* Boston: Albert Einstein Institute.
Hopmann, P.T. (2001). Bargaining and problem-solving: Two perspectives on international negotiation. In A. Crocker, F.O. Hampson and P. Aall (Eds.) *Turbulent peace* (pp. 445–468). Washington, DC: USIP Press.
Hunter, D., and G. Lakey (2003). *Opening space for democracy: Training manual for third-party nonviolent intervention.* Philadelphia: Training for Change.

Jabri, V. (1996). *Discourses on violence. Conflict analysis reconsidered.* Manchester: Manchester University Press.
Jerusalem Media and Communication Center (JMCC) (1989). "The intifada: An overview. The first two years." Jerusalem.
Karatnycky, A., and P. Ackerman (2005). How freedom is won: From civic resistance to durable democracy. *International Journal of Not-for-Profit Law* 7(3). www.icnl.org/knowledge/ijnl/vol7iss3/special_3.htm.
Kelman, H.C. (1996). The integrative problem-solving approach. In A. Crocker, F.O. Hampson and P. Aall (Eds.), *Managing global chaos: Sources of and responses to international conflict* (pp. 501–519). Washington, DC: USIP Press.
King, M. (2007). *A quiet revolution: The first Palestinian intifada and nonviolent resistance.* New York: Nation.
King, M.L., Jr. (1957). "Justice without violence." Speech delivered at Brandeis University on April 13, 1957. www.stanford.edu/group/King/liberation_curriculum/pdfs/justicewithoutviolence.pdf.
_____. (1964). *Letter from Birmingham jail: Why we can't wait* (pp. 76–95). New York: Signet.
Kuttab, J. (1988). An exchange on dialogue. *Journal of Palestine Studies,* 17(2), 84–108.
Lakey, G. (1968). The sociological mechanisms of nonviolent action. *Peace Research Review,* 2(6), 1–102.
Laue, J., and G. Cormick (1978). The ethics of intervention in community disputes. In G. Bermant, H.C. Kelman and D.P. Warwick (Eds.), *The ethics of social intervention* (pp. 205–232). Washington, DC: Halsted.
Lederach, J.P. (1995). *Preparing for peace: Conflict transformation across cultures.* New York: Syracuse University Press.
Levinson, C. (2010). Israel's foes embrace new resistance tactics. *Wall Street Journal,* 2 July. http://online.wsj.com/article/SB10001424052748704638504575318390063707222.html.
Martin, B. (2007). *Justice ignited: The dynamics of backfire.* Lanham, MD: Rowman & Littlefield.
McAdam, D., and S. Tarrow (2000). Nonviolence as contentious interaction. *Political Science and Politics* 33(2), 149–154.
McCarthy, R.M. (1990). The techniques of nonviolent action: Some principles of its nature, use, and effects. In R. Crow, P. Grant and S.E. Ibrahim (Eds.), *Arab nonviolent political struggle: Prospects for the Middle East* (pp. 107–120). Boulder: Lynne Rienner.
Miller, C.A., and M.E. King (2006). *Strategic nonviolent struggle: A training manual.* Addis Ababa: University of Peace.
Moser-Puangsuwan, Y., and T. Weber. (2000). *Nonviolent intervention across borders: A recurrent vision.* Honolulu: University of Hawaii Press.
Qumsiyeh, M. (2011). *Popular resistance in Palestine: A history of hope and empowerment.* London: Pluto.
Rabbani, M. (2001). Rocks and rockets: Oslo's inevitable conclusion. *Journal of Palestine studies* 30(3), 68–81.
Randle, M. (1994). *Civil resistance.* London: Fontana.
Rigby, A. (1991). *Living the intifada.* London: Zed.
_____. (1995). Unofficial nonviolent intervention: Examples from the Israeli-Palestinian conflict. *Journal of peace research* 32(4), 453–467.
_____. (2011). *Palestinian resistance and nonviolence.* Jerusalem: Palestinian Academic Society for the Study of International Affairs (PASSIA).
Rouhana, N., and S. Korper (1996). Dealing with the dilemmas posed by power asymmetry in inter-group conflicts. *Negotiation Journal* 12, 353–366.
Said, E.W. (2002). *The end of the peace process.* London: Granta.

Salem, P. (1997). A critique of western conflict resolution from a non-western perspective. In *Conflict resolution in the Arab world: Selected essays* (pp. 11–24). Beirut: American University of Beirut.

Scimecca, J.A. (1987). *Conflict resolution: The basis for social control or social change?* In D. Sandole and I. Sandole-Staroste (Eds.) *Conflict management and problem-solving: Interpersonal to international applications* (pp. 30–33). London: Pinter.

Sharp, G. (1973). *The politics of non-violent action.* Boston: Porter Sargent.

_____. (1989). The intifada and nonviolent struggle. *Journal of Palestine Studies, 19*(1), 3–13.

_____. (2005). *Waging nonviolent struggles: Twentieth century practice and twenty first century potential.* Boston: Porter Sargent.

Shatz, A. (2011). Is Palestine next? *London review of books, 33*(14), 8–14.

Stephan, M., and E. Chenoweth (2008). Why civil resistance works: The strategic logic of nonviolent conflict. *International Security, 33*(1), 7–44.

Summy, R. (1996). Nonviolence and the case of the extremely ruthless opponent. In M. Kumar and P. Low (Eds.), *Legacy and future of nonviolence* (pp. 118–138). New Delhi: Gandhi Peace Foundation.

Ury, W., R. Fisher, and B. Patton (1991). *Getting to yes: Negotiating an agreement without giving in.* London: Arrow.

Wallensteen, P. (2002). *Understanding conflict resolution. War, peace and the global system.* London: Sage.

Weber, T. (2001). Gandhian philosophy, conflict resolution theory and practical approaches to negotiation. *Journal of Peace Research. 38*(4), 493–513.

Wehr, P. (1979). *Conflict regulation.* Boulder: Westview.

Zartman, I.W., and L. Rasmussen (1997). *Peacemaking in international conflict: Methods and techniques.* Washington, DC: USIP Press.

_____, and J. Rubin (2002). *Power and negotiation.* Ann Arbor: University of Michigan Press.

The Activist and the Olive Tree: Nonviolent Resistance in the Second Intifada

Julie M. Norman

This essay uses the case of the Israeli-Palestinian conflict during the second intifada (2000–2009) to explore how nonviolent resistance functions as a form of conflict transformation by creating a space for diverse voices to be heard and a means for grassroots issues to be raised. Nonviolent resistance does not necessarily resolve conflict, but rather reframes it from a popular perspective and allows for increased community participation and ownership in processes of change. Thinking about conflict transformation in this way is especially useful in protracted conflicts like Israel-Palestine, where analyses often focus exclusively on the top-level peace process, rather than acknowledging the myriad of processes that might contribute to a just peace in the region.

Although the second intifada is characterized in the literature and media as mostly violent, many individuals, organizations, and communities continued to utilize nonviolent resistance[1] throughout this period. For organizational purposes, Palestinian nonviolent actions are explored through the framework of several dimensions of activism to illustrate how the repertoire of nonviolence expanded beyond the direct action approach often associated with it.

The discussion begins with a description of community-based nonviolent efforts utilizing direct action tactics, such as demonstrations, marches, and protests, primarily led by village popular committees. Then the role of civil society is discussed in terms of local nongovernmental organizations (NGOs) organizing direct actions, coordinating nonviolence trainings, organizing popular education campaigns, and supporting episodes of direct action in the West Bank; political parties mobilizing for popular resistance; and alternative media outlets amplifying the occurrence of nonviolent efforts in the local and international spheres. Finally, everyday acts of resistance that may not fit traditional notions of activism, but reflect acts of perseverance and determination that constitute a sort of subtle resistance, are examined. Considered collectively, these diverse modes of resistance constituted a cycle of nonviolent contention during the second intifada that brought attention to different issues and expanded participation at the local level, while creating new spaces for regional support and international solidarity.

Grassroots Direct Action

Direct action refers to strategic nonviolent tactics that deliberately challenge the authority of the oppressor. It is usually the most visible form of popular resistance and the approach typically associated with nonviolent activism. Nonviolent direct actions can include acts of omission, when people refuse to perform acts that they are required to do by practice, custom, or law; acts of commission, when people perform acts that they are not usually expected or allowed to perform; or combinations of the two (Sharp, 1973). Both acts of omission and acts of commission can be categorized in the areas of protest and persuasion, noncooperation, and intervention (Ackerman & Kruegler, 1994; Helvey, 2004; Sharp, 1973).

Popular resistance during the second intifada was largely rooted at the village level, where local communities used strategies of protest, noncooperation, and intervention to resist the occupation. There are several explanations for this localization of action; however, for many local communities, the decision to act was not so much a choice, but a necessity. Indeed, the majority of village-based resistance aimed to halt (or at least re-route) the construction of the separation barrier,[2] which has separated many village-based farmers from their agricultural land. The farmers, their families, and the communities themselves rely on the land for sustenance and livelihood, thus, prohibition of access instigated a number of grassroots resistance campaigns.

The majority of village-based direct action campaigns were (and continue to be at the time of writing) coordinated by local popular committees, consisting of individual volunteers from local communities with natural ties to the land and proximity to local residents. This proximity, in terms of geography and lived experiences, gives popular committees a degree of legitimacy and respect that may be difficult for non-community members to attain. The committees are not formal, thereby giving them considerable flexibility and freedom to communicate and associate with various groups and stakeholders. The membership of the popular committees varies, but often includes village elders, farmers, activists, students, and local political leaders. This diverse composition allows community members to collaborate on various objectives and actions in such ways that overcome political divisions plaguing other levels of Palestinian society.

Village popular committees undertake a variety of duties. For the sake of this discussion, it is important to note the committees' role in coordinating direct actions in terms of protest, noncooperation, and intervention. Regarding protest, popular committees are the primary organizers of sustained campaigns, usually consisting of weekly demonstrations following the Friday prayer. Villages throughout the West Bank have mobilized to organize and sustain these weekly marches, usually near the construction sites of the separation barrier. In terms of intervention, popular committees have organized episodes of civil disobedience — again focused on the separation barrier — by mobilizing villagers to physically block the destruction of olive groves and other land, or by taking control of the bulldozers and other equipment used for the wall construction. Finally, regarding noncooperation, popular committees have been instrumental in organizing boycotts of Israeli products, particularly those manufactured in settlements.

Each popular committee also performs other tasks in accordance with local grievances and needs, with several even pursuing legal cases in Israeli courts on behalf of villagers. Popular committees also typically handle villages' communications with Israeli authorities and sometimes settlers, maintain records and maps of land closures and seizures, act as spokespeople with the media, offer support to other villages, and coordinate actions, conferences, and events with other committees.

Case study: Bil'in

The village of Bil'in became a symbol of popular resistance in Palestine during the second intifada. It is a small farming village of approximately 1,700 residents, located 12 kilometers west of Ramallah, and just four kilometers east of the Green Line. The separation barrier's route cut off the village from over 2,000 dunams (approximately 500 acres) of its agricultural land, to allow for the expansion of the nearby Modi'in Illit settlement.

Starting in January 2005, Bil'in residents began participating in weekly demonstrations to protest the construction of the separation barrier, in which villagers marched from the mosque to the construction site. However, as the protest and persuasion techniques were having little effect on the wall's construction, leaders in the village decided that they needed to organize a popular committee, re-evaluate their work, and explore alternative tactics. As Ibrahim,[3] a member of Bil'in's popular committee, explains:

> We had to figure out how we wanted to continue, and what would be our aim. In the beginning, it was too simple, without any organization.... No one was thinking in terms of mapping or planning a strategy, but that need arose from our experience in the field. We felt we needed to decide on a strategy, aims, tactics, and methods [personal communication, 2007].

The popular committee was formed on February 20, 2005, including members from Fateh, Hamas, Islamic Jihad, Mubadara, and other parties, and with close communication with local (NGOs) and community-based organizations (CBOs). The committee decided to emphasize at the demonstrations that they were not against the soldiers, but against the occupation. Furthermore, they decided to focus on calling attention to the problem of land confiscation, in addition to the direct violence of the occupation that was visible at the demonstrations.

The popular committee also began to consider more creative noncooperation and intervention strategies. For example, on May 3, 2005, the Israeli Defense Forces (IDF) informed the village that the bulldozers would be coming to uproot a grove of olive trees in Bil'in. Rather than replanting the trees after the uprooting, an act of protest conducted by other villages, the popular committee, along with several Israeli activists, tied themselves to the olive trees and prevented their destruction. According to Ibrahim,

> It was like a day of revolution in how to resist. It communicated our real message, and it was successful, because the soldiers couldn't do anything, like arrest us or beat us. We weren't doing anything illegal, we weren't aiming at them, we didn't damage their property, and they couldn't claim it as a military zone since it was clearly our land. So this started a new way in our resistance [personal communication, 2007].

The popular committee continued to experiment with different types of actions. At several demonstrations, they used mirrors to reflect anti-occupation slogans onto the IDF soldiers and jeeps. At another protest, a group of activists distracted the soldiers while Tito Kayak, a Puerto Rican activist and climber, scaled a nearby Israeli surveillance tower and unfurled the Palestinian flag at its top. On another occasion, members of the popular committee dressed up like aliens from the film *Avatar* to create an analogy of a hostile takeover of native land by an outside force. These actions were successful in delaying the construction of the wall, and also in getting Bil'in's name in the news, calling media attention to the plight of villages affected by the wall, settlements, and land confiscation. The media attention subsequently increased international and Israeli activist support for the village, thus providing the weekly demonstrations with additional support and participation from the International Solidarity Movement (ISM) and Israeli groups such as Ta'ayush, Gush Shalom, and Anarchists Against the Wall.

Like the nearby villages of Budrus and Biddu, Bil'in's popular committee sought legal assistance through the Israeli court system, with the help of Israeli legal organization Yesh Din and Israeli human rights lawyer Michael Sfard. Although it took almost two years for the case to be heard, on September 4, 2007, the Israeli Supreme Court ordered the government to redraw the route of a 1.7-kilometer section of the wall near Bil'in because the original route was "highly prejudicial" to the villagers and not justified on security grounds (Asser, 2007). Although no immediate action was taken, the legal victory once again garnered regional and global media attention for Bil'in, which was one of the objectives of the popular committee. Raed, a videographer from Bil'in who heads the media section of the popular committee, notes, "Media is very important in Bil'in. The whole world sees the story of Bil'in, so it has changed the whole situation. The general media likes the story because we do creative, different things" (personal communication, 2007). According to Raed, the village has deliberately used media as a tool for resistance. Bil'in has also increased publicity by holding annual nonviolent activism conferences in the village for Palestinians, Israelis, and internationals, and assisting in organizing popular committees and resistance in other villages.

To be sure, Bil'in was not the only village to employ nonviolent resistance. Much of its success came from observing similar struggles in Budrus and Biddu, and the experiences of Bil'in later informed campaigns in Um Salamouna, Artash, and Ni'lin. It should also be noted that many direct actions took place without the institutional framework of a popular committee or village organization. For example, Yared, a young professional in Ramallah, explains how he and his friends decided to organize actions to protest Israel's 2006 offensive in Lebanon:

> We coordinated different activities each day for a month. Each day we met at 6 P.M. in Al-Manara [the city-center of Ramallah], and every day we did something unique. We played the national anthem, flew balloons, passed out [political] cartoons, organized a boycott by putting Israeli products on the street with a big "X" over them, and just did anything we could to increase public awareness. It was mainly just a group of friends who did this [personal communication, 2007].

Yared's experience is just one of many direct action initiatives that were not affiliated with any specific group, but still used tactics of protest and persuasion, and sometimes noncooperation and intervention. There were also numerous "spontaneous" occurrences of direct nonviolent action, including removals of roadblocks, re-planting of olive trees, demonstrations at checkpoints, and hunger strikes in prisons.

Clearly, direct action continues to be used as a nonviolent tactic in Palestinian resistance. The construction of the separation wall ironically created a political opportunity for resistance by providing a common cause for activists, a visible image of oppression to export internationally, and access to contact points with Israeli soldiers and police at construction sites. However, the separation barrier was also effective in its purpose of restricting movement and further isolating Palestinians from Israelis and from each other. Thus, Palestinians utilized other channels of nonviolence at the civil society level that complemented direct action.

Activism in Civil Society

In addition to grassroots campaigns, many Palestinian civil society organizations have been active in coordinating or supporting nonviolent resistance efforts throughout Palestinian history (Dajani, 1997). During the second intifada, civil society organizations facilitated nonviolent activism in the West Bank by coordinating and supporting resistance efforts, providing nonviolence trainings, and raising awareness locally and globally about the situation in Palestine.

Case study: Anti-apartheid wall campaign (Stop the Wall)

The Palestinian Grassroots Anti-Apartheid Wall Campaign, or Stop the Wall, is a coalition of Palestinian NGOs and popular committees that coordinate efforts on local, national, and international levels to resist the separation barrier and the occupation. Specifically, the campaign aims to halt the construction of the wall, dismantle the existing sections, return confiscated land to Palestinian owners, and compensate landowners for losses, in accordance with the 2004 ICJ ruling. A seven-member coordinating committee works with local popular committees and NGOs to support grassroots resistance, encourage NGO and national mobilization, facilitate research and documentation, and encourage international outreach and solidarity, especially in the form of boycott, divestment, and sanctions (BDS) on Israel.[4]

Although Stop the Wall aims for more organization and cooperation between popular committees, the coordinators view the initiative as a true campaign rather than an NGO. As Ahmed, a member of the coordinating committee, notes, "Stop the Wall is a campaign; we didn't want it to be an NGO, focusing on proposals and collecting money. We didn't want it to be like any organization just looking for profits. It had to be a grassroots struggle" (personal communication, 2007). Stop the Wall's resistance activities are also primarily land-based; the campaign emerged out of the Palestinian Environmental NGOs Network (PENGON), a collective of Palestinian environmental and agricultural NGOs, and its activities remain focused on supporting rural areas and agricultural villages. As Ahmed stated, "We needed to establish something national to support the farmers, especially those who depended on the land for generations" (personal communication, 2007). In the same way, Stop the Wall is committed to grounding its work in the local communities. Again, as Ahmed explained:

> The idea of Stop the Wall was to establish a network of popular committees and land defense committees. Each committee consists of 10 to 15 people who are the main contacts for Stop the Wall. They let us know what is going on locally, and we assist them by helping them get media coverage, sending internationals, and writing reports on our website [personal communication, 2007].

Ahmed pointed out that Stop the Wall goes beyond the strategies of protest and demonstrations. Indeed, the organization also conducts research on the effects of the wall and the occupation, assists villages and families in using the legal system to argue their cases, and encourages internationals to pressure their governments to support Palestinian rights. In 2005, the campaign also started a youth initiative, in which they offer courses at university campuses on the effects of the wall, the history of the Palestinian struggle, and the importance of strategies like boycotting, and they take youth on trips to other areas of the West Bank to see the effects of the wall. As Ahmed stated, "If we want to educate youth, we should teach them about the history of the struggle, about the leaders, and about why we have spent our lives fighting" (personal communication, 2007). In addition to the courses and trips, Stop the Wall involves youth in their research and documentation and supports students in organizing actions and campaigns at their universities.

Case study: Holy Land Trust

Holy Land Trust (HLT) is an NGO founded in Bethlehem in 1998 to encourage the use of nonviolence to resist the occupation, through community programs and local and international advocacy initiatives. HLT coordinates a number of projects, including the Palestine News Network (discussed in the following section), and travel and encounter programs for international visitors and activists. However, the projects most relevant to this section of the study consist of various nonviolence training programs. First, HLT organizes trainings for villages being affected by the wall and settlements. As Suheil, HLT's

Nonviolence Coordinator, explained, the trainings last three days and take place in the villages, so the people can see the situation on the ground and set up an action plan. The first day focuses on conflict analysis and applying different approaches to Israel-Palestine. The second day concentrates on understanding violence; as Suheil notes, "To understand nonviolence, you have to recognize violence. Some of the people practice nonviolence and don't know it is nonviolence. It's important to recognize violence and nonviolence so people can differentiate" (personal communication, 2007). The third day consists of exploring nonviolence in theory and practice, and the trainings conclude with developing an action plan and using role plays to see how proposed actions might play out in reality.

In addition to the village trainings, HLT offers short trainings on nonviolence in various youth centers and sports clubs, and helps to organize conferences and summer camps on nonviolence. HLT has also initiated a Training of Trainers (TOT) project, in which they provide in-depth nonviolence training to a group of 14 young people who work in pairs to provide nonviolence trainings and workshops in their respective local communities. According to Majdi, HLT's office manager, the goal of the TOT initiative is to spread the concept of nonviolent resistance to "build a nonviolent army in Palestine." As Majdi explained, "We don't just want to train people, we want them to lead, to develop an action plan, and to act" (personal communication, 2007). HLT thus focuses on nonviolence training and supports local villages in their direct actions and demonstrations.

Israeli and International Solidarity Organizations

Palestinian direct action in the West Bank has been supported by Israeli activist groups including Ta'ayush, Anarchists Against the Wall, Gush Shalom, the Israeli Committee Against Home Demolitions, and Peace Now, as well as by international groups such as the International Solidarity Movement (ISM), the Palestinian Solidarity Project, and Christian Peacemaker Teams (Norman, 2010). While the scope of this study does not allow for an in-depth discussion of these groups' participation, it is important to note their ongoing involvement in nonviolent direct action in the West Bank. Although Palestinian organizers have different opinions on the role of Israeli and international activists, most popular committees welcome their participation in a supportive capacity. In the immediate short-term, soldiers tend to use less violent measures when Israelis and internationals are present, and in the long-term, Israeli and international participation increases media attention and global publicity.

Political Parties

According to the majority of activists interviewed, Palestinian political groups have become increasingly institutionalized and dominated by elites who are often perceived as being out of touch with public sentiments. However, because most Palestinian parties emerged from political movement organizations that did rely on constituent mobilization in the past, these elements of contention still play a role in party dynamics, especially at the local level.

As noted previously, the majority of popular committees include representatives from various political parties. Despite the cleavages between parties at the top level, members of nearly all parties are represented in local events and joint actions, such as rallies and events on dates like May 15 (date of Israeli independence) and June 5 (date of the 1967 war and Israeli occupation of East Jerusalem, the West Bank, Gaza, the Sinai, and the Golan Heights). The parties also coordinate independent actions and support respective youth parties on university campuses. Indeed, many adult activists currently leading the popular committees first became involved in activism through the political youth movements.

Fateh remains one of the most prominent political parties, with Fateh Youth (formerly known as Al-Shabiba) constituting one of the main activist movements. According to Nidal, a spokesman for Fateh Youth, the organization aims to continue resistance against the Israeli occupation until a Palestinian state is declared, as well as develop Palestinian civil society and build Fateh membership. As Nidal indicates, Fateh Youth is instrumental in mobilizing young people through direct action strategies such as protest and persuasion:

> The main popular method of Fateh Youth resistance is demonstrations. In the beginning of the [second] intifada, Fateh Youth had demonstrations daily or weekly. Many of the actions were organized for the apartheid wall, checkpoints, campaigns to release prisoners, and solidarity with many people, especially Arafat, who was under siege, as well as people who were under curfew [personal communication, 2007].

According to Nidal, Fateh Youth coordination with other political movements varied, but at central campuses like Birzeit University, students participated in joint actions and demonstrations through June 2007, when Fateh and Hamas relations fractured.

While Hamas and Islamic Jihad, together referred to as the Islamic Block, openly support armed resistance, many of their members also support and participate in nonviolent actions. One Hamas official explained, "We need nonviolent resistance, first, because the world needs to hear us; second, because we are tired, we don't want to be in jail anymore, we want our prisoners to be released." (personal communication, 2007). As this statement illustrates, members of the Islamic Block participate in all forms of resistance, including nonviolent resistance, thus contributing to the wider sphere of protest and persuasion efforts.

Many smaller parties are also involved in popular resistance. Mubadara, headed by former Palestinian Authority minister of information Mustafa Barghouthi, organizes and actively participates in demonstrations against the wall. Many other activists subscribe to leftist parties like the Palestinian People's Party, which has advocated for land-based resistance through popular committees, and the Palestinian Popular Struggle Front, which has facilitated the Land Defense Committees, a sort of popular committee in rural areas. Political parties are distinct from popular committees and NGOs, but their contentious history in the Palestinian context still makes them influential actors in popular mobilization and participation, especially at the local level.

Alternative Media

According to Kriesi (1996), supportive organizations of social movements are institutions such as friendly media outlets, which "contribute to the social organization of the constituency of a given movement without directly taking part in the mobilization for collective action" (p.152). In Palestine, alternative media centers, documentary filmmakers, and participatory media initiatives contribute to this sort of consensus mobilization in that they often "work on behalf of the movement [and] their personnel may sympathize with the movement" (p. 152), but they utilize a more indirect approach to mobilization, through media. Though less direct, these efforts are still significant in the broader cycles of contention to raise awareness of both the issue and the movement, both locally and globally, thus using media as a persuasive tactic. The direct action campaigns and organizations mentioned above all rely heavily on media for drawing attention to violations, informing others about their efforts, and disseminating a call for nonviolent resistance.

Many Palestinians are critical of both the international mass media's coverage of Palestine, as well as Palestinians' efforts in negotiating that public sphere. As one activist noted, "Palestinians have failed in the media. We need to stop acting as victims and waiting for other countries to take action. Israel knows how to use the media, but Palestinians don't have much credibility.... We need to work more on owning our media" (personal communication, 2007). In response to this sentiment, several NGOs have launched their own independent news networks, including the Palestine News Network (PNN), launched in 2000 by Holy Land Trust; the International Middle East Media

Center (IMEMC), which grew out of the joint efforts of the Palestinian Centre for Rapprochement between Peoples (PCR) and the ISM in 2003[5]; Ma'an News Agency, launched in Bethlehem in 2005; and the Alternative Information Center (AIC), a Palestinian-Israeli activist organization that uses information for political advocacy.

These news groups have two main objectives, the first being to report on issues related to the occupation to tell another side of the Israel-Palestinian story that is often overlooked in the mainstream media. As Ghaleb, a reporter and producer for IMEMC, explains,

> We report on stories that you won't hear anywhere else. All the international news agencies have their correspondents based in Jerusalem, so they only hear one side of the news, or they only hear some of the stories.... We have a network of contacts who are actually in the field all over Palestine, and we try to present both sides of the story [personal communication, 2007].

The websites include updated news in multiple languages on developments within the West Bank and Gaza, and also maintain special sections on topics like refugees, prisoners, checkpoints, settlements, and incursions, while PNN and IMEMC host radio programs on timely issues and AIC produces publications based on more in-depth research.

PNN, IMEMC, and AIC also focus largely on nonviolent activism, which reflects their second objective of drawing attention to popular resistance efforts. As Majdi, one of the founders of PNN, stated:

> There are many kinds of nonviolent activities, but no one covers them. The [mainstream] media doesn't cover them regularly because they are not "exciting" without killing and shooting.... We want to show nonviolence, and we want to show it working. This is not for self-promotion, but to spread the message of nonviolence and publicize the activities. This is the power of nonviolence, and the media is essential for nonviolence [personal communication, 2007].

Ghaleb also noted that, like PNN, IMEMC aims to draw more attention to stories of nonviolent resistance:

> The mainstream news does not report on nonviolence, only violence. We do many nonviolent activities, but we are only in the news if someone dies, if there is blood. And this does not help the cause of nonviolence, because people just hear about the violence, and it reinforces it. It is good for people participating in nonviolence to see that their activities are being publicized. It reinforces what we are doing, and shows that it is making a difference [personal communication, 2007].

In documenting acts of nonviolence, as well as the violations and abuses that go unreported, these alternative news outlets thus contribute to both consensus formation and mobilization through their framings of both the issue and the movement, respectively. They provide affirmation and solidarity for local movement activists, while raising consciousness and prompting participation both locally and globally.

In addition to the groups mentioned above, individuals have also utilized media as a form of activism. For example, Raed, the media coordinator on Bil'in's popular committee, has documented the village's demonstrations with several objectives. First, as Raed explains, "Some of the footage has helped free people arrested in the demonstrations. Often the army will say they arrested someone for attacking the soldiers, but the footage often shows that was not the case, so the army has to release the activist" (personal communication, 2007). Second, Raed's footage has been important in getting the story of Bil'in out to the world, and attracting people from different countries to support the village. He has shared his footage with other news agencies, including Reuters, Al-Jazeera, Al-Arabiyya, and Israeli TV, and has also produced a documentary entitled *One Year of Peace and Resistance* that has been screened in several festivals, to draw attention to the situation in Bil'in and the village's nonviolent action campaign. In these ways, Raed identified media as a powerful form of resistance, commenting, "The camera isn't violent, but I can still use it as my weapon. It is a way to show what is happening in a nonviolent way" (personal communication, 2007).

Zeinab, another filmmaker, agreed, stating, "The best form of advocacy right now is the documentary, which helps the Palestinian story get out in the right way to the West.... When you see things you believe it" (personal communication, 2007). According to Zeinab, documentary media is a way of appealing to the international community by "sending our story in the right way" (personal communication, 2007) that appeals to universal values and uses the human rights frame. In these ways, documentary films function as tools for indirect mobilization by raising awareness, increasing solidarity, and prompting transnational activism.

Participatory media is a specific form of alternative media in which individuals and communities use photography, film, video, publications, websites, theater, and other forms of arts and media to share personal narratives and collective experiences, often with the goal of raising awareness about a specific issue or challenging dominant discourses in the mainstream media. Like alternative news networks and documentary films, participatory media projects can thus raise awareness, increase solidarity, and inspire action and movement participation through the introduction of new narratives. The Lajee Center in Aida Camp in Bethlehem is an example of just one of many community centers using media such as photography, film, and radio for creative advocacy.

Various sectors of civil society contribute to the cycle of nonviolent contention in Palestine. While some activists criticize the partial shift of activism from local communities to organizations, it is helpful to recognize the role of these campaigns, NGOs, political parties, and media outlets in both directly and indirectly contributing to popular resistance. These organizations' work further underlines the fact that, in addition to grassroots direct action, other nonviolent efforts are simultaneously focusing on mobilizing local populations and appealing to international networks, thus broadening the space for popular participation.

Sumoud

The majority of this essay has focused on direct action campaigns and civil society organizations like NGOs, media outlets, and youth groups that utilize the approaches of protest, persuasion, noncooperation, and intervention. However, it is also important to note the presence of everyday acts of resistance in Palestine, conducted by individuals and communities, employing the nonviolent tactic of *sumoud*, or steadfastness.

The development of consciousness and the will to resist can occur outside the scope of popular committees and civil society, particularly among peasant and rural communities. As Scott (1985) explains in *Weapons of the Weak*, daily experience is one of the most organic sources of consciousness development that leads to everyday acts of resistance. These acts reflect the tactics of relatively powerless groups, tactics such as "foot dragging, dissimulation, desertion, false compliance, pilfering, feigned ignorance, arson, sabotage, and so on" (p. xvi). As Scott continues, in contrast to more visible social movements, these forms of struggle "require little or no coordination or planning; they make use of implicit understandings and informal networks; they often represent a form of individual self-help; they typically avoid any direct, symbolic confrontation with authority" (p. xvi).

Everyday acts of resistance are often more a reflection of individual resilience and survival strategy than a deliberate effort to be part of a greater collective movement. Scott also explains, "Where institutionalized politics is formal, overt, concerned with systematic, *de jure* change, everyday resistance is informal, often covert, and concerned largely with immediate, *de facto* gains" (p. xv). Despite what may be more humble intentions however, everyday acts of resistance can have a powerful transformative effect when accumulated over time. As Scott writes, "such kinds of resistance are often the most significant and the most effective over the long run" (p. xvi). Indeed, although revolutions and social movements flow largely from dramatic large-scale processes, such movements are created and sustained by countless individual acts, both seen and unseen, that form the foundation for larger cycles of contention.

It is clear that everyday acts of resistance are complementary to, and indeed, inherent in, larger social movements. In the case of Palestine, this type of resistance includes staying on one's land and refusing to be moved. Within the West Bank, there were seemingly countless stories of daily acts of resistance and examples of sumoud during the second intifada. At the village level in particular, Palestinian farmers and their families have stayed on their land despite harassment from soldiers, abuses from settlers, and land confiscation from the separation wall and encroaching settlements and outposts. In this section, I provide two brief case studies to reflect the everyday land-based resistance tactics employed by Palestinians in West Bank villages.

Nahalin is a village near Bethlehem where the local Palestinian community has resolved to remain, despite Israeli threats of land confiscation. Alex, whose family's land is targeted for confiscation, has pursued various avenues to hold on to the land, including taking a case to the Israeli courts and calling for international solidarity. However, his main form of resistance is encouraging Palestinians to stay on the land. According to Alex, "Nonviolence is connected to the land. Without land, there is no future. Land is worth nothing without a people, and a people is worth nothing without land. So the land and the people should be connected" (personal communication, 2007). Alex started an organization to involve Palestinians, Israelis, and internationals in land-based resistance. The idea is to support local farmers, reconnect people with the land, and nurture a sense of self-sufficiency in Palestine. According to Alex, this type of land-based activism is useful in several ways. First, working the land is therapeutic for people: "When people dig, their frustration comes out. It helps them relax, and helps them think in another way" (personal communication, 2007). Second, working the land renews people's sense of hope by engaging them in something active and constructive. Third, in keeping the land populated and making it productive, Alex and others prevent it from being confiscated. In these ways, he and other villagers in Nahalin have made working the land a form of community empowerment and nonviolent resistance.

Ghwein is another small village consisting of eight families who live in caves on the southern border of the West Bank. The people are mainly shepherds and rely on the surrounding land for grazing. However, in the past 20 years, a number of settlements and outposts have been built in the area, including the large settlements Karmel, Mo'an, and Susya. The settlers, with the approval of the army, have taken much of the land in the region, including over 100 dunams (25 acres) from Ghwein, significantly reducing the land available for grazing. It has also limited access to the land on which the villagers produce beans and grains to feed the livestock, and perhaps more importantly, it has cut off the village from several wells and water sources.

The residents' very presence on the land is a form of resistance, according to Khaled, the director of a volunteer organization in Hebron that assists Ghwein with food, clothes, books, and medical care. Khaled notes that if the villagers left the area to avoid the encroaching settlements, Israel would take the land *ala tul*, meaning quickly and completely (personal communication, 2007). Ghwein is thus one of many villages in the West Bank in which people's steadfastness and determination to remain on their land function as a form of resistance.

Synthesis

This essay has described the state of nonviolent activism in the West Bank during the second intifada by providing examples of direct action campaigns; civil society-based initiatives coordinated by village popular committees, NGOs, dialogue groups, political parties, and media outlets; and everyday acts of resistance. It is important to note that these categories are not distinct, as many nonviolent efforts occur at various levels and employ multiple strategies; rather, these categories serve as an organizing framework for examining the scope of nonviolent resistance activities. It is also important to emphasize that these categories, and the examples discussed, are by no means exhaustive, but are instead a sampling of the nonviolent initiatives taking place in Palestine.

This mapping of nonviolent activities during the second intifada reveals several trends. First, it is evident that nonviolence was in fact utilized as a form of resistance during the second intifada. Although nonviolence never became as widespread of a phenomenon as it did during the first intifada, nonviolent actions were taking place consistently. Second, it is clear that there was a broad scope of nonviolent activities, with various groups and individuals becoming engaged in nonviolence in different ways. At the same time, within that scope, it is evident that the many actions were coordinated through organized groups, sometimes creating a tension between the organization and institutionalization of activism.

Third, while the breadth of nonviolent actions was notable during the second intifada, nearly all activists noted that most campaigns remained relatively localized and never constituted a full-fledged nonviolent movement to challenge the occupation. Indeed, the majority of actions were undertaken to address specific local grievances, such as the seizure of village land, or were conducted to raise awareness about Palestine outside the region, in a sort of boomerang approach to activism. The lack of a unified movement can be attributed to various causes, including political constraints from both Israel and the Palestinian Authority, international framings of nonviolence, and organizational shortcomings (Norman, 2010).

Nevertheless, despite its limitations in directly challenging the occupation, nonviolent resistance still had an impact at the local, regional, and international levels by expanding the space for popular participation. Indeed, nonviolent actions created opportunities for engagement in the struggle that many felt had been hijacked by armed groups or politicians. Many activists emphasized this point, noting that, "If you use just military action, you only have a few members, but with nonviolence you can get a lot of people involved" (personal communication, 2007). One activist used a series of concentric circles to illustrate this phenomenon, noting, "Just a very small percentage of the population will be willing to be suicide bombers or martyrs. Just slightly more will be willing to use guns. Then maybe using stones will bring slightly more. But with nonviolent resistance ... every person in the society can participate" (personal communication, 2007).

To be sure, at the local level, nonviolent methods, whether employed through direct actions, community organizations, media outlets, or sumoud, allowed for individuals from many different backgrounds to participate in the struggle. Regionally, nonviolent actions allowed for joint efforts between Palestinian and Israeli activists, organizations, and human rights groups. Internationally, nonviolent campaigns allowed for the direct participation of international activists, and also created new spaces for indirect support networks and solidarity groups to form and act in their own countries and communities. Furthermore, the nonviolent campaigns launched during the intifada are continuing to expand in the post-intifada context, with continued village demonstrations, growing BDS campaigns, additional legal cases, and increasing global awareness.

In these ways, nonviolent resistance during the second intifada was an important force in creating new spaces to work for a just peace in Israel-Palestine. First, nonviolent resistance broadened the scope of actors who were working to transform the conflict. Moving beyond top-level policymakers and government officials, nonviolence allowed for participation at all levels, both inside and outside the region. These grassroots movements and civil society networks helped ensure that diverse voices were heard and could influence, pressure, and persuade decision-makers in new ways. Second, nonviolent resistance brought attention to community issues and manifestations of the conflict at local levels, which might be overlooked in typical detached negotiations. Nonviolence thus provided a space for the inclusion of diverse actors and agendas that may not be a part of traditional conflict resolution processes, but are integral in transforming conflict dynamics.

NOTES

1. I use the terms "nonviolent resistance," "unarmed resistance," "civil resistance," and "popular resistance" interchangeably in my discussion. The term "nonviolence" is perhaps the most common word for Western readers; however, the Arabic word for nonviolence (*la'anf*) often has negative connotations, implying submission, passivity, and even normalization. For this reason, many Palestinian activists prefer the term "popular resistance" (*muqau'ama sha'abia*) to refer to actions and strategies considered to be "nonviolent" by activists elsewhere. For the purpose of this essay, both nonviolence and popular resistance refer to a set of tactics and behaviors that intend to change the other side's actions and policies without the use of arms.

2. In 2002, Israel began construction of the 723-kilometer long separation barrier, taking the form of a 6-to-8 meter concrete wall in some areas and barbed wire and electric fence in others. Though erected for "security purposes," the separation barrier was not built directly on the Green Line separating 1967 Israel and the West Bank, but rather snakes around, and sometimes through, Palestinian villages and towns within the West Bank. The route of the separation barrier was contested in the Israeli High Court of Justice in February 2004, with the court ruling that the route was illegal and needed to be changed, yet that ruling was not implemented. On July 9, 2004, the International Court of Justice (ICJ) in the Hague likewise ruled against the legality of the separation barrier and its route, calling for a cessation of construction, dismantling built portions, and compensating affected communities. The court's rulings are non-binding however, and the recommendations went unheeded. For more on the separation barrier, see http://www.btselem.org/english/Separation_Barrier/Index.asp.

3. All interviews were confidential. Names of participants have been changed or withheld by mutual agreement.

4. The Anti-Apartheid Wall Campaign started in October 2002, when construction of the wall first began. As the founder and coordinator of the campaign explained,

We started by visiting people in the affected areas to try to get a real sense of what was going on ... and started to bring things together.... We decided that the only way to respond was through resistance and confrontation. We decided on three main dimensions of work. First, documentation and research. Second, organizing local committees to function as local contact groups and to organize local activities. And third, contacting international delegations and sending them to affected villages [personal communication, 2007].

5. IMEMC grew out of the PCR, an action-oriented NGO that has functioned as a dialogue group and an activist organization, and was the primary Palestinian group involved in the development of ISM. Indeed, IMEMC grew out of the Palestine Media Alert Project that PCR coordinated with ISM. In 2001, PCR started utilizing ISM activists' stories, photos, and footage as alternative information sources on their website, to counter the stories given to the mainstream media by Israeli military reporters, then moved the reports and images to the ISM website in 2002.

REFERENCES

Ackerman, P., and C. Kruegler (1994). *Strategic nonviolent conflict: The dynamics of people power in the twentieth century.* Westport, CT: Praeger.

Asser, M. (2007). "West Bank village hails victory." http://news.bbc.co.uk/2/hi/middle_east/6979923.stm (accessed 5 September 2007).

Dajani, M. (1997). *The concept of civil society*. Jerusalem: PASSIA.
Helvey, R. (2004). *On strategic nonviolent conflict: Thinking about the fundamentals*. Boston: Albert Einstein Institution.
Kriesi, H. (1996). The organizational structure of new social movements in a political context. In D. McAdam, J.D. McCarthy, and M.N. Zald (Eds.), *Comparative perspectives on social movements: Political opportunities, mobilizing structures, and cultural framings*. New York: Cambridge University Press.
Norman, J.M. (2010). *The second Palestinian intifada: Civil resistance*. London: Routledge.
Scott, J.C. (1985). *Weapons of the weak*. New Haven: Yale University Press.
Sharp, G. (1973). *The politics of nonviolent action*. Boston: Porter Sargent.

"If You Use Nonviolence, I Will Respond with Nonviolence": The 2007 Pattani Protest in Southern Thailand[1]

Janjira Sombatpoonsiri

In studies of nonviolent action or civil resistance, there is a dearth of examples of reciprocal "nonviolent conflict," in which all parties to the conflict opt for nonviolent methods. The majority of the literature focuses on the way in which the so-called powerless employ nonviolent methods to overthrow a dictator, oust a foreign occupier, or change racial discrimination policies (Sharp, 1973; Ackerman & Kruegler, 1994; Zunes et al., 1999; Schock, 2005; Martin, 2007; Roberts & Ash, 2009; Stephan, 2009; Stephan & Chenoweth, 2011). Although Sharp (2005, p. 413) acknowledges cases of "counter-nonviolent action" staged by the state apparatus, little attention has been paid to these cases. The 2007 Pattani demonstration, however, provides such a case study, even amid a larger backdrop of armed conflict between the Thai state and Malay Muslim militants.

Thailand's southernmost provinces — namely Pattani, Yala, and Narathiwat — have been the site of armed and unarmed struggle between the Thai state and the Malay Muslims since the annexation of the Patani Kingdom into Siam (the former name of the Kingdom of Thailand) in 1909.[2] The "colonization" — which was followed by series of abuses by Thai authorities and cultural assimilation policies — has been responded to with waves of resistance by both Malay Muslim elites and ordinary people. Prior to the 1990s, the

Thai state relied heavily on scorched-earth military policies which only played into the hands of the Malay Muslim separatist groups (Bang-Nara, 1973; Surin, 1985; Chaiwat, 1986, 2005; Serajul Islam, 1998). The 1990s saw the Thai government's shift to a political approach in dealing with the southern unrest (Mark & Somkiet, 2008). Nevertheless, the armed resistance was re-ignited when former Prime Minister Thaksin Shinnawatra returned to heavy-handed security measures and changed the existing power structure in the area (Kasian, 2006; McCargo, 2006). Many believe that the militants' raid on the army depot in Narathiwat province in 2004 started the re-emergence of armed struggle which, until December 2010, took approximately 4,500 lives ("Statistics of Southern Thailand Unrest," 2010). Despite the initiation of some measures for long-term conflict transformation, such as the appointment of the National Reconciliation Commission in 2004 and the re-establishment of the local governance body (the Southern Border Provinces Administration Centre, or SBPAC) in 2007, the armed conflict lingers on.

Despite the perception that the conflict in southern Thailand is strictly violent, methods of nonviolent action have been employed by ordinary Malay Muslims in their resistance against injustice inflicted by the Thai state. The history of nonviolent action can be dated back to the period of early occupation, when, among other examples, Thai officials deployed from Bangkok faced massive noncooperation from Malay Muslim elites. Later, in 1948, Hayi Solung Abdulkader, the then spiritual leader, proposed seven demands to the Thai government in regard to the exercise of political, economic, and cultural autonomy in the old Patani Kingdom, threatening to boycott the next election if the government did not meet these demands (Surin, 1985, pp. 158–61). The first recorded mass demonstration took place in 1975–1976 for 45 days; it was attended by roughly 10,000 Malay Muslims and was dissolved by military force despite the fact that the majority of participants remained peaceful (Arong, 1973, p. 12; Chaiwat, 2001, pp. 195–211). During the 1990s, two nonviolent protests were carried out in response to government policies that banned the wearing of headscarves by women in schools and universities, and the registration of the most respected mosque as a tourist site (Chaiwat, 2005, pp. 60–100).

Even when the armed conflict re-escalated in 2004, nonviolent protest remained a crucial means for Malay Muslim villagers to voice their grievances. While the protest at Takbai in Narathiwat province in October 2004 ended with bloodshed — six protesters were shot dead and 78 deaths were caused by suffocation during detainee transportation to the army camp (National Reconciliation Commission, 2006, p. 47; International Crisis Group, 2007, p. 6; Janjira & Naree, 2007, p. 16) — nonviolent protesters were not deterred. Some estimates register 36 protests in the first half of 2007; the number reached its peak between May 31 and June 4, with the largest mass demonstration held within the terrain of the Pattani provincial mosque (Srisompop, 2007). Based on in-depth interviews with protest organizers and protesters, local authorities handling the demonstration, and mediators,[3] and through the collection of protest materials, official documents, and news reports, this essay describes in detail this event and analyzes its politics of nonviolent conflict.

The 2007 Pattani Protest: An Overview

On May 31, 2007, between 8,000 and 10,000 Malay Muslims from the southernmost provinces of Thailand staged a mass demonstration in front of the provincial mosque in downtown Pattani, the capital of the province. The demonstration was led by a coalition of university students from Bangkok and Pattani, dubbed the Student Network to Protect the People. Students, on behalf of the demonstrators, proposed 10 demands to the army and government, focusing on the withdrawal of military and paramilitary troops — which protesters claimed was an underlying cause of southern unrest. They also requested that authorities allegedly involved in at least 21 cases of unlawful detention, torture, and extrajudicial persecution of Malay Muslim villagers between February and June 2007, be held accountable for their misconduct (Student Network to Protect the People, 2007a, 2007b). The final incident that was perceived as the catalyst of the mass protest was the killing of a family and the rape of the daughter, Nurhayadi Jehloh, in Yala province on May 22, 2007 (student leader A, personal communication, January 20, 2008; student leader B, personal communication, January 20, 2008; Ramdon, 2007, p. 12; Crisis Group, 2007, pp. 10–3).

On the one hand, student leaders believed that the cases of state abuse precipitated the widespread outrage among Malay Muslims, who might resort to violence to resist injustice. Accordingly, they explained that staging a nonviolent protest was necessary to provide people a channel to demand justice from the state (student leader A, personal communication, January 20, 2008; student leader B, personal communication, January 20, 2008). On the other hand, state authorities perceived the demonstration as masterminded by the armed resistance groups, their aim being to worsen the image of the Thai state among Malay Muslims and galvanize the mass support to further their course of resistance. High-ranking officials, therefore, associated students with the militant movements and claimed villagers were paid or deceived to participate in the protest ("Pickets Emerged around Pattani," 2007).

In the first two days of the demonstration, there was a lack of communication between protesters and authorities, as student leaders concentrated on dealing with the increasing number of participants and organizing activities to keep numbers at critical mass (Ramdon, 2007, p. 10). Tension was heightened on June 2, when villagers from other districts in Pattani province traveled to the city center of Pattani to attend the protest — but their entry into the city area was prevented by cordons of soldiers and riot police ("Bombing in Bannagsta," 2007). Concurrently, official negotiations were initiated by the Pattani governor, the chief commander of the Pattani metropolitan police station, the chief of the Pattani military unit, and protest organizers. Politicians and representatives from civil society provided assistance as mediators and negotiation conveners ("Buddhists-Muslims," 2007). On June 3, Buddhist and Muslim residents in the city organized a counter-rally, requesting that protesters end the demonstration because they were obstructing traffic in the city and damaging local business ("Bombing in Bannagsta," 2007; "Buddhists-Muslims," 2007; "Schools in the South Burned Down Again," 2007).

The following day, the negotiation concluded as stakeholders agreed to establish the Commission to Investigate Cases of Injustice. The commissioners included key figures of the government, parliamentary members, the southern army chief, the southern police commander, governors of three southern provinces, human rights lawyers, and peace activists (Internal Security Operation [ISO], 2007). The demonstration was, subsequently, discontinued ("Schools in the South Burned Down Again," 2007). While state authorities and mediators claimed that the halting of the protest was the result of negotiation, student leaders insisted that it was their initial plan to terminate the demonstration on the fifth day (student leader A, personal communication, 2008).[4]

Despite the discrepancy in the perception of how the protest was brought to a bloodless end, information derived from authorities present at the protest site and student leaders underscores the argument that methods of nonviolent action utilized by Malay Muslim protesters and the nonviolent response of the Thai authorities was crucial in the resolution of the situation without the use of violent means.

Nonviolent Actions

During the course of the five-day mass demonstration, protesters carried out a wide range of nonviolent street actions, using strategic protest sites and maintaining leadership and nonviolent discipline. Due to the nonviolent character of the protest, authorities were compelled to respond with a non-confrontational style of policing. When tension caused by the lengthy stand-off rose, student leaders sought a channel to communicate with the authorities. Similarly, the authorities were conscious of the political necessity of dealing with peaceful protesters through a process of communication and negotiation.

Nonviolent actions staged by protesters

The existing community structure and students' mobilization serves as an explanation for the large number of Malay Muslims participating in the Pattani protest. According to student leaders, their initial intention was not to stage a demonstration, but rather to organize a workshop seminar on issues of justice and human rights violations (student leader A, personal communication, January 20, 2008; Ramdon, 2007, p. 13). However, as they arrived at the provincial mosque, the venue of the workshop, they found thousands of villagers expecting them. Villagers told students they were outraged by stories of state abuse of their fellow Malay Muslims over the past six months, especially the alleged rape in Yala province. When the news that students would raise such injustices to state officials was spread in coffee shops, Islamic sermons on Friday, and daily family conversation, villagers from different areas came to the mosque. It was the existing village structure and communitarian culture which facilitated the assembly of people at the mosque without much organized mobilization (student leader A, personal communication, January 20, 2008; Bahroon, 2007, pp. 78–9; Scott, 1990).

The Pattani provincial mosque was used as a protest site due to its religious, political, and historical meaning. While it is common knowledge that mosques are religious sites, the president of the Pattani Islamic Committee affirmed that the use of mosques for public assembly is typical within Muslim communities (personal communication, January 5, 2008). This view confirms Chaiwat's (2001; 2010) assertion that the stark boundary between religious and secular life for Muslims barely exists. Historically, the Pattani provincial mosque was the site of the 45-day demonstration in 1975–1976, remembered as the most crucial nonviolent Malay-staged uprising against the Thai state. Student leaders pointed out that such a historical connection encouraged them to use the mosque again as a protest site (student leader A, personal communication, January 20, 2008; Ramdon, 2007, p. 13).

Student leadership, nonviolent discipline, and the implementation of security measures prevented the state's coercive response. In terms of leadership, seven students were selected as representatives from several universities. They constituted members of an ad hoc board for decision-making, which initiated seven rules to maintain the discipline of protesters. These rules included: the following of rules of protest introduced by the ad hoc board; staying within the security area, which was divided into four zones, each zone monitored by 30 to 40 students; the prohibition of any act of sabotage done to public property; the hygienic maintenance of the protest site; and the preservation of peaceful behavior. The ad hoc board, in addition, put together plans for daily activities, ranging from public speeches and collective praying, to cultural and theatrical performances (such as traditional Malay group singing, and Malay/Southern folk musical theater performance, or *Likae Hulu*), as well as leaflet distribution and rallies. Key student leaders also represented protesters in the negotiations with officials (student leader A, personal communication, January 20, 2008; student protester C, personal communication, January 20, 2008).

The collective chanting of *Allahu Akbar* ("God is Great") constituted the vital symbolic action of the Pattani nonviolent protest. The purpose of the chanting, a student leader explained, was to boost the morale of protesters and create a sense of solidarity. Expressed differently, the Islamic chanting became the protesters' marker of identity, reminding them of their position of being a Malay Muslim living in a Thai-Buddhist state.[5] For the Thai authorities, from a Buddhist background, such chanting was unfamiliar, its spiritual meaning non-existent in their worldview. This possibly explains why the Thai authorities felt that protesters were intimidating while they were chanting (former Pattani governor, personal communication, January 4, 2008; former Pattani deputy governor, personal communication, January 6, 2008; former chief of the Pattani military unit, personal communication, January 23, 2008).

For security purposes, roughly 200 male students teamed up as security guards. They were divided into four teams according to the arrangement of the protest site, encircling protesters in each zone to prevent the infiltration of agitators. One student leader pointed out that such a presence potentially provided a positive image of villagers, who, as mentioned previously were often perceived by the authorities as sympathizers of militant groups (student leader A, personal communication, January 20, 2008). Apart from escorting protesters during the rally, these security guards were also assigned to accompany those wanting to leave the protest site for their homes (student leader A, personal communication, January 20, 2008).

The public relations campaign launched by student leaders was crucial in countering the state's attempt to defame the protesters. Beginning on the second day of the demonstration, students from the security team went to four mosques in Pattani city and talked to residents to determine public opinion of the protest. According to both a student leader in charge of a security team and a mediator, people in one neighborhood were too afraid to show their support for the protest. Nevertheless, students constantly received food and water from residents in Pattani city. Some locals were even in tears after hearing stories of their Malay Muslim fellows in remote areas being abused by the military (student leader A, personal communication, January 20, 2008;

student leader B, personal communication, January 20, 2008; student protester D, personal communication, January 20, 2008; Niraman, 2007).

Student leaders were aware that negotiation and bargaining with authorities was also needed in order to abate the heightened tension caused by the stand-off. The official process of negotiation can be a mechanism to end protest without bloodshed, but it can also reproduce the imbalance of power among the conflict parties, thus silencing the protestors. Consequently, official negotiation potentially undermines the root causes of the conflict. In the case of the Pattani protest, the negotiation concentrated on the protestors' demands. Some could not be met — for example, the withdrawal of troops or the revocation of the emergency decree, which had to be dealt with on the national policy level. Yet, local authorities conceded to the request for the investigation of 20 alleged cases of state abuse and set up the Committee to Investigate Cases of Injustice. In addition, they guaranteed that protest leaders and participants would not face charges or subsequent threats, since the protest was staged peacefully and within the constitutional right of freedom of expression ("The Path to the Pattani Provincial Mosque's Seizure," 2007, p. 11).[6]

Despite its potential to address underlying causes of the conflict in southern Thailand, the Committee to Investigate Cases of Injustice was short-lived. It had no budget from the government, and there was no will from state authorities to accomplish the mandate. A student leader revealed that while the students attended meetings at their own expense, state representatives were always absent. As the committee became increasingly idle, key figures resigned (ISO, 2007). Accordingly, a student leader viewed the establishment of the committee as merely instrumental, aimed at the time to disband the demonstration without the use of force, rather than a legitimate means to address the injustice that stands at the heart of the conflict (student leader A, personal communication, January 20, 2008).

Bargaining, in the context of the Pattani protest, connotes the process wherein authorities and protesters sought to communicate with one another to find common ground on logistical issues that could facilitate and prolong the use of nonviolent methods during the demonstration. These issues ranged from the provision of food and water, health services, and access to office facilities (such as a printer for leaflets and statements distributed at the protest site). The bargaining process was most evident during the rally on the fourth day of the protest. A protest leader in charge of public relations and students from the security team, together with around 300 protesters, announced that they would march from the provincial mosque to the biggest shopping mall in downtown Pattani, a distance of 1 kilometer. When student leaders informed authorities of their plan, authorities initially prohibited the rally, claiming they could not provide the adequate security for the marchers and that provocateurs might take the opportunity to attack them and then blame authorities for such action. As student leaders insisted on going ahead with the march, the authorities asked if they could walk from the mosque to a petrol station at the entrance of downtown, instead of the shopping mall. Student leaders agreed. When they reached the petrol station, they began further bargaining with authorities to be allowed to march to the intersection near the shopping mall. They explained that there were more communities living close to downtown, and contacting them was important to provide them with a better understanding of the aims and demands of protesters. By allowing them to do so, the authorities could also show their benign image to Malay Muslims (student leader B, personal communication, January 20, 2008). The authorities agreed, but on the condition that the use of megaphones and speakers, and the distribution of leaflets, was prohibited. The march then continued without the use of speakers or megaphones, as promised to the authorities. Instead, they collectively chanted "Allahu Akbar." This example demonstrates the way in which a bargaining process enables the continuation of the struggle between conflict parties in which minor concessions are made in order to facilitate the nonviolent protest.

The state's non-confrontational response

The ways in which local authorities dealt with the Pattani protest can be classified as military, service offer, and negotiation and bargaining. The first is characterized by the presence of troops at the protest site and other security measures. Approximately 200 soldiers, riot police, and paramilitary units (*Taharn Phran*) were stationed around the Pattani provincial mosque and intersections downtown (former deputy commander of the Pattani metropolitan police station, personal communication, January 31, 2008). Riot control equipment was prepared for the potential dispersion of the protest, yet the deputy commander of the Pattani metropolitan police station assured that force would not be used against peaceful protesters (former deputy commander of the Pattani metropolitan police station, personal communication, January 31, 2008; "Why was the Pattani Protest Brought to an End?" 2007). Each day, before the beginning of protest activities, the authorities checked the bags and belongings of newcomers in order to preclude any chance of the infiltration of agitators (former deputy commander of the Pattani metropolitan police station, personal communication, January 31, 2008; former chief of the Pattani Military Unit, personal communication, January 4, 2008). Another measure included the deployment of female paramilitary units in handling female protesters. In doing so, authorities could avoid physical contact between male soldiers and female protesters, which could be perceived by Muslim communities as a cultural offense (former chief of the Pattani Military Unit, personal communication, January 4, 2008). Despite the military dimension of policing in the Pattani case, it was the service offer and practice of negotiation and bargaining that set the scene for the state's non-confrontational response to the demonstration.

Authorities' offering of service for protesters opened a window of communication between protesters and state agents, thereby paving the way for the negotiation process. Local authorities made sure that throughout the five days of protest, water and electricity were provided for protesters and food was offered. When the march to the business area of Pattani was carried out, the authorities also arranged for a minivan to escort marchers if needed and to transport those who fainted to the medical service center (former deputy commander of the Pattani metropolitan police station, personal communication, January 31, 2008; former chief of the Pattani Military Unit, personal communication, January 4, 2008). At some stages, authorities allowed students to access computer and printing facilities to reproduce leaflets distributed at the protest site (president of the Pattani Islamic Committee, personal communication, January 5, 2008; Soraya Chamjuree, personal communication, January 6, 2008). Reportedly, when the protest was over, officials even offered transportation for protesters to return to their homes ("Analysing the Pattani Demonstration," 2007).

However, students turned down offers such as water and food, afraid they might be poisoned (student leader A, personal communication, January 20, 2008; student leader B, personal communication, January 20, 2008). While the genuine intention of the authorities in providing service was highly doubted by protesters, the offer for service in many ways opened up an opportunity for communication between protest leaders, authorities, and mediators. These daily issues were petty enough for protest leaders and authorities to find common ground for agreement. At the same time, the constant contact challenged existing prejudices among conflict parties.[7] Thai authorities were seen as individuals who might not always be allied with the Thai state ideology, and were disassociated from the misconduct of other state officials. Authorities could likewise observe that Malay Muslim dissidents were not necessarily sympathetic to armed resistance groups. In this sense, the offer of service enabled circumstances that made possible the formal negotiation process.

The formal channel of negotiation became the instrument to dissolve the demonstration without the use of force. The establishment of the Committee to Investigate Cases of Injustice enabled local authorities to fulfill the protesters' demand for the state to investigate alleged cases of human rights violations, while bypassing other demands related to security policies. The former Pattani governor pointed out that the establishment of the committee was meant to deal with the psychology of the crowd, lessening the anger of the people at the time by convincing them that their demand was taken care of by the state. This psychosocial approach to official negotiation let the authorities address the situation without the use of force, thus avoiding a crackdown which would have only played into the hands of militants and undermined the effort to stabilize the southernmost region (former chief of the Pattani military unit, personal communication, January 4, 2008).

Officials' willingness to make a concession with protesters in regard to details of their street activities fostered the nonviolent aspect of the protest instead of halting the protest. This was a bargaining process facilitated by dialogue. As delineated earlier, the most evident example of the bargaining process can be discerned from the staging of the march on June 3, when student leaders agreed to march without megaphones and instead chanted, "Allahu Akbar." The security authorities were unsure of how to deal with the chanting protesters. The former Pattani governor commented that the protesters' activities distinguished them from a "Thai" identity, and to him, the demonstration would have been more legitimate had the participants worn yellow T-shirts to display their loyalty to the king or waved the flag of Thailand (personal communication, January 4, 2008). The then deputy governor of Pattani province similarly noted that the expression of "Thai-ness" was completely absent in the Pattani protest, thus confirming the officials' perception that the demonstration was masterminded by militants. Therefore, as a state representative in the negotiation process, he reminded student leaders that the southernmost provinces belong to Thailand, and that separatism was not an option (personal communication, January 6, 2008). These comments reflect the culturally entrenched nature of the conflict, manifest through the 2007 Pattani demonstration. The bargaining process, in this sense, allows not only the continuation of nonviolent struggle between Thai authorities and Malay Muslim protesters, but also the ongoing clash and the need to come to terms with differing Thai and Malay identities.[8]

The non-confrontational policing of the Pattani protest should be contextualized in the government's political approach to solving the southern Thailand conflict at the time. The coup d'état in 2006 that toppled former Prime Minister Thaksin Shinnawatra ironically made possible the policies that recognize and tackle problems of injustice underlying southern unrest. The interim government under the leadership of General Surayut Chulanon re-established the SBPAC, the key local governance body founded in the 1990s and dissolved during the Thaksin administration.[9] Other crucial moves (a nationally televised apology for victims of a 2004 protest, the revocation of a blacklist for suspected insurgent sympathizers, and an order which highlighted the nonviolent movement in the south)[10] were conducted in parallel with the Thai army's nonviolent counter-insurgency strategy of "winning the hearts and minds" of Malay Muslims.

Within the framework of this strategy, high-ranking authorities from Bangkok were aware that political momentum would shift to militant groups if any violence was carried out against unarmed protesters. General Sonthi Boonratklin, chair of the National Security Council that spearheaded the coup d'état in 2006, stressed that the use of force to disperse protesters was strictly prohibited. Furthermore, the prime minister pointed out that because of existing injustice, it should not be assumed that all protesters were manipulated by militant groups ("Analysing the Pattani Demonstration," 2007). The image of the Thai state perceived by the Malay Muslim population would be further tarnished, worsening the legitimacy of the state to govern the region ("Bombing in Bannagsta," 2007). Aree Wong-Araya, then interior minister shared this viewpoint, stating that "...the Government has to handle [the protest] without the use of force. We need to win over the mass, and hinder the hatred [of Malay Muslims toward the Thai state]. Otherwise, we will not have anyone on board with us" ("Twenty Two Corpses," 2007).

Conclusion

This essay offered a thorough account of a nonviolent encounter between Malay Muslim protesters and Thai state authorities between May 31 and June 4, 2007. The protestors manifested consistent employment of nonviolent action, strong leadership, and discipline in undertaking street demonstrations to express their grievances and demand justice — despite the operation elsewhere of armed resistance groups and a pending threat of military crackdown. By maintaining the nonviolent characteristic of the protest, demonstrators weakened any possible state justification for a military crackdown and earned them legitimate ground for their struggle, as well as sympathy from facets of society that may have previously ignored or discounted their grievances.

The state's non-confrontational methods of protest policing indicated that — regardless of its monopoly on violent means — it can rely on nonviolent counter-action as a political response to nonviolent action staged by the people. Aware of the potential for slowing political momentum for militant groups by resisting the urge to respond violently, local officials in Pattani province and policymakers from Bangkok implemented measures of service offering and negotiation and bargaining. They believed that these measures could work to win the hearts and minds of the Malay Muslim population, thereby supplying the state with more legitimacy to govern the southernmost region. Due to these characteristics, the 2007 Pattani demonstration exemplifies a type of nonviolent conflict in which nonviolence is used by all sides of the conflict in the pursuit of their struggle. The case, perhaps more importantly, demonstrates that nonviolence can serve as an alternative to the heightened armed conflict in southern Thailand.

NOTES

1. The essay is based on the author's master's degree research paper submitted to the International Studies Program (Peace and Conflict Resolution), University of Queensland, Australia. It is also part of a research project on "Violence, Nonviolence, and Thai Society," funded by the Thailand Research Fund.

2. Throughout this essay, the spelling of Patani refers to the original spelling of the Patani Kingdom, while that of "Pattani" refers to Pattani as a province of Thailand after the annexation in the early 19th century.

3. For safety reasons, the names of interviewees are not revealed. Ranks of authorities are indicated, but names of student leaders and protesters are replaced with pseudonyms.

4. However, there is a discrepancy between that interview and students' final statement. While the student leader insisted that the termination of the protest on the fifth day was their initial plan, their final statement points out that the emergence of the Buddhist counter-rally and their concern about a clash between the two groups was the reason for them to call off the demonstration (Student Network to Protect the People, 2007c).

5. Numerous references in the literature regarding the southern Thailand conflict demonstrate how the Malay identity of people in the old Patani Kingdom is closely tied with being a Muslim. The kingdom was once a cradle of Islam in Southeast Asia. In the southernmost provinces, when people identify themselves as Malay they implicitly refer to themselves as Muslims. The same logic can be applied to understand the way in which Malay Muslims in southernmost provinces perceive somebody as being Thai, in that being Thai is implicitly attached to being Buddhist. For further discussion about the politics of identity in southern Thailand, see Surin (1985, pp. 229–58); Scupin (1998); Horstmann (2004); and Alisa and Dusadao (2005).

6. This agreement was made and recorded in written form prior to the end of the protest. However, a student leader claimed that despite the agreement, one of the leaders was detained in an army camp when he returned to his hometown in Narathiwat province. It was also reported that an imam was shot dead by an unidentified militant the day after he gave a speech supporting the protesters.

7. Existing literature in protest policing also suggests that contact between protest organizers and police officers can bridge the gap of perception, thereby decreasing the possibility of authorities' use of force to break down the demonstration. See Porta (1996, 1997); Porta & Reiter (1998); McPhail, Schweingruber, & McCarthy (1998); and Schweingruber (2000).

8. Numerous studies on the southern Thailand conflict point out that the clash of Thai and Malay Muslim identities is not the fixed feature of the conflict. Thai society, at times, accommodates practices of Muslim and Malay-ness as a cultural identity, while Malay Muslims negotiate their identity in order to co-exist with the Thai nation-state. Therefore, negotiated identity demonstrates both resolved and ongoing cultural struggles between the Thai state and Malay Muslims in the south (Chaiwat, 2005, pp. 60–77).

9. However, the renewed SBPAC operated under the command of the Internal Security Operation Centre (ISOC). In December 2010, parliament passed a bill for SBPAC to be directly subordinate to the prime minister, not the army (

10. The political approach of General Surayut soon shifted to the military-oriented approach after June 2007, when the military search-and-cordon operation to uproot networks of militant groups was implemented (Danai, 2008).

REFERENCES

Ackerman, P., and C. Kruegler (1994). *Strategic nonviolent conflict: The dynamics of people power in the twentieth century.* Westport, CT: Praeger.
Alisa, H., and L. Dusadao (2005). *Research paper on the identity of Malay Muslims: Areas of conflict and negotiation.* Bangkok: National Reconciliation Commission.
Analysing the Pattani demonstration. (2007, June 28). *Khao Sod,* p. 10.
Arong, S. (1973). *The problem of the conflict in southern border provinces of Thailand.* Bangkok: Pithak Pracha.
Bahroon. (2007, June 12). Observations on the demonstration at the Pattani provincial mosque. *The Nation Weekly,* pp. 78–79.
Bang-Nara, A. (1973). *Patani: From past to present.* Bangkok: Saeng Tien Club.
Bombing in Bannagsta: 20 young men dead and 3 injured. (2007, June 3). *Kom Chad Luk,* p. 5.
Buddhists-Muslims. (2007, June 4). *Matichon,* pp. 12, 15.
Chaiwat, S. (1986). *Islam and Violence.* Tampa: Department of Religious Studies, University of South Florida.
_____. (2001). The nonviolent crescent: Eight theses on Muslim nonviolent action. In A.A. Said, N.C. Funk and A.S. Kadayifci (Eds.), *Peace and conflict resolution in Islam: Precept and practice.* New York: University Press of America (pp. 195–211).
_____. (2005). *The life of this world: Negotiated Muslim lives in Thai society.* Singapore: Marshall Cavendish.
_____. (2010). Movements of sacred topographies: Mosques as sites of violence/nonviolence in southern Thailand. Paper presented at the International Peace Research Association Commission, Sydney, Australia.
Danai, M. (2008). *Policies and strategies in resolving southern Thailand unrest implemented by the administration of General Surayut Chulanon.* Bangkok: World Bank.
Horstmann, A. (2004). Ethnohistorical perspectives on Buddhist-Muslim relations and coexistence in southern Thailand: From shared cosmos to the emergence of hatred? *Sojourn,* 18(1), 76–99.
Internal Security Operation, 4th Region. (2007). The establishment of the Committee to Investigate Cases of Injustice, Order 214/2007.
International Crisis Group. (2007). *Southern Thailand: The impact of the coup.* Retrieved from www.crisisgroup.org/en/regions/asia/south-east-asia/thailand/129-southern-thailand-the-impact-of-the-coup.aspx.
Janjira, S., and C. Naree (Eds.). (2007). *Takbai in the air: The unrecognized memory.* Bangkok: Peace Research Institute, Mahidol University, and Pusaidad Publishing.
Kasian, T. (2006). Toppling Thaksin. *New Left Review,* 39, 5–37.
Mark, T., and B. Somkiet (2008). The comparative study of national security policies in 30 years. In Chaiwat S. (Ed.), *Imagined land.* Bangkok: Matichon Publishers (pp. 53–105).
Martin, B. (2007). *Justice ignited: The dynamics of backfire.* Lanham, MD: Rowman & Littlefield.
McCargo, D. (2006). Thaksin and the resurgence of violence in the Thai south. *Critical Asian studies,* 38(1), 39–71.
McPhail, C., D. Schweingruber, and J.D. McCarthy (1998). Policing protest in the United States: 1960–1995. In D. Porta and H. Reiter (Eds.), *Policing protest: The control of mass demonstrations in Western democracies.* Minneapolis: University of Minnesota Press (pp. 49–69).
National Reconciliation Commission. (2006). *Report of the National Reconciliation Commission: Overcoming violence through the power of reconciliation.* Bangkok: National Reconciliation Commission.

New Era of SBPAC. (2011, February 11). *Thairath*, p. 2.
Niraman, S. (2007). *The Report of the Pattani Protest*. Bangkok: Special Committee on the Investigation and Study of Southern Border Province Insurgency, the National Assembly.
The path to the Pattani provincial mosque's seizure. (2007, June). *Kampong*, pp. 10–11.
Pickets emerged around Pattani: The governor led negotiation with picketers, being afraid of worsening situation. (2007, June 2). *Khom Chad Luk*, p. 10.
Porta, D. (1996). Social movements and the state: Thoughts on the policing of protest. In D. McAdam, J. McCarthy, and M. Zald (Eds.), *Comparative perspectives on social movements*. Cambridge: Cambridge University Press (pp. 62–92).
_____. (1997). The policing of protest. *African Studies, 56*(1), 97–127.
_____, and H. Reiter (Eds.). (1998). *Policing protest: The control of mass demonstrations in Western democracies*. Minneapolis: University of Minnesota Press.
Ramdon, P. (2007, June). Student leaders talked openly about their mission to "seize" the Pattani provincial mosque. *Kampong*, pp. 10–12.
Roberts, A., and T.G. Ash (Eds.). (2009). *Civil resistance and power politics: The experience of non-violent action from Gandhi to the present*. Oxford: Oxford University Press.
Schock, K. (2005). *Unarmed insurrections: People power movements in nondemocracies*. Minneapolis: University of Minnesota Press.
Schools in the south burned down again. (2007, June 4). *Thai Rath*, p. 19.
Schweingruber, D. (2000). Mob sociology and escalated force: Sociology's contribution in repressive police tactics. *The Sociological Quarterly, 41*(3), 371–389.
Scott, J. (1990). *Domination and the arts of resistance*. New Haven: Yale University Press.
Scupin, R. (1998). Muslim accommodation in Thai society. *Journal of Islamic studies, 9* (2), 229–258.
Serajul Islam, S. (1998). The Islamic independence movements in Patani of Thailand and Mindanao of the Philippines. *Asian Survey, 38*(5), 441–456.
Sharp, G. (1973). *The politics of nonviolent action*. Boston: Porter Sargent.
_____. (2005). *Waging nonviolent struggle*. Boston: Porter Sargent.
Srisompop, C. (2007). Forty months of violence: The extreme of reasoning and reconciliation. Retrieved from www.deepsouthwatch.org/matcharticle.php?id=16.
Statistics of southern Thailand unrest, from January 4, 2004 to December 28, 2010. (2010, 29 December). *Isara News*. Retrieved from http://www.deepsouthwatch.org/node/1200.
Stephan, M.J. (Ed.). (2009). *Civilian jihad: Nonviolent struggle, democratization, and governance in the Middle East*. New York: Palgrave Macmillan.
Stephan, M.J., and E. Chenoweth (2011). *Why civil resistance works: The strategic logic of nonviolent conflict*. New York: Columbia University Press.
Student Network to Protect the People. (2007a). Ten Demands.
_____. (2007b). Summary: Incidents that the Network of Students to Protect the People Requests the Investigations.
_____. (2007c). Statement: June 4, 2007.
Surin, P. (1985). *Islam and Malay nationalism: A case study of the Malay-Muslims of southern Thailand*. Bangkok: Thai Khadi Research Institute, Thammasat University.
Twenty-two corpses. (2007, June 2). *Matichon*, p. 15.
Why was the Pattani protest brought to an end? (2007, June 4). *Muslim Thai*. Retrieved from www.muslimthai.com/main/thai/content.php?category=72&id=308&page= content.
Zunes, S., R.L. Kurtz, and S.B. Asher (Eds.). (1999). *Nonviolent social movements: A geographical perspective*. Oxford: Blackwell.

"We Want Freedom!" Nonviolent Conflict to Curb Corruption

Shaazka Beyerle[1]

> The protesters and bloggers over nearly a decade now have made a conscious effort to downplay sectarianism in their rhetoric and demands, focusing on democracy, human rights, accountability, corruption [Parker, 2011].

The valiant voices rising from the Middle East since 2011 are a potent reminder that in the trajectory of civil resistance and people power, the distinctions between nonviolent conflict, conflict resolution, and peacebuilding begin to blur. When unarmed citizens rise up against persistent oppression, endemic corruption, and poverty, they are engaged in a conflict they ultimately seek to resolve by forcing autocrats from power, holding national and local governments accountable, and changing unjust political, social, and economic systems. They generate collective people power through civil resistance — as mentioned previously in this section — by strategically utilizing peaceful weapons, including varieties of noncooperation, protests, digital mobilization, blogging, strikes, monitoring, boycotts, dilemma actions, graffiti, leafleting, symbolic acts, cultural expressions, humor, social and economic empowerment initiatives, creation of parallel institutions, and yes, negotiation.[2] To succeed, they must enforce nonviolent discipline; build unity across socio-economic, ethnic, and religious groups; articulate shared grievances and goals; develop both a sense of collective identity and ownership of the struggle; and finally, win people over from the oppressor's side. Cumulatively, these elements create conditions conducive to post-conflict reconciliation rather than violent revenge and civil strife.

This essay will:

- examine the historical record and dynamics of civil resistance to combat oppression and corruption;
- identify the linkages between corruption and violence;
- explore synergies among peacebuilding, conflict resolution, anti-corruption strategies, and nonviolent conflict;
- move from the conceptual to the practical by outlining the limitations of conventional approaches to fighting corruption and presenting cases of civil resistance to curb corruption in situations of violence and post-conflict transformation;
- distill general lessons learned for practitioners in the peacebuilding, conflict resolution, and anti-corruption realms;
- conclude with an alternative paradigm of conflict, justice, and positive peace that draws together these conceptual and practical strands.

People and Power

> The strike, the boycott, the refusal to serve, the ability to paralyze the functioning of a complex social structure — these remain potent weapons against the most fearsome state or corporate power [Zinn, 2000].

Traditionally, power has been viewed as a force (good or bad) exercised by a few at the top, over the many. In essence, it is considered monolithic, quite fixed, and not easily shifted (Sharp, 2005). But the reality is very different. The pioneering nonviolent conflict scholar, Gene Sharp (2005), explains that while power can indeed be found at the top of institutions and governing bodies, it is also dispersed throughout society. In his "social view of power," powerholders are "dependent on the population's goodwill, decisions and support." Mohandas Gandhi applied this dynamic to fight the British colonial occupation of India, saying, "Even the most powerful cannot rule without the cooperation of the ruled" (as cited in Ackerman & DuVall, 2001).

Although the terms "people power" and "civil resistance" are often used interchangeably, for purposes of this essay, I draw the following distinctions. People power refers to political, social, and economic pressure that is exerted by significant numbers of people organized together around shared grievances and goals. Civil resistance — also called nonviolent conflict/struggle/resistance — is the process through which the grassroots challenges oppression and injustice.[3] Civil resistance expresses people power through the sustained, strategic application of a variety of nonviolent tactics that are designed to:

- disrupt oppression and systems of corruption, making the status quo more and more untenable;
- undermine the legitimacy of unaccountable and corrupt powerholders, entities, systems, and their enablers, and weaken their sources of support and control;
- win support of sectors, groups, institutions, and people over to the civic campaign or movement, including from the public and from within autocratic and corrupt systems, such as political figures, honest officials, security forces;
- strengthen citizen participation and their capacity for mobilization.

The efficacy of civil resistance is not a matter of theory. In 2011 it rigorously unfolded across the Middle East, with nonviolent victories (thus far) over entrenched dictators in Tunisia and Egypt. According to Mary King (2011), a leading nonviolent conflict scholar, the events "were years in the making." Though largely ignored by the international community, during the previous decade there was ongoing citizen dissent in the region, following a rich and relatively unknown history of civil resistance throughout the twentieth century (King, 2007; Stephan, 2010). In Egypt, the historic April 6, 2008, general strike (or the Facebook Revolution) was organized by youth, which evolved into the April 6 movement. The anti-corruption campaign shayfeen.com (meaning "we see you") spawned the Egyptians against Corruption movement. As well, the Bahrain Youth Society for Human Rights had been actively studying civil resistance and engaging in nonviolent actions well before the onset of the island-nation's nonviolent uprising began last year, which at the time of this publication remains defiant in spite of severe repression. In May 2006, a group of young men and women, communicating through text messages, launched the Orange Movement against political corruption in Kuwait. Their nonviolent tactics, which included leafleting the parliament, enlisted public support and participation, and resulted in early parliamentary elections in which legislation to change electoral districts (to prevent corruption) became a major campaign issue and was later adopted. For over two months in 2005, spontaneous protests over the assassination of Lebanese prime minister Rafiq al-Hariri grew into the Intifada for Independence, a civilian uprising that led to the resignation of the prime minister — and what had seemed impossible: the withdrawal of Syrian forces that had occupied the country for over 30 years. Lastly, as mentioned by Norman in this volume, Palestinian nonviolent resistance to the Israeli occupation — through popular committees in the West Bank — continues to grow in spite of repression. It has united local Palestinian political factions, including Hamas and Fateh, and is joined by hundreds of Israelis who take part in the protests. Efforts are under way to build a national movement.

These campaigns and movements are the latest manifestation of a long chain of civil resistance that has undermined oppression, injustice, and corruption. A 2008 study conducted by Maria Stephan and Erica Chenoweth found that in the last century, violent campaigns succeeded historically in only 26 percent of all cases, compared to 53 percent in the case of nonviolent, civilian-based campaigns. Moreover, subsequent investigation found a high correlation between nonviolent campaigns and a democratic outcome five years later. A quantitative analysis of transitions from authoritarianism to democracy over the past three decades found that civil resistance was a key factor in driving 75 percent of political transitions, and such transformations were far more likely to result in democratic reform and civil liberties than violent or elite-led, top-down changes. Of the 35 countries subsequently rated "Free" according to a Freedom House index, 32 had a significant "bottom up" civil resistance component (Karatnycky & Ackerman, 2005). In other words, civil resistance not only has a greater chance of success than violent conflict, but it also lays the foundation for a more peaceful and fair aftermath. Thus, the historical record confirms what Gandhi (1938) understood decades ago: the form of struggle impacts the outcome. He wrote, "The means may be likened to a seed, the end to a tree; and there is just the same inviolable connection between the means and the end as there is between the seed and the tree."

Corruption, Violence, and Peace

Corruption is intimately linked to violent conflict, human insecurity, and oppression, and as such, is directly relevant to scholars and practitioners in the peacebuilding and conflict resolution realms. In a checklist on the "root causes of conflict and early warning indicators," the European Commission includes the corruption troika of bribery in bureaucracies, collusion between the private sector and civil servants, and organized crime. At an aggregate level, corruption has been found to be positively correlated with higher risks of political instability (Le Billon, 2003). Human Rights Watch (2007) cites a direct relationship between corruption and political violence, in which state officials use stolen public revenues to pay for political violence in support of their ambitions. A 2004 report of the United Nations Secretary-General's High-level Panel on Threats, Challenges and Change states that "corruption, illicit trade and money-laundering contribute to State weakness, impede economic growth and undermine democracy. These activities thus create a permissive environment for civil conflict" (pp. 20–21). Finally, corruption also creates an overall climate of impunity (Kaufmann, 2006). Human rights organizations link corruption to repression, as it impedes government accountability and can motivate officials and security forces to commit abuses for financial or other forms of gain (Ganesan, 2007).

There are multiple ways in which corruption is linked to violent conflict, some direct and some indirect. Corruption is often a venal legacy of violent strife, and is embedded into the political, social, and economic fabric of the society. War economies, by their nature, function through malfeasance; the parties in the conflict depend on fraud, bribery, and criminal groups to expedite the smooth functioning of the system (Scharbatke-Church & Reiling, 2009). Arms traffickers and transnational organized crime add to the deadly mix by readily providing weapons: the global illicit arms trade is estimated at $200 million to $300 million annually (United Nations, 2010).

Moreover, corruption can draw out or perpetuate bloody confrontations. Violent groups themselves engage in illicit activities to acquire weapons and supplies. According to a confidential source, Al Qaeda has access to emeralds mined in the North-West Frontier Province[4] of Pakistan, from which it has been deriving approximately $150 million per year. Nowhere is this process more wrenchingly evident than in the Democratic Republic of the Congo, where approximately 3.5 million lives have been lost since the onset of war in 1998 and hundreds of thousands of girls and women have been systematically raped (Global Witness, 2004; UNICEF, 2008). The military, rebel groups, and various foreign allies have plundered the country's diamonds, gold, timber, ivory, coltan, and cobalt, not only to finance their atrocities, but also ultimately to enrich themselves, which has become an end unto itself (Global Witness, 2004). Over the past decade, violent confrontations over the Casamance region have broken out among The Gambia, Guinea-Bissau, and Senegal, and between Cameroon and Nigeria in the oil-rich Bakassi peninsula for an equal length of time. A 2007 USAID report concluded that corruption, more often than not, played a key role in fomenting and protracting these conflicts.

When corruption is endemic—whereby a complex system of graft permeates the political system, economic spheres, and basic provision of services in a country—it can stimulate social unrest and foment violent conflict. For example, in the Niger Delta, insurgent groups are amassing weapons and recruiting young men from an impoverished, angry, and frustrated population that experiences little benefit from oil wealth while living amidst horrendous environmental degradation from its extraction and processing (UNDP, 2006).

In the post-conflict context, corruption can function as an inhibitor of sustainable peace, the latter needing human security and stability to take root and flourish (Ahtisaari, 2009). First, graft can allow the entrenchment of the political status quo that operated during the conflict (Le Billon, 2007). Second, it undermines the new government's legitimacy, rule of law, and capacity for reconstruction, economic development, and the provision of basic public services. For ordinary citizens, the horrors of war are replaced with grueling hardship, to which pervasive malfeasance adds another layer of tangible injustice, such as in Afghanistan. In a 2010 poll, 83 percent of Afghans said corruption affects their daily lives (United States Government, 2010). As a result, the Taliban is recruiting new members from among the marginalized population oppressed through unrelenting graft and poverty.

Corruption can be an enabler of state-capture in post-conflict or fragile democracies. Tragically on the rise in Central America, narco-corruption refers to the interrelationship between transnational drug cartels and state security forces, as well as the infiltration of organized crime interests into politics, governance, and the actual functioning of institutions. Countries such as Mexico and Guatemala are now being called narco-states. As of February 2012, during the first six years of Mexican President Felipe Calderon's administration, drug-related violence has taken over 45,500 lives (BBC, 2012). The chief of the United Nation's Office of Drugs and Crime (2010) has asserted, "Corruption, poverty and poor criminal justice capacity make Guatemala extremely vulnerable to organized crime." Not coincidentally, the country is experiencing the worst violence since the cessation of the 36-year civil war in 1996. Approximately 5,000 people are murdered each year due to organized crime and gangs, now compounded by Mexican drug cartels expanding south across the border (Dudley, 2010; Sanchez, 2007). Narco-corruption, of course, is not limited to the Americas. According to a confidential communication, the drug trade in Afghanistan also serves as the main source of financing for the private armies of local warlords, which are connected to parts of the post-conflict government. The Taliban is in on the game as well, exchanging drugs for weapons (Starkey, 2008).

A vicious cycle can develop, whereby authoritarian and/or ineffectual governance paired with endemic corruption results in the further de-legitimization of authority and rule of law, leading to fragmented tyrannies — which in turn reinforces authoritarian and/or ineffectual governance, impunity, and poverty (Zunes, 2008). In contrast, civil resistance has the potential to activate an anti-corruption cycle. Nonviolent social movements and grass-roots civic campaigns can challenge the corruption-violence nexus, creating an alternative loci of power, thereby empowering the civic realm to continue to wage strategic civic campaigns and movements.

To target corruption is to touch simultaneously the myriad of injustices to which it is linked, from violence and poverty, to impunity, human rights abuses, authoritarianism, unaccountability, and environmental destruction. Thus, fighting malfeasance is not a superficial solution that avoids the underlying problem; it can be a direct attack on oppression and the propensity for aggression, thereby impacting prospects for conflict resolution and peacebuilding.

Beyond Dichotomies

> Nonviolent resistance should instead be seen as an integral part of conflict transformation, offering one possible approach to achieving peace and justice, alongside other methods of conflict intervention focusing on dialogue, problem-solving and the restoration of cooperative relationships (e.g., mediation, negotiation, restorative justice, etc.) [Dudouet, 2008].

In recent years, new scholarship has emerged that transcends dichotomous views of the realms of civil resistance, conflict resolution, peacebuilding, and anti-corruption that reveal fundamental similarities and synergies.

(Nonviolent) conflict and negotiation

Amy Finnegan and Susan Hackley wrote a seminal analysis in 2008 on the interface between the fields of negotiation and civil resistance during an asymmetric conflict in which one side is being oppressed by the other. In such cases, there are a number of similarities and synergies.

Both are action-oriented processes to get the other side to act in a way or to do things that one wants. For an oppressed group, this involves getting the oppressor side to meet its demands and change practices that are harmful or unjust. Second, civil resistance and negotiation require strategic analysis and planning, as well as the sequencing of actions or tactics. This can involve the identification of ways to strengthen the best alternatives of one's own side while weakening the alternatives of the opponent. Third, the processes of nonviolent conflict and negotiation are skills-based, which can be learned and honed through experience. Finally, power analysis — the examination of power asymmetry and leverage — is central to waging nonviolent conflict and successful negotiation (Finnegan & Hackley, 2008).

Negotiation can support nonviolent movements and campaigns. Through the lens of civil resistance, it can be considered a tactic that can be used both during and at the cessation of a struggle. Negotiation can also help achieve interim goals and small victories, build unity across groups, and maintain harmony within a movement itself. Toward the end of a struggle, negotiation is sometimes the means through which key demands are met. Finally, in some instances, there can be strategic benefits to negotiation, even when the probability for gains is low. Bernard Lafayette (2008), a leader in the U.S. civil rights movement and an educator in Kingian nonviolence, explains that negotiation can provide opportunities to interact with the oppressor's side — including making contact, gathering information, conveying messages, and beginning to shift support of some toward the movement or campaign. As importantly, negotiations can be used in some instances to build legitimacy for both the civic initiative and nonviolent direct action, demonstrating that the oppressed group made an effort to reach out to the oppressor's side, which in turn can build support, engage citizens, and delegitimize the oppressors.

On the other hand, nonviolent conflict can create conditions of ripeness for negotiation (Lafayette, 2008). In "Letter from a Birmingham Jail," Martin Luther King, Jr. eloquently encapsulated the breadth of this dynamic: "Nonviolent direct action seeks to create such a crisis and foster such a tension that a community which has constantly refused to negotiate is forced to confront the issue..." (1963, p. 34). Subsequently, civil resistance can further negotiations by creating leverage. This involves exercising people power and equalizing imbalances. In the negotiation field, this is viewed as improving the people's BATNA (best alternative to a negotiated agreement) and reducing the oppressors' BATNA (Finnegan & Hackley, 2008).

Civil resistance and conflict transformation

Over the past six years, Véronique Dudouet and Howard Clark have been at the forefront of exploring the duality of nonviolent conflict and conflict transformation in situations of power asymmetries and injustice.

Both civil resistance and conflict transformation share a commitment to achieving justice and social change through nonviolent methods (Dudouet, 2008). As importantly, neither field shirks from conflict. For many conflict transformation scholars, "the existence of groups making demands and exerting pressure for social justice is intrinsic to the very idea of conflict transformation" (Clark, 2005, p. 2). Thus, both realms view citizens as active agents of positive change rather than passive recipients of top-down conflict resolution interventions that often involve external actors.

Civil resistance by definition involves contention, but its capacity to generate power and ultimately succeed rests on maintaining a nonviolent character. As well, both civil resistance and conflict transformation converge over what exactly is being transformed. The shift is not from violent conflict to the cessation of violent conflict, or what Kingian practitioners call a "negative peace" that perpetuates injustice and even less overt forms of aggression. Instead, the shift is from violent conflict to nonviolent conflict to end the oppression and gain rights and justice, thereby laying the foundation for reconciliation and what is known as "positive peace," defined as "the presence of justice" (Lafayette & Jehnsen, 1995, p. 37). Last but not least, both realms emphasize the importance of power relations, power imbalances, and power structures (Clark, 2005).

Asymmetrical power conflicts involving oppression, by their nature, generate hostility and are latent sources of violence. An Iranian dissident (confidential communication) explained this dynamic as a series of social choices. People living under unjust conditions—in which the oppressors not only refuse to change but will use intimidation and violent force to maintain the status quo—must first decide whether they will remain apathetic and continue to suffer, or fight to achieve change. If they choose to fight, they must then decide whether or not to use violent or nonviolent methods. By choosing the latter, the conflict has already transformed.

In addition, civil resistance entails "constructive confrontation"—that is, the conflict shifts from the negative to the positive. Bridging the two fields, Gene Sharp and William Ury encapsulate the process:

> We need more conflict, not less, to really uncover and address a lot of issues that are still not being addressed properly in this world.... [I]t's about transforming conflict from its often destructive forms of violence and war to more constructive forms such as nonviolent action and negotiation [quoted in Finnegan & Hackley, 2008].

Finally, expanding upon the Gandhian insight that means determine ends, Kingian practitioners see the process as a continuum in which nonviolent conflict is necessary to end oppression and achieve positive conflict transformation that ultimately leads to social harmony and reconciliation. Under conditions of collective societal violation, they explain that aggression is a common impulse. If that aggression is directed toward the oppressors, it will produce violent behavior and continue the negative status quo. Nonviolent conflict channels societal aggression away from physically harming or seeking revenge on the perpetrators and toward changing the unjust system. While justice should be sought and the behavior of the perpetrators is not accepted, Kingian practitioners maintain the necessity of treating them as human beings (Lafayette & Jehnsen, 1995).

Anti-corruption and Peacebuilding

Anti-corruption and peacebuilding have been, up until fairly recently, characterized as a "tale of two communities" (June & Heller, 2009). Traditionally, the former focused on technocratic and legislative policies and reforms, while the latter attempted to promote dialogue and reconcile competing groups and interests. And neither realm factored the role of civil resistance and people power into the equation.

In a landmark essay on the nexus of corruption and conflict, Cheyanne Scharbatke-Church and Kirby Reiling (2008) observed: "As conflicts are riddled with corruption, peacebuilding work should be appropriately riddled with anti-corruption efforts" (p. 4). Similarly, the anti-corruption realm needs to better comprehend post-conflict dynamics when dealing with graft in such settings (June & Heller, 2009). There is a convergence of challenges, such as abuse of power, impunity, and societal trust. Both seek longer-term goals of social justice and transparent, accountable governance. Finally, the anti-corruption and peacebuilding communities emphasize change at the socio-political level (e.g., institutional practices, social norms) and at the individual level (e.g., knowledge, skills, and attitudes) (Scharbatke-Church & Reiling, 2008).

Civil resistance to target corruption and gain accountability

"The greatest enemy of corruption is the people" (Klitgaard, Maclean-Abaroa, & Parris, 2000). For regular citizens, the experience of corruption is the denial of basic freedoms and rights. For the international community, these outcomes present geopolitical crises and humanitarian calamities. Into such settings enter negotiators, foreign policymakers, donors, multilateral institutions, and relief agencies, with the Herculean challenges of ending violent conflicts, engaging in peacebuilding, fostering social and economic development, and cultivating democratic governance, rule of law, and accountability. Yet their efforts are often stymied, and corruption squanders much of aid money.

Systematic anti-corruption efforts are relatively new, having emerged over the past two decades. Notwithstanding some advances, change has been modest (Hussmann & Hechler, 2008; International Council on Human Rights Policy & Transparency International, 2009). A major literature review found "few success stories when it comes to the impact of donor supported anti-corruption efforts" (Norwegian Agency for Development and Cooperation, 2009, p. 9). As a result, a paradigm shift is under way in the international anti-corruption community: corruption cannot be fully challenged without the involvement of citizens.

Traditional, top-down strategies are based on the assumption that once anti-corruption structures are put in place, illicit practices will change. Institutions accused of corruption are often made responsible for enacting change.

But those benefiting from graft are much less likely to stand against it than those suffering from it. It's not surprising that even when political will exists, it can be thwarted, because too many individuals have a stake in the crooked status quo. In contrast, civil resistance has a strategic advantage as it consists of extra-institutional methods of action to push for change when power holders are corrupt and/or unaccountable, and institutional channels are blocked or ineffective.[5] This involves generating political will, demanding specific measures, and reinforcing new patterns of administration and governance centered on accountability to citizens. Thus, top-down and bottom-up approaches are not mutually exclusive. Civic campaigns and movements can complement and reinforce legal and administrative mechanisms, which constitute the anti-corruption infrastructure needed for long-term transformation of systems of graft and abuse.

Over the past 15 years, citizens have been proving they are not passive onlookers of elite-driven, anti-corruption initiatives, but rather drivers of accountability, reforms, and participatory democracy. This author has conducted an international research project documenting nonviolent, grass-roots campaigns and movements to fight graft and abuse, demand accountability, and win rights. Over 30 cases were identified, of which 18 were studied in-depth. Key findings include:

- Bottom-up initiatives can be found around the world, among democracies, semi-democracies, and authoritarian regimes.
- They are prevalent in societies enduring poor governance, poverty, illiteracy, repression, and violence, the latter two perpetrated by the state, organized crime, paramilitary groups and gangs — in contrast to the deeply ingrained misconception that civil resistance is only possible when there is political space, a somewhat educated population, and a nonviolent setting.
- Organization and planning usually precede action, even when a scandalous event first arouses public indignation.
- Taken together, these characteristics confirm that skills and strategy generally matter more than pre-existing conditions.
- Women and youth are playing galvanizing roles in many campaigns, notably in Muslim settings.
- "Defining methods" (Shock, 2012), around which a host of nonviolent tactics revolve, are common.
- Success in one struggle or context inspires new applications, knowledge-sharing, and campaigns locally and even across borders and continents.
- People power can be amplified through engagement with selected

powerholders, and support and allies can be drawn from within corrupt institutions and systems, which can be a source of information, access, and constructive negotiations.
- Finally, these civic initiatives are usually multidimensional in focus, and may not necessarily be framed in terms of corruption. This reflects the reality that graft and abuse do not occur in a vacuum; they are linked to other forms of oppression and injustice.

From this research, two civic initiatives are profiled here, which illustrate the connections between corruption and violence on the ground, and concomitant obstacles for peacebuilding. As importantly, they demonstrate the power of citizens to resist graft and oppression nonviolently in spite of a legacy of armed conflict and severe conditions of aggression, impunity, and inequity.

Afghanistan: Post-conflict, grass-roots empowerment curbs corruption and improves development

Unfettered malfeasance in war-torn Afghanistan is now considered a clear threat to peace, counterinsurgency, reconstruction, and development (Hussmann, 2009). It is undermining government legitimacy and national and international efforts for reconstruction, poverty reduction, and the provision of basic public services. For citizens, it adds a crushing burden to their daily lives. According to NATO Secretary-General Anders Fogh Rasmussen:

> In many ways, corruption in Afghanistan is a bigger detractor to stability and progress than the insurgency. Many Afghans face violence at the hands of the insurgency. But every Afghan experiences corruption, sometimes at the hands of Government officials, whom they are expected to trust over the insurgents [NATO, 2010].

In 2007, Pajhwok Ghoori and Lorenzo Delesgues decided they didn't simply want to produce reports on corruption while sitting in Kabul. They determined to involve those most affected by the dire conditions — everyday people — and the way to start was at the local level.[6] Integrity Watch Afghanistan (IWA) began going into rural settings and listening to people. Based on the collective grievances heard, IWA sought to make aid and service provision accountable to citizens and to give them a say over the reconstruction of their communities.

IWA realized that if the citizen campaigns were characterized as anti-corruption, they could fail and create additional tensions. As project information and site access were needed, doors would have closed on them, and those benefiting from graft could easily retaliate. Hence, the campaigns were framed as getting projects done according to plan. This enabled IWA to negotiate with the various players: donors (international military, foreign governments, multilateral development institutions), the confusing mix of international and Afghan contractors and subcontractors, and the national and local governments. IWA needed a baseline of cooperation so communities could monitor projects and secure a "statement of work" for each project, consisting of blueprints, donors, budgets, work plans, technical characteristics, etc. These negotiated outcomes also provided a measure of reassurance to villagers, which was particularly important for overcoming their fear of taking action. Even if not genuine, at the very least the agreements with state institutions created leverage, emboldened citizens, and expanded civic space, or the arena for public expression.

Inspired by the pioneering social audit strategies and tactics of the *Mazdoor Kisan Shakti Sangathan*, or "Right to Information," movement in India, as well as the successes of nonviolent social movements and the social accountability initiatives developed by the Aga Khan Foundation, IWA created a defining nonviolent method: community monitoring. Each initiative or campaign lasted for the life-cycle of a development project, normally one year. Once a community decided to engage in the campaign, the first step was to elect two local monitors (who volunteered their time), and to choose the development project it wanted to monitor. IWA then trained the monitors and conducted a community survey, which provided "strategically designed data." This information was directly relevant to donors, thereby enabling the campaigns to gain their attention and receptivity. The third step was for each village to select the development project it wanted to monitor. Thus, from the outset, the tactics began building ownership and practical experience in grass-roots democracy. Nonviolent discipline was strongly emphasized. Delesgues reported that villagers "understood the arguments for nonviolence. Coming out of war, they wanted to try something different." As violence is also prevalent in the post-conflict context, he added: "Because people know its consequences, they are more reluctant to engage in violence."

The communities played an integral role in the process. They found technical specialists to provide expertise, used their collective knowledge to help the monitors, participated in assemblies, solved problems, and overcame obstacles such as being blocked from work sites and dealing with uncooperative officials, donors, and contractors. The next step was collecting and assessing information. Every week, monitors conducted site visits and interacted with the project implementers. This ongoing tactic not only disrupted potential corrupt practices, but the development of personal relationships also enabled them to win support for the community. The local monitors subsequently presented their findings at weekly village meetings, which also built accountability into the monitoring process and maintained enthusiasm and unity. A locally recruited IWA staff person in each district serves as the focal point for the monitoring campaigns, meeting weekly with monitors and addressing and solving problems. The training and regular village visits are an illustration of how external actors can support civic initiatives without controlling or directing them.

When the monitors found problems, the communities demanded changes. First they would use dialogue to come to a resolution. If that didn't work, they would increase pressure by inviting project implementers or state officials to community meetings or site visits, and through independent assessments. If the villagers were not satisfied with the outcome, they would flex their civil resistance muscles through other collective actions, such as protests, letter-writing, and sit-ins.

What began with 10 communities has expanded to over 200 in 2011. The positive track record has captured the attention of the media, public, and donors. Delesgues estimated that in approximately one-third of the cases, the problems were solved through strong community pressure. In about another third, villagers didn't find problems or the project implementers were cooperative in addressing issues. Among the remaining third, no change was achieved. Either the problems weren't detected, access to the project site proved impossible to secure, or the communities were not sufficiently mobilized to wield people power.

IWA, together with the dozens of community monitoring campaigns, are making history in more ways than one. Fifty years after the U.S. civil rights movement, these communities are unknowingly recreating the Kingian six-step strategy for nonviolent campaigns: personal commitment, education, information gathering, negotiation, direct action, and reconciliation — the latter as donors and even some government officials now recognize and even support the role of empowered citizens in reconstruction and development (Lafayette & Jehnsen, 1995).

Guatemala: Civil resistance to undermine the corruption-violence nexus

In Guatemala, innovative grass-roots civil resistance movements have been undermining the corruption-violence nexus at the community level, maintaining resilience in the face of brutal repression and fostering social and economic development.[7] One particularly poignant case is in Santa Lucia Cotzumalguapa, a mid-size town populated largely by indigenous people, and which suffered great losses during the civil war. It was the cradle of the organized peasant movement and the site of persecution and mass murder of peasants, church members, and unions by state forces, sponsored by sugar plantation (*Finca*) owners. Every guerrilla faction had a presence there as well. Dozens of the organized paramilitary groups have since been transformed into hit-men operations, and it is now situated in a geographical spot convenient to cross-border narco-trafficking, from Colombia up to Mexico for the North American market.

Reflecting a collective "outcry of despair," a local citizens' movement emerged in the aftermath of the civil war. Its objectives were to recover the community and local government from the hands of drug lords and organized crime, promote economic and social development, create a collective sense of worth and empowerment, challenge the climate of impunity, prevent electoral fraud, and defend hard-won gains along the way. Organizers built a strong coalition that included women, youth, and community groups. In spite of the legacy of repression, they initially built alliances with Finca owners (which later broke down) to support an honest candidate in the local elections and kick out a drug lord from the local government (Samayoa, 2008).

Over the years, they conducted a wide range of nonviolent actions, such as civil disobedience; solidarity demonstrations; literacy, education, and development programs; radio call-in programs; theater; art festivals; and recreation projects aimed at youth, who are often the targets of organized crime recruitment. Their successes wrought severe counter-attacks. By 2007, 11 community leaders had been murdered, four attempts were made on the life of an honest mayor, slandering and defamation cases were lodged, electoral fraud was orchestrated, and the police, prosecutors, and judges favored the drug cartels — an odious confirmation of the extent of corruption and state capture.

In spite of this extreme intimidation, citizens refused to be subdued. Solidarity demonstrations and civil disobedience persisted. People engaged in new methods to disrupt the corrupt status quo, such as monitoring the actions and spending of the new authorities in power, as well as criminal activities, reporting the latter to the newly instituted International Commission against Impunity in Guatemala (though it appears the case will not be taken on). However, in 2011 the Inter-American Commission on Human Rights accepted the case of the first assassination in the town.

A significant dimension was added to the struggle: the international community. Guatemalan human rights defenders drew world attention to the struggle. They garnered support for civic initiatives from the United Nations Development Programme and the Friedrich-Ebert-Stiftung. A security plan was devised, bolstered by human rights organizations that brought international observers and nonviolent accompaniment to protect people at risk. Santa Lucia Cotzumalguapa became the host of national and international meetings, thereby sending a message to the corrupt power holders that the country and the world were watching and stood together with the townspeople. Finally, homegrown, grass-roots solidarity and coordination networks have been established with other indigenous communities engaged in civil resistance both in Guatemala and across borders. They share information, experiences, and strategies, send out alerts, and even have come to one another's aid, for example, by blocking a road.

In extending the arena of resistance from the local to the regional and international, the community is increasing its capacity of people power, the foundation being strength in numbers. From unity within, they are building a broader front involving allies at all levels. In confronting a system of violence, graft, and impunity involving the state and transnational organized crime, in essence, the citizens' movement is now creating its own alternative system — one of civil resistance that involves national and transnational networks, solidarity, and action. In seeking to overcome marginalization and poverty through education and development initiatives, for women and youth as well as the town at large, the movement calls to mind Gandhi's (1945) "constructive programme in the nonviolent effort," in which equality, education, and economic self-reliance were core elements. Finally, the people of Santa Lucia Cotzumalguapa embody what Gandhi observed decades ago, "Strength does not come from physical capacity. It comes from an indomitable will" (as cited in Ackermann & DuVall, 2000).

Engaging (Nonviolent) Conflict: An Alternative Paradigm for Justice and Peace

> Nonviolence is aggressive and assertive toward changing the institutionalized policies, practices, and conditions that deny people their full dignity as human beings.... Violence is the violation of peoples' integrity, dignity, and self-respect through the exercise of stronger physical, psychological, or economic forces without regard to them as human beings. The opposite of this violence is not nonviolence but a seemingly peaceful status quo that tolerates the brutal and sometimes subtle victimization of people.... Nonviolence comes from a long tradition of disturbing the peace and challenging contemporary conditions [Lafayette & Jehnsen, 1995].

The discourse of traditional conflict resolution and peacebuilding has been based, in part, on what can be called a "statist" model — state actors or elites, top-down, monolithic power, and externally prescribed "solutions" or interventions. But change and peace are not easily imposed from above, and stronger parties rarely, if ever, give up power willingly; they must be pressured to make concessions. That impetus can come from the grass-roots. Given the historical record of nonviolent movements, civil resistance turns traditional concepts of conflict resolution and peacebuilding upside down, by demonstrating that:

- Not all conflict is bad; conflict is normal and sometimes desirous and necessary for change to occur. Civil resistance targets oppression and injustice, thereby mitigating the propensity for violent strife.
- Not all peace is good. Negative peace — peacefulness without justice — is itself a violation of human rights and dignity (Lafayette & Jehnsen, 1995).
- To win positive peace, it is often necessary to fight, albeit in a nonviolent manner.
- Those at the bottom have power as well as those at the top. People are often engines of change through civil resistance, which shifts power relations, expands civic space, overcomes difficult conditions, and exerts pressure on powerholders.

In conclusion, civil resistance contributes to creating outcomes on the ground needed for sustainable peace. It provides an alternative paradigm of conflict that transcends various approaches and articulates the dynamic relationships among states, institutions, elites, civil society, and last but not least, citizens. It actively engages conflict through collective action in order to end oppression and win freedom, justice, and human dignity, thereby reducing the propensity for violent conflict to emerge. The ultimate lesson is to respect the needs and wishes of people on the ground and to include them in the process. There is an inherent wisdom among those who risk their welfare and lives for the common good. As this essay is written, their voices cry out from many parts of the world — such as these valorous citizens from Syria, whose demands and vision encapsulate the linkages between corruption and violence on the one hand, and civil resistance and positive peace on the other hand:

> No to mayhem, no to corruption, no to sectarianism, no to arms, no to trial, no to violence. Yes to freedom, yes to peace, yes to national unity, yes to reform, yes to change, yes to cooperation [Syrian Revolution Digest, 2011].

Notes

1. The research conducted by the author and cited in this essay was made possible through a grant from the United States Institute of Peace (USIP) and support from the International Center on Nonviolent Conflict (ICNC), where the author is a senior advisor. The views expressed here do not necessarily reflect those of USIP or ICNC, which do not advocate specific policies. The author wishes to thank Daryn Cambridge, director, Knowledge and Digital Strategies, ICNC, for his constructive review of this essay.

2. Nonviolent conflict and civil resistance are used interchangeably in this essay.

3. There are many terms for nonviolent conflict because it is a social phenomenon that can reflect culturally specific nuances and references. Thus, different groups refer to it in different ways. For example, in Palestine, the common term is "popular resistance," and in Burma, "political defiance" came to describe civil resistance. What remains constant are two fundamental notions: unity of people and active refusal to acquiesce to an oppressor or unjust status quo.

4. The province is now known officially as Khyber Pakhtunkhwa, though it is still commonly referred to as the North-West Frontier Province.

5. This conceptualization is based on the definition of social movements by Schock, 2008, p. 186–207.

6. The section on Afghanistan is based on conversations and interviews conducted with Lorenzo Delesgues, co-founder, Integrity Watch Afghanistan, in October 2010 and April 2011.

7. The section on Guatemala is based on personal communications with Claudia Samayoa, co-founder, Unit of Protection of Human Rights Defenders (UDEFEGUA), and a member of the Advisors Council for Security to the President of Guatemala from 2008 to 2010.

References

Ackerman, P., and J. DuVall (2000). *A force more powerful: A century of nonviolent conflict.* New York: Palgrave.

Ahtisaari, M. (2009, April 6). Violence Prevention: A Critical Dimension of Development conference. Presentation, Washington, DC, World Bank.

BBC. (2012, February 12). Mexico drug war deaths over five years now total 47,515. Retrieved from http://www.bbc.co.uk/news/world-latin-america-16518267.

Clark, H. (2005). *Campaigning power and civil courage: Bringing "people power" back into conflict transformation.* London: Committee for Conflict Transformation Support. Retrieved from http://www.c-r.org/ccts/ccts27/review27.pdf.

Dudley, S.S. (2010, July). How Mexico's drug war is killing Guatemala. *Foreign policy.* Retrieved from http://www.foreignpolicy.com/articles/2010/07/20/How_Mexicos_Drug_War_Is_Killing_Guatemala.

Dudouet, V. (2008). Nonviolent resistance and conflict transformation in power asymmetries. Berlin: Berghof Research Management.

Finnegan, A., and S. Hackley (2008, January). Negotiation and nonviolent action: Interacting in the world of conflict. Boston: Harvard University, Program on Negotiation, Harvard Law School. Retrieved from http://www.pon.harvard.edu/events/negotiation-and-nonviolent-action/negotiation-and-nonviolent-action-interacting-in-the-world-of-conflict/.

Gandhi, M.K. (1938). Hind Swaraj or Indian Home Rule. Chapter 16. Retrieved from http://www.mkgandhi.org/swarajya/coverpage.htm

_____. (1945, November 13). Constructive Programme, Its Meaning and Place. Retrieved from http://www.mkgandhi.org/cnstrct/cnstrct.htm.

Ganesan, A. (2007). Human rights and corruption: The linkages. Human Rights Watch. Retrieved from http://hrw.org/english/docs/2007/07/30/global16538.htm.

Global Witness. (2004, June). Same old story: A background study on natural resources in the Democratic Republic of Congo. Global Witness. Retrieved from http://www.globalwitness.org/media_library_detail.php/118/en/same_old_story.

Human Rights Watch. (2007, October). Corruption, godfatherism and the funding of political violence. Human Rights Watch. Retrieved from http://hrw.org/reports/2007/nigeria1007/5.htm.

Hussmann, K. (2009, October). Working towards common donor responses to corruption.

OECD DAC Network on Governance-Anti-Corruption Task Team. Retrieved from http://www.oecd.org/dataoecd/26/1/45017423.pdf.

_____, and H. Hechler (2008, January). Anti-corruption policy making in practice: Implications for implementing UNCAC. *U4 Brief*, I. Retrieved from http://www.cmi.no/publications/file/2915-anti-corruption-policy-making-in-practice.pdf.

International Council on Human Rights Policy and Transparency International. (2009). *Corruption and human rights: Making the connection*. Geneva: International Council on Human Rights Policy. Retrieved from http://www.ichrp.org/files/reports/40/131_web.pdf.

June, R., and N. Heller (2009). Corruption and anti-corruption in peacebuilding: Toward a unified framework. *Life & Peace Institute, 14*(3/4), 10–13.

Karatnycky, A., and P. Ackerman (2005). *How freedom is won: From civic resistance to durable democracy*. New York: Freedom House.

Kaufmann, D. (2006, October). Human rights, governance and development: An empirical perspective. *Development Outreach*. Retrieved from http://siteresources.worldbank.org/EXTSITETOOLS/Resources/KaufmannDevtOutreach.pdf.

King, M. (2007). *A quiet revolution: The first Palestinian intifada and nonviolent resistance*. New York: Nation Books.

_____. (2011, February). Egypt and Tunisia: The untold story. *Waging nonviolence*. Retrieved from http://wagingnonviolence.org/2011/02/egypt-and-tunisia-the- untold-story/.

King, M.L., Jr. (1963/2005). Letter from a Birmingham jail. In B. Lafayette Jr. and D. Jehnsen. The nonviolence briefing booklet (pp. 33–42). Galena, OH: Institute for Human Rights and Responsibilities.

Klitgaard, R., R. Maclean-Abaroa, and H.L. Parris (2000). *Corrupt cities: A practical guide to cure and prevention*. Oakland: ICS Press.

Lafayette, B., Jr. (2008, July). Kingian nonviolent conflict reconciliation training of trainers workshop. Providence, RI: Center for Nonviolence and Peace Studies, University of Rhode Island.

_____, and D. Jehnsen (1995). *The nonviolence briefing booklet*. Galena, OH: Institute for Human Rights and Responsibilities.

Le Billon, P. (2003). Buying peace or fueling war: The role of corruption in armed conflicts. *Journal of International Development, 15*, 413–426.

_____. (2007). What is the impact: Effects of corruption in post-conflict. Boston: The Nexus: Corruption, Conflict and Peacebuilding Colloquium, The Institute for Human Security, The Fletcher School, Tufts University. Retrieved from http://fletcher.tufts.edu/corruptionconf/pdf/LeBillion.pdf.

North Atlantic Treaty Organization [NATO]. (2010, September). NATO-ISAF takes steps to prevent corruption. NATO-News. Retrieved from http://www.nato.int/cps/en/SID-2E863892-94136853/natolive/news_66201.htm.

Norwegian Agency for Development and Cooperation [NORAD]. (2009). Anti-corruption approaches: A literature review. Oslo: NORAD. Retrieved from http://www.norad.no/en/Tools+and+publications/Publications/Publication+Page?key=119213.

Parker, N. (2011, February). In Bahrain, Sunni activist's plight seen as cautionary tale. *Los Angeles Times*. Retrieved from http://articles.latimes.com/2011/feb/25/world/la-fg-bahrain-sunnis-20110225.

Samayoa, C. (2008). Presentation and unpublished materials. Athens, Greece: Thirteenth International Anti-Corruption Conference.

Sanchez, M. (2007, September). Drug gangs fuel political violence. Al Jazeera International video report. Retrieved from http://bravenewfilms.org/blog/12242-guatemala-s-drug-gangs-fuel-political-violence-09-sep-07.

Scharbatke-Church, C., and K. Reiling (2009). Lilies that fester: Seeds of corruption and peacebuilding. *New Routes Journal of Peace Research and Action, 14*(2–4), 4–9.

Schock, K. (2008). People power and alternative politics. In P. Burnell and V. Randall (Eds.), *Politics in the developing world* (pp. 186–207). New York: Oxford University Press.

_____. (2012). Land struggles in the global South: Strategic innovations in Brazil and India. In G.M. Maney, R.V. Kutz-Flamenbaum, D.R. Rohlinger, and J. Goodwin (Eds.), *Strategies for social change.* Minneapolis: University of Minnesota Press.

Sharp, G. (2005). *Waging nonviolent struggle.* Boston: Porter Sargent.

Starkey, J. (2008, April). Drugs for guns: how the Afghan heroin trade is fuelling the Taliban insurgency. *The Independent.* Retrieved from http://www.independent.co.uk/news/world/asia/drugs-for-guns-how-the-afghan-heroin-trade-is-fuelling-the-taliban-insurgency-817230.html.

Stephan, M. (Ed.). (2010). *Civilian jihad: Nonviolent struggle, democratization and governance in the Middle East.* New York: Palgrave.

_____, and E. Chenoweth (2008). Why civil resistance works: The strategic logic of nonviolent conflict. *International Security, 33*(1), 7–44.

Syrian Revolution Digest. (2011, May 9). Daily E-bulletins.

United Nations [UN]. (2004, December). A more secure world: Our shared responsibility. Report of the Secretary-General's High-Level Panel on Threats, Challenges and Change, New York: UN Doc a/59/565, p. 7.

_____. (2010, March). Eradicating arms trafficking will further peace in Central Africa, say UN officials. United Nations News Center. Retrieved from http://www.un.org/apps/news/story.asp?Cr=weapons&Crl=&NewsID=34134.

United Nations Development Programme [UNDP]. (2006). Niger Delta human development report. UNDP Nigeria. Retrieved from http://hdr.undp.org/en/reports/nationalreports/africa/nigeria/nigeria_hdr_report.pdf.

United Nations International Children's Emergency Fund [UNICEF]. (2008, April). V-Day put rape in Democratic Republic of the Congo front and center. UNICEF Press Release. Retrieved from http://www.unicef.org/infobycountry/drcongo_43541.html.

United Nations Office of Drugs and Crime (UNODC). (2010, March 17). UNODC assists Guatemala to tackle organized crime. Retrieved from http://www.unodc.org/unodc/en/frontpage/2010/March/unodc-assists-guatemala-to-fight-organized-crime.html.

United States Agency for International Development [USAID]. (2007, September). Conflict prevention and anti-corruption overview. *USAID West Africa.* Retrieved from http://www.usaid.gov/missions/westafrica/cprevention/overview/index.htm.

United States Government. (2010). Facebook posting. United States Embassy—Kabul. Retrieved from http://www.facebook.com/topic.php?uid=34734118909&topic=15934.

Zinn, H. (2000, January). A Flash of the possible. *The Progressive.* Retrieved from http://www.thirdworldtraveler.com/Zinn/FlashofPossible_Zinn.html.

Zunes, S. (2008, October). Presentation. Athens, Greece: Thirteenth International Anti-Corruption Conference.

The Roots of Resistance: Victims' Responses to Genocide

Laura K. Taylor

Past genocide research has attempted to understand the roots of evil (Staub, 1989), highlighting the conditions and processes through which ordinary people can commit atrocious acts of violence (Browning, 1992; Harff, 2000). This line of research is perpetrator-focused, directed primarily toward understanding how individuals and groups reach the "final solution" to escalate violence to genocidal levels (Valentino, 2000). A second trend in genocide studies focuses on victims and survivors, primarily documenting their experiences and stories of survival (Miller & Miller, 1993; Levi, 1996).[1] These narratives are complemented by recent political psychological literature on victims' positive or constructive responses to violence, such as post-traumatic growth (Calhoun & Tedeschi, 2009) and altruism born of suffering (Staub & Vollhardt, 2008), through a lens of resilience (Luthar, Cicchietti, & Becker, 2000; Masten, Best, & Garmezy, 1990; Rutter, 1995).

Yet, looking across the cases of modern genocides of the 20th century, a question not adequately addressed by either of these approaches in the scholarly literature remains: Why don't the victims resist?[2] This question has been raised both by victims (Gourevitch, 1998: 23; Hatzfeld, 2006) and philosophers (Todorov, 1996). For example, through what processes are thousands of Armenians marched to their death guarded only by two Ottoman gendarmes (Miller & Miller, 1993)? The dearth of scholarly attention to this third line of genocide prevention research may be explained by a lack of conceptual clarity on resistance and resilience, reluctance to blame the victims, assumption of lack of victim agency, a selection bias toward survivors, preference toward perpetrator motivations, and greater interest in armed revolt. These biases, however, shape our understanding of resistance and obscure the range of victims' responses to genocidal violence. This question also opens a critique of the traditional ways in which social scientists have conceptualized and "measured" resistance.

To address this, this essay expands the scope of resistance to examine the range of responses and the conditions underlying different manifestations of protest against genocide. It emphasizes two aspects of the definition of resistance: from the psychological perspective, (a) the "opposition to an attempt to bring ... thoughts or feelings into consciousness," and (b) "the act or power of resisting, opposing, or withstanding" (Webster's English Dictionary, 1966).

Unlike the previous essays in this section, this one approaches nonviolence and genocide from the psychological perspective of the survivors of genocide. It highlights the conditions and the individual and group processes which may contribute to passivity and/or alternate forms of resistance, such as withstanding or opposing dehumanizing messages — and argues that in situations of genocide, these modes should be characterized as nonviolent resistance. To do so, it constructs a relevant theory aimed at describing patterns of victims' responses to genocidal violence and extracting a useful model. Applying the theory to three cases studies of modern genocide, the essay documents the patterns of relationships between individual attitudes and behaviors and systematic oppression and widespread targeted killing. This analysis informs the development of a more dynamic heuristic of resilience and resistance.

Theoretical Review

Three areas of research were reviewed to develop a theory about the roots of resistance: (1) experimental psychology applied to perpetrator and bystander actions during genocide, (2) clinical, developmental, and political psychology applied to understand patterns of trauma and resilience, and (3) anthropological-sociological analysis of how oppressed peoples respond to systemic domination.

The first trend in the existing literature, previously applied toward understanding perpetrator and bystander responses, would suggest a theory of obedience. The early experimental work of Milgram (1974) and Zimbardo (1973) demonstrates the depth and speed at which social processes of obedience are enacted. An extension of this theory would suggest that victims do not resist because they are following orders of those perceived to be in control or authority (Milgram, 1974). But how do these processes change over time? For example, how and why did the prisoners' behaviors change over the course of the six-day Stanford prison experiment?[3] Zimbardo et al. (1973) notes the ease with which normal, healthy U.S. college students became prisoners demonstrating "passivity, dependency, depression, helplessness and self-deprecation" and adopted "attitudes and behaviors which helped sanction their victimization" (p. 89). Prisoners adopted the jail's de-individuating language, spoke 90 percent of the time about cell topics not their outside lives, and exhibited only one helping incident among them. Over time "the prisoners came to initiate acts far less frequently and responded (if at all) more passively to the acts of others — they simply *behaved less*" (p. 85).

One possible explanation is that the changes in the prisoners were influenced by the experiment's dehumanizing conditions, such as the lack of privacy, small cells, solitary confinement, uniforms with no underclothes, hair covered in a nylon sack, and being referenced by prisoner number not by name (pp. 73–76). A second explanation is the escalating hostility of guards including verbal commands, forced physical exertion, isolation, direct aggressive behavior, creative cruelty, and harassment (pp. 80–81). A third possibility is that the prisoners internalized the oppressive narratives of the guards. Taken together, these studies suggest obedience is achieved as dehumanizing messages are incorporated internally into the prisoners' narratives and enforced by escalating hostility by authority figures.

A second approach from clinical, developmental, and political psychology examines the theory of resilience at an individual level. Resilience is conceptualized as an individual trait (Herman, 1992) or process that is defined as successful adaptation despite adversity (Rutter, 1985) and overcoming hardships and trauma to achieve developmental competencies (Masten, Best & Garmezy, 1990; Werner, 1993). In the clinical literature, terror can distort reality, "including depersonalization, derealization, and change in sense of time" (Herman, 1992, p. 43). However, resilient individuals often have high sociability, task-oriented coping, and an internal locus of control (p. 58). Herman describes resilient combat veterans as those who maintained social connection and active coping, despite extremely stressful conditions.

Departing from resilience as a trait, developmental psychology conceptualizes resilience as a process, taking into account transactions between individuals and their environments over time (Luthar, Cicchietti, & Becker, 2000; Masten, Best, & Garmezy, 1990). Past literature has considered deep breaches in trust—for example, severe child abuse and neglect—but has only more recently been applied to a limited extent in contexts of widespread collective violence. In these settings, political psychology has identified factors such as ideological commitment, family cohesion, and social support as protective aspects that buffer individuals from the negative consequences of ongoing political violence (Barber, 2001; Barber & Olsen, 2009; Punamaki, 2006). This theoretical orientation suggests that individual resilience can be facilitated by individual traits (e.g., internal locus of control) and social support (e.g., family cohesion). However, the psychological literature has not adequately considered the larger, societal systems of power that can define a social ecology of extreme political violence (Bronfrenbrenner, 1979; Cummings et al., 2009).

Third, an interactive theory considers the dynamic relationships and "hidden transcripts" between those who attempt to resist and those who attempt to rule. Scott (1990) demonstrates how the institutionalization of relationships is fused with personal terror, the essence of totalitarian domination (Arendt, 1968, p. 162). One of the key tools of domination is the creation of a system in which "personal dignity becomes a mortal risk" (Scott, 1990, p. 37) and solidarity becomes the "fugitive political conduct of subordinate groups" (p. xii). Examining hidden transcripts, Scott suggests high threat from above produces high compliance among the oppressed, but also yields more covert reactions (p. 109). These hidden transcripts are at odds with public obedience and are specific to the social site and set of actors (p. 5). Scott notes broad patterns or a "family of responses" (p. 21); this essay adopts a similar approach in documenting modes of resistance across cases of modern genocide.

Recalling the two aspects in the definition of resilience — opposition to thoughts/feelings and active withstanding — these three theoretical foundations suggest a preliminary model that conceptualizes resistance in three ways: internal thoughts, individual acts, and social acts (Figure 1). Within this frame-

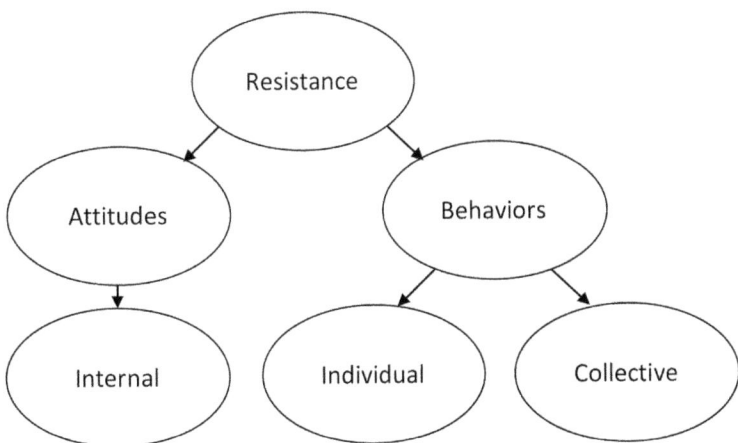

Figure 1

work a series of distinct hypotheses are derived. First, a theory of obedience would suggest that we would observe few physical acts, some verbal questioning of authority figures, and signs of internalization of the dehumanizing message, such as high mood fluctuations. This would indicate that victims do not resist in either form of the current definition: they let thoughts of their oppressors into their consciousness and do not act or have the power to oppose. Second, a theory of individual resilience suggests that certain individual and social conditions, such as task-oriented coping and social support, would buffer an individual from harm. With these conditions present, the theory would predict that we would see collective acts of withstanding domination, but does not directly address internal forms of resistance. The third theoretical approach suggests a more complex set of hypotheses. In the face of oppression, an internal form of resistance would be to maintain personal dignity, or the assertion of one's humanity. Differing from the obedience theory, while acts of submission may be observed in public, this theoretical approach calls attention to the more subtle and subversive modes, including verbal exchange among victims, that counteract the dominate narrative. This approach covers both aspects of resistance noted in the original definition and necessitates a contextual analysis of the system of oppression and the spaces of resistance.

Methods and Preliminary Models

To address a weakness in the current theory on comparative genocide — the lack of theoretically-based investigation of resilience and resistance — the paper will test the relevance of the theoretical model in Figure 1 in cases that have variation on the independent and dependent variables. Data collection will be primarily from survivors' narratives and interviews.

Case selection: Variation of the independent variables

The essay will test the usefulness of the model of resistance on three cases: the Holocaust, Cambodia, and Rwanda. Within the universe of cases of genocidal violence in the 20th century, these were selected as a critical case and two least-similar cases, respectively.[4] First, the theoretical model will be tested on the paradigmatic case of the Holocaust, focusing on the peak of violence in the death camps (1941–1945).[5] Second, Cambodia (April 1975 to January 1979) demonstrates the heterogeneous nature of political ideology and state capacity in genocidal regimes. While Pol Pot's rhetoric was similar to the other cases in terms of providing a dominating discourse about racial purity (Kiernan, 2008), the Khmer Rouge lacked totalitarian control of the territory and capacity to inflict its discourse across the population. On the other hand, the systematic population movements of displacement and confinement parallel systems within Nazi Germany's work, concentration, and death camps. This latter point is not present in Rwanda (April to June 1994). While the killing was systematic, the violence perpetrated in Rwanda did not develop into highly bureaucratic and industrial killing structures. Yet, the efficiency of death was achieved quickly (Gourevitch, 1998). While Rwanda differs in many respects — in particular the speed of violence, from other cases of genocide — it shares similarities with the Holocaust that are absent from Cambodia, such as pre-existing cleavages within the population.

Brief overviews of each case are presented in the following paragraphs and summarized in Table 1. This table highlights key variation among the three cases and differentiates between various contextual conditions. It simplifies the heterogeneous nature of each factor by collapsing them over time to depict a parsimonious set of comparisons across the three cases (George & Bennett, 2005).

	Holocaust/Germany	Cambodia	Rwanda
State-sponsored genocidal violence	Yes	Yes	Yes
Totalitarian ideology /governance	Yes	No (aspiration)	Partial
Dominating discourse	Yes	Yes	Yes
Control by center / elites	Yes	Partial	Partial
Fractures within elites	No	Yes	Yes
Pre-existing cleavages	Yes	Partial	Yes
War and revolution	Yes/concurrent (territorial expansion)	Yes/prior civil war (nation building)	Yes/prior and concurrent civil war (consolidate power)
External support / protection / ability to flee	No	Yes	Yes / Partial
Bureaucratic killing/camps	Yes	Yes	No
Widespread displacement	Partial	Yes	Yes

Table 1. Variation of conditions and causal factors of genocidal violence

Brief history of war and resistance: The Holocaust (1941–1945)

In her 2003 work *War and Genocide: A Concise History of the Holocaust*, Doris Bergen traces the rise of Hitler and the Nazi party, along with the escalating violence in a time of war. She explains the Holocaust as the result of three preconditions: the *timber*—rampant anti-Semitism and a prejudiced post-war Europe following the Great Depression; the *spark*—Hitler's extermination policies amid a campaign for territorial expansion; and *favorable conditions*—lack of intervention by foreign powers fatigued from the Great War. In 1941, the extermination policy of a Final Solution is formally established in the Wannsee Conference. Together Hitler and the Nazi elite make policy shifts that change the nature of destruction: they require Jews to wear the Star of David on their clothing; they transport the victims to their killers; they establish gas chambers for more "efficient" killing; and they target all of Europe's 11 million Jews. The impact of this strategy: approximately 75 percent of the victims were killed after 1943.

For the victims, Bergen (2003) identifies key barriers to resistance including fear of reprisals, divisions within communities, and fatigue from years of war (p. 200). Moreover, the war trapped the victims within German-held territory, and after 1941 it was practically impossible for Jews to flee (p. 142). In this context, however, she documents numerous cases of resistance, which she defines as any actions—individual or group, armed or unarmed—taken with the intent to thwart the Nazi goals (p. 193). Although Bergen uses a fairly inclusive definition of resistance, which includes armed modes, she excludes internal resilience, such as holding onto dignity as an attempt to thwart the Nazi goal of an "anti-human order maintained through the bureaucratic application of death" (Des Pres, 1980, p. 13).

Brief history of war and resistance: The Pol Pot regime (1975–1979)

The following two sections analyze the contexts according to Bergen's three identified preconditions for the Holocaust. There is weak evidence for relevant pre-existing cleavages as "timber" in Cambodia. While there is documented antipathy against the ethnic Vietnamese and Chinese (Chandler, 1983, p. 161), prior prejudice toward Buddhists or Muslim Cham is less clear. Another distinction in the Cambodian case is that the Khmer Rouge extended their political aims from national and racial purity to ideological purity. Pol Pot attempted to essentialize ideas, not just identities. This goal also shifted the targets and forms of repression, due to the regime's enormous fear of ideological subversion. The category of "enemy" was unbounded and potentially all-inclusive. However, this ideological fear was often framed in nationalistic/ethnic terms: "Cambodian bodies with Vietnamese brains" (Locard, 2004, p. 181). The goal of ideological purity meant that everyone in Cambodia could be a target of genocidal violence.

Second, like the Holocaust, there was a "spark" of destabilizing crisis (Harff, 2000) and a context of war and revolution in Cambodia. Both countries used war as nation building; however, Hitler's aim was territorial expansionism, while Cambodia was more focused on consolidation and strengthening the center's control. Third, "favorable conditions" for genocidal violence were also present in the case of Cambodia: U.S. and formal colonial powers (e.g., France and Japan) withdrew from Southeast Asia in 1975, and a regional policy of isolation from neighbors largely continued until the Vietnamese invasion in 1979 (Chandler, 1983, p. 188). Internally, there was also weak historic civic engagement in Cambodia to organize resistance; Chandler notes that in the 1930s the French attributed Cambodian obedience to their "reverence for authority" (p. 162). The lack of organized civil society and isolation from regional neighbors created favorable conditions for the Khmer Rouge to conduct a genocidal campaign.

Finally, state strength shaped the modes and forms of resistance during the genocide in Cambodia. Whereas Hitler's Germany was a totalitarian regime, penetrating all aspects of life, the Khmer Rouge in Cambodia is an example of a strong but brittle state. It was too weak to trust the people it consumed, but strong enough to impose its will (Chandler, 1983). However, the Pol Pot regime did have totalitarian aspirations, asserting "absolutely everything belongs to the *Angkar*" (Locard, 2004, p. 372). The Khmer Rouge never fully achieved centralized control; for example, each region had its own military force. However, in many areas of the country, the regime dominated personal, private, and public life — for example, enforcing group marriage ceremonies, communal eating, and dividing families through separate living areas for men, women, and children. These policies were enforced with terror (Kiernan, 2008) and required obedience and loyalty (Kiernan, 2008, p. 225; Chandler, 1983, p. 192).

Brief history of war and resistance: Rwanda (1994)

Like the Holocaust, the 1994 genocide in Rwanda has become a paradigmatic case. Like Cambodia, structural differences in the state and society add comparative clarity to understand modes of resistance. First, prior to colonialism there were distinctions among Hutus, Tutsis, and Twa, yet categorization was fairly plastic and was not the organizing factor to violence or conflictive clashes. In 1933, the Belgian census formalized "ethnic" identities which also had direct implications for governance. As "timber," these cleavages were maintained through the ID card system and violence between the Tutsi diaspora, Tutsi civilians, and the Hutu-led authoritarian state continued through the 1970s and 1980s. Second, in the 1980s, an economic crisis with the fall of coffee and tea prices left the Rwandan government dependent on external sources of funds. As a "spark," this economic destabilization created conducive conditions for the Rwandan Patriotic Front (RPF) to launch a civil war from 1990 to 1993. During peace negotiations to end the civil war, a split in the Hutu elite positioned the *akazu* in opposition to President Habyarimana (Gourevitch, 1998, p. 81). The *akazu* bankrolled the Hutu Power machine, including the media and *interahamwe* (pp. 85, 95). The third structural factor, "favorable conditions," was also present in 1994. The international community was politically invested in the Arusha peace process and proved unable to muster the political will to intervene militarily, based on the ongoing war in Bosnia and the humiliation of the U.S. military in Somalia in 1992 (Power, 2001).

In 1994, Rwanda was a strong but brittle state and, similar to Cambodia, genocide was used to consolidate state power through an approximation of totalitarian control. Unlike Cambodia, however, a history of authoritarian rule had created a strong, centralized government that could control most aspects of people's lives. However, following the crash of Habyarimana's plane, the government collapsed and the military took over when the genocide started. Also differing from Cambodia in timing and motivation, the armed struggle waged against the genocidal regime in Rwanda was initiated externally by the Tutsi RPF from Uganda, not by internal members.

Variation of the dependent variable

Variation on the dependent variable, resistance, includes both attitudinal and behavioral responses. According to the theoretical model above, there are three modes of resistance: internal, individual, and solidarity. There is also variation in more active forms of resistance. Behavioral changes can be both individual and social/collective. Personal changes in behavior reflect an individual choice to counteract the state-sponsored violence. However, a collective behavioral challenge, such as social support and solidarity, may vary based on the conditions noted above.

Data collection. The current case studies relied primarily on survivor memoirs and interviews. Recognizing that internal feelings are impossible to measure precisely, compounded by the noise introduced by memories and retrospective accounts, the current essay adopts the perspective that "there is no way of knowing what provokes survivors' behavior unless we accept [their attitudes] at face value" (Des Pres, 1980, p. 44). Systematic data collection included immersing in a particular case and generating an inductive list of victim responses, including positive and negative, and protective and harmful reactions. Factors that survivors identified as important, as well as those which fit the three theoretical approaches above, were included. Compilations of survivors' experiences were also used, keeping in mind the original author bias (George & Bennett, 2005, p. 100). A limitation in the current data is that only those who survived can tell their stories. Therefore, the resistance examples that emerge from the data are biased toward those that helped individuals live. "The stories survivors tell are limited, of course, but they possess the kind of certainty, wholly human and involved, that moral resistance needs" (Des Pres, 1980, p. 49).

Rethinking Resistance, Testing the Model

Structures and struggles for survival: The Holocaust

In *An Anatomy of Life in the Death Camps*, Des Pres (1980) writes that survival is "the capacity of men and women to *live* beneath the pressure of protracted crisis, to sustain terrible damage in mind and body and yet be there, sane, alive, *still human*" (p. v, emphasis added). Survival is more than the physical aspects of eating and breathing; it necessitates humanity and dignity (Todorov, 1996, p. 21). Des Pres gathered multiple stories so that "these scattered voices might issue in one statement" (p. vi). The individual memoirs tell a collective story which highlights the major themes of resistance (p. 38). In the death camps three types of resistance emerge: (1) covert acts of humanity and attitudes of dignity, (2) concrete physical acts, and (3) social bonding and an ever-present camouflage that reveals the duality of behavior in the extreme (Scott, 1990).

Humanity, the "capacity of the individual to remain a subject with a will" (Todorov, 1996, p. 16), and dignity, "inward resistance to determination by external forces," were forged in covert ways (Des Pres, 1996, p. 67). The camps were structured to uproot victims, giving them no place in the world, and to make them superfluous, asserting the victims no longer belonged to the world at all (Arendt, 1968, p. 173). To defy the camps' design, a form of internal resistance was to regain or re-root a sense of self. When people first arrived to the camps, "the old self fell apart, not able to root itself in new ground" (Des Pres, 1980, p. 78). Literally stripped of their identity, they were immediately forced to shave hair, be naked in extreme temperatures, wear ill-fitting uniforms, and be tattooed with a number that became the sole means of interacting with the official camp hierarchy. Destroying differentiation, individuality, and a unique identity are mechanisms that totalitarian regimes use to create an atmosphere of terror (Arendt, 1976, p. 151).

To protect themselves emotionally from this terror, those living in the camps experienced a subject-object split (Des Pres, 1980, p. 82). Regaining the severed sense of self and dignity was critical for survival and to repair this split. One example of how this was practiced was to use each other's names, because "only a man is worthy of a name" (Levi, 1996, p. 42). This exchange of affirming one another's humanity and selfhood can also been seen in a second example: sharing stories. "Despite the prohibition, we exchanged a visit and we talk and we talk ... full of words, memories and of another pain ... 'longing for one's home'" (p. 55). Keeping memories alive was a means to resist the camps' structure and to keep rooted in one's own home and history. At the same time, sharing words and stories kept survivors rooted in the social world, in a larger humanity.

Second, individual concrete acts gave survivors the physical strength needed to sustain themselves each day. An individual example of physical resistance is washing. "At 4:30, a 'coffee'—a light mint infusion without nourishment and with a repulsive taste—was distributed. We often took a few swallows and used the rest for washing" (Donat in Des Pres, 1996, p. 64). The physical act of washing had symbolic importance: it allowed victims to remain visibly human (Levi, 1996, p. 40).

Third, the camps were designed to fracture human relationships, and yet victims engaged in social acts and solidarity despite the fear (Des Pres, 1980, p. 199). Totalitarian regimes impose domination through enforcing two strategies: loneliness and isolation. Loneliness separates the individual from social intercourse, while isolation removes him or her from the political sphere (Arendt, 1968, p. 173). Loneliness and isolation were overcome in secretive and subtle ways. Social interaction was found in a clandestine holiday celebration or singing songs in Yiddish or one's native language (Levi, 1996). It also includes a range of behaviors such as pilfering, sabotage, and "organizing," or stealing from the Ka-Be. A survivor from Buchenwald accounts how during roll call they would push together to prop up weak prisoners who could no longer stand; "others pressed close on either side and supported me with the weight of their bodies" (Des Pres, 2003, p. 117). Regardless of the way the transcript is voiced or expressed, the creation of a space for this hidden transcript is itself an achievement (Scott, 1990, p. 118). The first step was social interaction; through this, life in the camps was rebuilt by overcoming loneliness. Scott (1990) calls the culmination and cultivation of these social acts of resistance "infrapolitics," or the cultural underpinning of a more visible political action (p. 184). Infrapolitics represents a second step in which solidarity undermines the political isolation imposed by totalitarian policies.

Support for the initial theoretical model is found in the types of resistance in the Holocaust death camps (Table 2). The various individual stories and memoirs highlight the internal covert maintenance of dignity, the individual acts for daily existence, and the solidarity forged through hidden communication and collective infrapolitics of resistance. However, the Holocaust case study also reveals the need for a more dynamic heuristic to adequately capture the relationship between survival and multiple types of resistance during genocidal violence.

		Holocaust	Cambodia	Rwanda
Attitudes				
	Internal	Cultivate sense of self	Keep memories alive	Not fear death
		Use names	Maintain emotions	
		Maintain dignity		
Behaviors				
	Individual	Wash face/hygiene	Hide identity	Hide identity
			Steal food	Pay for protection
			Flee	Flee and run
	Collective	Tell stories	Silence	Throw stones
		"Organize" food		Talk about the dead
		Celebrate holidays		Live in small teams

Table 2. Contextual examples of survivors' modes of resistance in each case study

Structures and struggles for survival: Cambodia

In *Children of Cambodia's Killing Fields: Memoirs by Survivors* (1999), brief vignettes of survivors' strategies for resistance demonstrate the shifting forms of coping with genocidal violence. Mounting feelings of hopelessness were accompanied by deep hunger and intense fatigue (Pran, 1999, p. 47). "We rarely played or had long conversations because we lacked the energy and tried to conserve it for the next day's work quota" (p. 48). Yet, survivors' stories from the killing fields of Cambodia reaffirm the three types of resistance in the Holocaust: internal covert acts of humanness, individual concrete physical acts, and solidarity through infrapolitics.

First, even in an environment of starvation and brutal violence, survivors report internal resistance. Darith Keo explains his experience: "Even during the darkest days of captivity I clung to the good memories of my early childhood. They would help me make it through the times of hard labor. I would remember the rustling of mango leaves in the back of our house. Taking a shower in the rain. How warm I felt inside when I came back in the house and my mom would wrap me in a blanket. My first day of preschool" (Pran, 1999, p. 164). The things that were denied to him during the genocide — food, hygiene, warmth, family contact, and education — were kept alive in Keo's memories. In a second example, Sophea Mouth shares how maintaining emotions defies "Angka's ... attempt to destroy all my compassion for another human being." Mouth held compassion "deep inside," despite public behavior of compliance. He retained the capacity to feel in order to resist the dehumanizing and isolating ideology of the Khmer Rouge. These covert acts of cultivating memories and emotional responses help individuals retain a sense of humanity in the face of genocidal terror.

Second, victims in Cambodia also countered the rules of the Pol Pot regime with individual acts that enabled their physical survival. During the initial population displacement and period of more targeted killing, victims would hide military belongings and college degrees to obscure connections to the former Lon Nol government or being labeled as a "new" person (Pran, 1999, pp. 43, 164). By hiding former identities, individuals increased their chances for survival. A second form of physical survival was to steal food. "Every day and night we prayed and thought only about food…. Everyone became a burglar, and if we were caught, death was certain" (p. 55).

Third, Ben Kiernan (2008) documents various types of resistance which included irony, silence, and mocking humor (pp. 246–250). "Terror minimized meaningful vertical communication," so individuals found ways to subvert, through horizontal stories and interactions (p. 64). Facing material danger, threat of physical harm, and an onslaught of revolutionary messages jamming the airwaves, silence became an example of resistance. "Peasants, soldiers, and intellectuals had their quiet ways of mocking their conditions and CPK [Communist Party of Kampuchea] responsibility for them" (p. 247). In an ironic twist to Pol Pot's isolating policies, silence was added to the list of prohibited acts (p. 249). Analyzing the hidden transcripts in Cambodia highlights how victims resisted by choosing intentional silence rather than affirming their allegiance to the Khmer Rouge.

Structures and struggles for survival: Rwanda

There are similar themes in the ways victims resisted in Rwanda as in the other cases, yet because of the speed and method of genocidal violence new patterns also emerged. Previous modes of survival in Rwanda, such as seeking sanctuary in churches, proved ineffective in the face of genocide. Gourevitch (1998) and Hatzfeld (2006) offer complementary sets of stories of survival in the Rwandan genocide. Set in urban and rural contexts, respectively, there is a certain degree of overlap in how individuals found a way to survive (Table 2).

First, there is a notable silence in survivors' stories about internal forms of resilience. Despite the history of conflict between the Hutus and Tutsis, the victims still could not fully comprehend the scale and scope of genocide. "We heard [the Hutu killers], we did say to ourselves that things weren't going well, but still, we couldn't actually believe it" (Hatzfeld, 2006, p. 11). Once the truth set in, many victims experienced an internal collapse. Telling his story to Gourevitch (1998), Nkongoli explained that some were resigned to die, full of fear, who had been "psychologically prepared to expect death just for being Tutsi. They were being killed for so long that they were already dead" (p. 23). However, some were able to move from disbelief and despair to begin to fan embers of resilience. After being left for dead, Francine Niyitegeka accounts how she was "not afraid of death anymore.... I finally brought myself back to life, returned to the business of survival, and rejoined my team" (Hatzfeld, 2006, p. 38).

Second, as the genocide unfolded, the number of options for individual resistance shrank. At the beginning, mistaken identities and hiding allowed some to survive. When these methods did not work, victims tried to pay for protection and to flee to refuge. In Nyamata, Marie-Louise Kagoyire, the wife of a shopkeeper, was able to combine resources for protection and passage to Burundi from a Hutu neighbor (Hatzfeld, 2006, p. 128). Flight, or running from the perpetrators, also took on a literal sense in rural areas of Rwanda. "That's how young people with nimble legs that could cleave the air tried to save themselves. As for others, their only chance was to dash onward until they ran out of breath, hoping not to be cut down before the end" (p. 100). These individual acts increased the chances of physical survival.

Third, new forms of solidarity had to be created during the genocide in Rwanda. For example, seeking sanctuary in churches, a method used in past cycles of inter-group violence, did not protect victims during the 1994 genocide. "A great crowd had already gathered, because it's part of Rwandan custom to take refuge in God's houses when the massacres begin," explained Cassius Niyonsaba (Hatzfeld, 2006, p. 13). The perpetrators of the genocide exploited this custom. For example, a Hutu Power mayor advised the Tutsis to seek sanctuary in the church. "They did, and a few days later the mayor came to kill them" (Gourevitch, 1998, p. 18). Solidarity was thus forged through new forms of communication and relationships in an attempt to resist the loneliness and isolation imposed by Hutu Power violence. In Rugarama Hill, "We would describe the bodies we had seen during the day, and how they had been cut; we'd determine who hadn't emerged from the marsh, and thus discover who had been caught that day" (Hatzfeld, 2006, p. 199). Each small group developed their own way to communicate. "At times we even had the heart for teasing," said Innocent Rwililiza in Kayumba Hill (p. 101), whereas in Cyugaro, "we did not argue, we teased no one, we did not mock the women who had been raped, because all the women expected to be raped," explained Jean-Baptise Munyankore. In contrast to the memories and stories about the past shared in the death camps of the Holocaust and Cambodia, the communication described by survivors in Rwanda was primarily focused on their day-to-day experiences. These verbal exchanges were facilitated as survivors formed small groups or pseudo-family units in the marshes. "To avoid dying together, we divided into small teams. We'd place three children here, two children farther along, two more somewhere else" (p. 198). While they were "forced to live 'everyone for himself' during our flights through the swamp" it was "'all for all' in our evening camp" (p. 71).

In conclusion, the types of resistance in the case of Rwanda do not completely match the methods in the Holocaust and Cambodia. These survivors' stories highlighted the role of initial disbelief, mistaken identity, paying for protection, flight, and new patterns of communication and relationships as collective responses when places of sanctuary were betrayed. This is not to say that internal resistance was *not* present in Rwanda, but it was not as prevalent as in memoirs of those who survived the bureaucratic death camps of the Holocaust or the killing fields of Cambodia.

Synthesis

There is mixed support for the hypotheses generated by the three initial theories. First, the theory of obedience may partially explain why victims are initially caught in cycles of genocidal violence. The history of political exclusion leading to weak civic engagement in Cambodia and the disbelief of the scale and speed of violence in Rwanda provide two examples. However, the obedience theory falls short in explaining the complex sets of attitudes and behaviors over time. For example, the survivor narratives from the Holocaust and Cambodia also contradict the prediction of internalizing the oppressors' dehumanizing message. Keeping memories alive, washing one's face, and telling stories of the past are important ways the victims resist internally and socially and maintain their humanity. Finally, across each case there are a number of individual and collective examples of physical acts of resistance which cannot be explained by the obedience theory.

The second theory of individual resiliency also partially explains patterns of resistance to genocidal violence. Task-oriented coping can be understood as the concrete physical acts for daily survival, such as stealing food. This theory predicts social support is an important construct, helping explain the pseudo-family units formed in Rwanda and the social connections forged in the death camps around shared holidays and singing in one's mother tongue. However, this theory does not capture the internal and symbolic forms of resilience, such as regaining a sense of self or washing to remain more visibly human.

Third, the interactive theory on the hidden transcripts of resistance most completely describes the observed patterns of victims' responses to genocidal violence. For example, attention on the conditions of genocide helps to explain why fleeing was evident in Cambodia and Rwanda but not in the Holocaust. This theory accounts for the link between stronger totalitarian ideologies and more internal, covert patterns of resilience, such as in the case of Cambodia. However, this theoretical approach does not fully explain (a) the individual's path from disbelief to despair to resistance or (b) the overall relationship between genocidal violence, victims' responses, and survival.

An interactive heuristic

By examining how the existing theories can explain the paradigmatic case of the death camps in the Holocaust and the least-similar cases of Cambodia and Rwanda, a more dynamic heuristic is proposed. Rather than static models of resistance (Figure 1) or discussing victims as a monolithic group, it is necessary to chart an individual's trajectory of resistance. It is also necessary

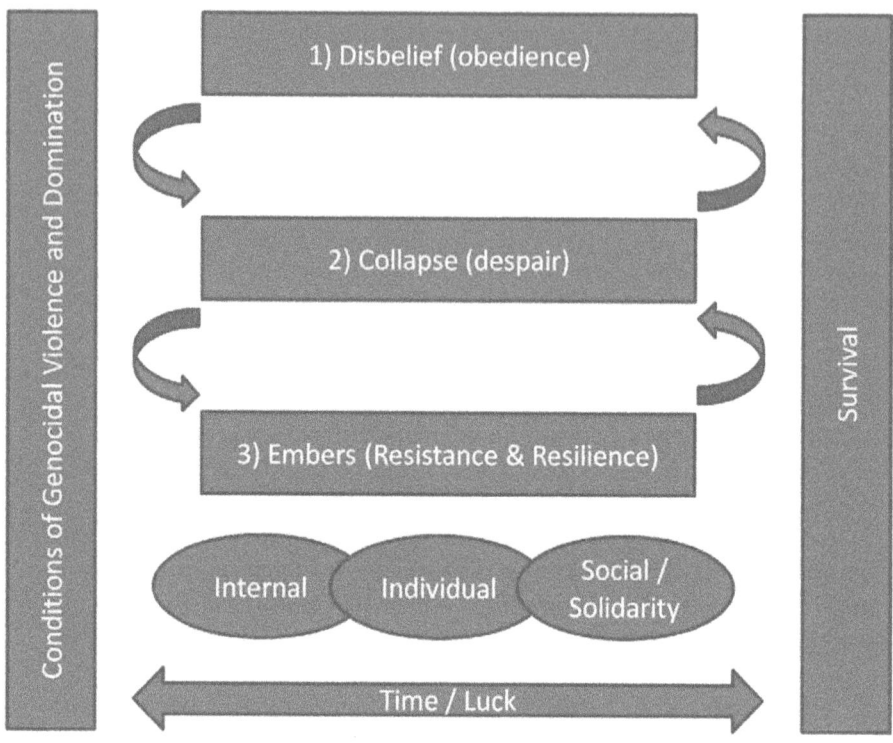

Figure 2

to understand how the forms of nonviolent resistance are crafted to defy the conditions of violence and the methods of domination (Table 1). These two dimensions are incorporated into a revised heuristic (Figure 2), which also includes one of the key insights gained from the case studies: the fundamental role of time and chance. This heuristic highlights that resistance is a necessary, but not necessarily sufficient, condition for survival in settings of genocidal violence. In a context of a "final solution," a strategy for survival may not be possible. Instead, survival is determined by time and chance, and life is practiced through daily resistance and struggle against the structures of oppression.

"All things human take time," (Des Pres, 1980, p. 89). When time is taken into account, seemingly contradictory descriptions within survivor memoirs become more comprehensible. For example, Levi (1996) first describes the Ka-Be where "all are enemies or rivals" but later is "bound by a tight bond of alliance" with his friend Alberto (pp. 42, 138). Tracing the survivors' narratives across time in the case studies, three stages emerge. First is a feeling of disbelief in which victims' get caught in the genocidal system.

This temporary paralysis may prevent them from fleeing during brief windows of opportunity. However, once caught in the setting that seems to lead to death, individuals may quickly pass to the second stage: collapse or breakdown. During genocidal violence, the attack on selfhood proved too powerful for many; for example, the highest death rates in the Holocaust were among newcomers to the camps. In Rwanda, Nkongoli said some people were resigned to death; they were "already dead." Symptoms of the second phase of despair include uncertainty, grief, terror, shock, and moral disgust. "The prisoner discovers a world without pity and finds that he can actually live in such a world" (Todorov, 1996, p. 41). In this stage, the dominance of the genocidal regime seems to prevail; the desire for life is largely silenced.

Yet, with time and chance, it is possible for victims to enter the third stage of reintegration and recovery (Des Pres, 1980, p. 77; Bergen, 2003, p. 202). The embers of humanity have not been extinguished, "and it takes only the smallest relief from brutality for the flames of conscience to flare again" (Todorov, 1996, p. 41). The transition can be precipitated through social bonds, suggested by resilience theory, or through an interaction which they are "jarred back with the same horror that earlier had paralyzed them" (Des Pres, 1980, p. 86). Des Pres describes this "flare of humanity" as a psychological turn from passivity to action, from horror to the daily business of staying alive (p. 87). However, time in the death camps was a luxury, and for many the psychological turn never came. But for those who reached the third stage, it was marked by healing and inner repair. For example, survivors' actions in the camps were fueled by the attitude: "They might make it, they probably won't, but they will not stop trying" (p. 188). Within this stage a desire to live was cultivated.

Time and chance also were prevalent in survivors' stories from Rwanda. Paul Rusesabagina described that he "had merely been able to work for [refugees at the Hotel Milles Collines] protection until the time came when they were saved by someone else" (Gourevitch, 1998, p. 123). However, Gourevitch notes, "had the RPF not been pounding Hutu Power from across the valley, there would have been no [UN] convoy—and probably no survivors" from the hotel (p. 144). This sentiment was echoed in the rural areas. "If the liberators of the RPF had taken another week to arrive, not one Tutsi in Bugesera would still be alive" stated Mukamanzi (Hatzfeld, 2006, p. 82). The killing during the 100 days of violence was intense; however, the comparatively quick end to genocide also allowed those who could struggle to live each day to survive.

Finally, the heuristic emphasizes the overlapping nature of forms of resistance—treated as distinct constructs in the initial model. During genocide, the struggle for survival "could only be a social achievement, not an individual accident" (Weinstock in Des Pres, 1980, p. 122). The individual assertion of dignity was integrally linked with concrete acts of mutual support that provided for physical needs. Claiming dignity was also linked with solidarity and breaking through social loneliness and political isolation through the hidden transcripts of infrapolitics. With the goal of maintaining dignity, internal, individual, and social modes of resistance took shape through reciprocal, concrete mutual support and subversive communication of individual will.

In addition to tracing an individual resistance trajectory over time, the heuristic depicts the overall relationship of conditions, victims' responses, and survival. For example, the case of Cambodia demonstrates the interplay between the method of oppression and the mode of subversion. First, the Khmer Rouge goal of ideological purity introduced a more pervasive and indiscriminant threat of persecution; anyone could be accused of being an enemy for having disloyal thoughts. In response, to avoid affirming the Center's rhetoric, silence was turned into a form of resistance. More internal forms of resistance, as shown in Mouth's story of keeping compassion deep inside, were emphasized.

Second, because identity did not determine victims' fate, patterns of bonding were not different in Cambodia. For example, in the death camps, Levi and Alberto find mutual support with a fellow Italian from the POW camp who shares food with them, and Yiddish songs were shared at times in the barracks among co-ethnics. However, when family units were systematically torn apart by the Khmer Rouge, the lack of pre-existing cleavages or established identity groups in Cambodia meant there was not a ready identity group for support or solidarity. While social identity was a reason for being targeted in the Holocaust, it may also have served as an organizing form of resistance. This does not appear to be present in the narratives of Cambodian survivors.

Third, the different conditions of war and relationships with regional neighbors provided an escape valve for Cambodian survivors to flee that was not available to those under attack in the Holocaust. The case of Cambodia shows how the heuristic improves understanding of resistance responses by studying the structural conditions of genocidal violence.

In summary, the revised heuristic redefines the relationships among the existing theories. First, the center of Figure 2 opens analytical space for individual transitions across three stages and overlapping modes of resistance. For example, in the Holocaust, the heuristic captures not only the destruction of self in the initiation into camp life, but also the reconstruction of self within the camp "unreality." The arrows up and down suggest that victims' resistance is not linear and unidirectional, but shifts as the conditions change. Second, the revised heuristic suggests that the daily resistance practices only partially mediate the relationship between genocidal conditions and survival; however these are necessarily not sufficient causes. Third, the model positions time and chance as an essential component for survival in the face of totalitarian domination. Testing existing theory in three cases results in a heuristic that more adequately describes survivors' mechanisms of resistance amid cases of modern genocide.

Conclusion

As "genocide scholars often don't pay attention to attempts to oppose genocidal regimes" (Kiernan, 2008, p. xiv), the essay examined the roots of victims' resistance. These modes discussed are often overlooked because they are not recognized as successful. The "real behavior of survivors goes unobserved because it [is] covert, un-dramatic and not at all in accord with our expectation of heroism" (Des Pres, 1980, p. 172).Yet, although victims' resistance cannot overturn genocidal policies, they are not ineffective (Kiernan, 2008, p. 3). Whereas a traditional focus of resistance focuses on active, military resistance movements, this essay demonstrates the importance of the nonviolent dimensions, namely personal dignity and individual and collective hidden transcripts of subversion.

Toward this end, one must "make the structure of survival visible," as survivors are trapped in a world of total domination (Des Pres, 1980, pp. v, 13). Escalation of genocidal violence is paralleled by escalating resistance. However, the forms of resistance shift depending on the conditions of oppression: the more comprehensive the means of domination, the more subtle and internal the means of confronting that terror (Scott, 1990, pp. 3, 109). In the case of the Holocaust and Cambodia, for example, victims' "dignity and selfhood were beyond the enemy's reach" (Des Pres, 1996, p. 202). Levi (1996) wrote, "we still possess one power, and we must defend it with all our strength for it is the last — the power to refuse our consent" (p. 41). These more subversive or internal forms are no less powerful. Thus, the paper argues we must examine both aspects of resilience, (a) the "opposition to an attempt to bring ... thoughts of feelings into consciousness" and (b) "the act or power of resisting, opposing, or withstanding" (Webster's English Dictionary, 1966).

NOTES

1. This essay understands victims as those targeted by the perpetrators of genocide. Although there is frequently a distinction made between victims and survivors in the clinical psychological literature, this essay uses them interchangeably.

2. An online search of relevant journals (*Genocide Studies and Prevention, Holocaust*

and Genocide Studies, Human Rights Review, Journal of Conflict Resolution, Journal of Genocide Studies, Journal of Human Rights and *Journal of Peace Studies*) confirmed the dearth of theory or empirical literature on "resistance" during genocide. The handful of relevant articles that appeared focused on rescuers or armed revolts. For an exception, see a cross-case comparative study on resistance during genocidal violence (Bhavnani & Backer, 2000). None of the journals covered topics that linked "resilience" to genocide studies.

3. Five of the original sample of prisoners had to be released early due to extreme emotional responses. The entire study was ended after six days, rather than running the full 14 days because of ethical concerns for the welfare of the remaining seven participants.

4. Case selection was determined by instances of genocide as a social/political phenomenon, not as a legal category or definition. Scholarly debate surrounding Cambodia are irrelevant to the current argument (for a more complete discussion, see *Searching for the Truth: The Magazine of the Documentation Center of Cambodia,* 2001). Therefore, throughout the paper, genocide and genocidal violence will be used interchangeably.

5. Refining theory based on paradigmatic case is particularly important in genocide studies in which the Holocaust serves, in many respects, as the "definition" of genocide.

References

Arendt, H. (1968). *Totalitarianism: Part three of the origins of totalitarianism.* San Diego: Harcourt Brace Jovanovich.

Barber, B.K. (2001). Political violence, social integration, and youth functioning: Palestinian youth from the Intifada. *Journal of Community Psychology, Special Issue: The impact of violence on children at home, community, and national levels, 29*(3), 259–280.

_____, and J.A. Olsen (2009). Positive and negative psychosocial functioning after political conflict: Examining adolescents of the first Palestinian intifada. In B.K. Barber (Ed.) *Adolescents and war: How youth deal with political violence* (pp. 207–237). New York: Oxford University Press.

Bergen, D. (2003). *War and genocide: A concise history of the Holocaust.* Lanham, MD: Rowman & Littlefield.

Bhavnani, R., and D. Backer (2000). Localized ethnic conflict and genocide: Accounting for differences in Rwanda and Burundi." *Journal of Conflict Resolution, 44*(3), 283–306.

Bronfrenbrenner, U. (1979). Contexts of child rearing: Problems and prospects. *American Psychologist, 34*(10), 844–850.

Browning, Christopher. (1992). *Ordinary Men: Reserve Police Battalion 101 and the Final Solution in Poland.* New York: HarperCollins.

Calhoun, L.G., and R.G. Tedeschi (2009). *Facilitating post-traumatic growth: A clinician's guide.* Mahwah, NJ: Lawrence Erlbaum Associates.

Chandler, D. (1983). *A history of Cambodia.* Boulder, CO: Westview.

Cummings, E.M., M.C. Goeke-Morey, A.C. Schermerhorn, C.E. Merrilees, and E. Cairns. (2009). Children and political violence from a social ecological perspective: Implications for research on children and families in Northern Ireland. *Clinical Child and Family Psychology Review,* 12, 16–38.

Des Pres, T. (1980). *The survivor: An anatomy of life in the death camps.* New York: Oxford University Press.

_____. (2003). The will to survive. In D. Neiwyk (Ed.), *The Holocaust: Problems in European civilization* (pp. 113–118). Boston: Houghton Mifflin.

George, A.L., and A. Bennett (2005). *Case studies and theory development in the social sciences.* Cambridge: MIT Press.

Gourevitch, P. (1998). *We wish to inform you that tomorrow we will be killed with our families: Stories from Rwanda.* New York: Farrar, Straus, and Giroux.

Harff, B. (2000). The etiology of genocides. In I. Walliman and M. Dobkowski (Eds.), *Genocide and the modern age: Etiology and case studies of mass death* (pp. 41–59). Syracuse: Syracuse University Press.
Hatzfeld, J. (2006). *Life laid bare: The survivors in Rwanda speak* (Linda Coverdale, Trans.). New York: Other.
Herman, J.L. (1992). *Trauma and recovery.* New York: Basic.
Kiernan, B. (2008). *The Pol Pot regime: Race, power, and genocide in Cambodia under the Khmer Rouge, 1975–1979 (3d edition).* New Haven: Yale University Press.
_____. (2008). *Genocide and resistance in Southeast Asia: Documentation, denial and justice in Cambodia and East Timor.* New Brunswick, NJ: Transaction.
Levi, P. (1996). *Survival in Auschwitz.* New York: Touchstone.
Locard, H. (2004). *Pol Pot's little red book: The sayings of Anghkar.* Chiang Mai, Thailand: Silkworm.
Luthar, S.S., D. Cicchietti, and B. Becker (2000). The construct of resilience: A critical evaluation and guidelines for future work. *Child Development, 71*(3), 543–562.
Masten, A.S., K.M. Best, and N. Garmezy (1990). Resilience and development: Contributions from the study of children who overcome adversity. *Development and Psychopathology, 2,* 425–444.
Milgram, S. (1974). *Obedience to authority: An experimental view.* New York: Harper & Row.
Miller, D., and L.T. Miller (1993). *Survivors: An oral history of the Armenian genocide.* Berkeley: University of California.
Power, S. (2001, September). Bystanders to genocide. *Atlantic Monthly.*
Pran, D. (1999). *Children of Cambodia's killing fields: Memoirs by survivors,* selections. New Haven: Yale University Press.
Punamaki, R. (2006). *Resiliency in conditions of war and military violence: Preconditions and developmental processes.* Lanham, MD: Jason Aronson.
Rutter, M. (1995). Psychosocial adversity: Risk, resilience and recovery. *Southern African Journal of Child & Adolescent Psychiatry, 7*(2), 75–88.
Scott, J. (1990). *Domination and the arts of resistance: Hidden transcripts.* New Haven: Yale University Press.
Searching for the truth: The magazine of the Documentation Center of Cambodia. (2001).
Staub, E. (1989). *The roots of evil: The origins of genocide and group violence.* New York: Cambridge University Press.
_____, and J. Vollhardt (2008). Altruism born of suffering: The roots of caring and helping after victimization and other trauma. *American Journal of Orthopsychiatry, 78*(3), 267–280.
Todorov, T. (1996). *Facing the extreme: More life in the concentration camps* (Arthur Denner and Abigail Pollak, Trans.). New York: Metropolitan.
Valentino, B. (2000). Final solutions: The causes of mass killing and genocide. *Security Studies* 9/3 (Spring): 1–59.
Webster's third new international dictionary of English language, unabridged (1966). Chicago: Encyclopedia Britannica.
Werner, E. (1993). Risk, resilience, and recovery: Perspectives from the Kauai Longitudinal Study. *Development and Psychopathology. Special Issue: Milestones in the development of resilience, 5*(4), 503–515.
Zimbardo, P., et al. (1973). Interpersonal dynamics in a simulated prison. *International Journal of Criminology and Penology, 1,* 69–97.

SECTION II — IN FROM THE MARGINS

Voices from the Diaspora: Reconciliation and Capacity Building in Refugee Communities from the Great Lakes Region of Africa

Barbara Tint, Julie Koehler, Vincent Chirimwami, Marie Abijuru, Sa'eed Mohamed Haji, Djimet Dogo, Carmina Rinker Lass and *Mindy Johnston*

> *This family from the Great Lakes, a Hutu family, was living upstairs in an apartment, and there was a Tutsi family living downstairs. The Hutu family was so scared; overnight they just moved out without telling people. Everyone was wondering why they broke the contract. They preferred to break the contract and pay the fine than share space with the Tutsi family. I didn't know about it. Both families are our clients—not only clients, but they even work for us. They are community leaders, and I didn't know until we came to this project; this issue came out during the dialogues. I didn't know. I was so stunned, that wow, those people, when they come here, when you see them, they are openly talking as if there is no problem. At the same time, they are so scared of each other, they have to move away from each other.*

So begins the African Diaspora Dialogue Project (ADDP) and the collaboration between the Conflict Resolution Graduate Program at Portland State University (PSU) and the Immigrant and Refugee Community Organization's Africa House. Hutu and Tutsi refugees from the genocide in Rwanda and the ongoing conflicts in Burundi, Democratic Republic of Congo (DRC), were arriving in the United States with great trauma behind them and great challenges ahead. From 2007 to 2011, with generous support from and collaboration with the Andrus Family Fund, we[1] worked intensively within these communities to build capacity toward a more reconciled and unified post-conflict African diaspora. We worked with groups from the Great Lakes region (Burundi, Congo, DRC), Somalia, Liberia, and Ethiopia. Our goals were to assess community needs, conduct a series of dialogue groups with selected participants, and then to train participants to become dialogue facilitators to carry this work deeper into their communities. This capacity-building dimension was critical to our efforts, as our goal was for the impact of the project to endure and be sustained beyond our involvement.

This essay will focus, specifically, on this work with groups from the Great Lakes region. We highlight issues particular to diaspora populations, discuss the phenomenon of latent conflict in the Great Lakes communities, describe the dialogue and training process undertaken in ADDP and offer insights related to the benefits and challenges of capacity building in these kinds of efforts. The essay includes excerpts from interviews with community members who became trained dialogue facilitators.

Dynamics of the Diaspora

> When the music changes, so does the dance. — African proverb

Diaspora populations around the world present an ever-growing global force; they are driven from their countries by civil wars, ethnic conflicts, famine, rural underdevelopment, lack of opportunity, forced or voluntary displacement, and political complexities. Diaspora communities include refugees, immigrants and political asylees whose official status may differ, but whose experiences in the diaspora are very much the same. As migrant populations increase, so does the need for services to accommodate these communities and the challenges they face. Particular to the challenges facing diaspora populations worldwide are the unaddressed issues of historical conflict that drove them from their homes.

Regardless of the circumstances that propel people into the diaspora, almost all migrants struggle to rebuild their lives. They share the common experience of undergoing a life-altering transition, typically forced and stemming from adversity. They endure various degrees of trauma, including separation from family, isolation, breakdown of community, discrimination in their new environment, and loss of identity, status, and livelihood. As they resettle, their ability to lead successful lives is challenged by new cultures, religions, climates, educational systems, economic hardships, employment difficulties, languages, and social and political barriers. They are often minorities in their adoptive countries and neighborhoods, which adds an additional challenge with racism they may not have previously encountered. Communities in the diaspora face a continuous battle in trying to manage this trauma and loss, maintain their traditional heritage and culture, and adapt to a new environment.

In addition to the challenges inherent in the refugee experience, there are vital issues related to the exporting of historical native conflict into the resettlement experience. While resettlement efforts address issues such as housing, education, employment, health care, language, and other issues vital to successful integration, little has been done to address the reality that former enemies are now living next door to each other in apartment complexes, that new arrivals are reluctant to visit service agencies staffed by someone from a conflicting tribe, or that people are being ostracized by the very community members whom they thought would provide support in the new land. Many in the diaspora are still living with the memories and consequences of the internal conflict and politics of the motherland; historical challenges and conflicts are imported with the communities themselves and are typically left unaddressed. Inter-communal conflict in these communities becomes a major obstacle to successful resettlement and to the development of a unified diaspora community. These conflicts are powerful forces as people transition into the diaspora. While mutual interdependence has the potential to unify people across conflict lines, increased fear, trauma, and insecurity related to resettlement can also harden the barriers between conflicted people and groups.

It is also true that along with the loss and transition that diaspora communities face, for some, their new lives provide opportunities they would not have had at home. This might include educational opportunities, greater freedom from persecution, shifting gender roles (which are often empowering to women and challenging for men), and the ability to start fresh in a new context. Whether the changes are painful, liberating, or both, for most diaspora community members, the transition from one context to the next is rarely a smooth or predictable journey.

Identity associations within diaspora populations are dependent, to some degree, on the size and make-up of that community in the host environment (Hume, 2008). Diaspora community members often need each other in different ways than they did in the home context. Their shared experience of loss, transition, adjustment challenges, and new minority status shifts the relational dynamics. Smaller communities feel a greater need to join together for a greater sense of unity, connection, and security. While this is challenging in circumstances of community difference, it also provides a great opportunity for mutual interdependence, as reconciliation can be fueled by this shared need in a new land.

For example, a pan–African identity is more prominent in smaller diaspora communities, in which many regions might be represented, but with only a handful of individuals from any particular country, region, or ethnicity. Conversely, in areas with larger African populations, identity and associations tend to develop along more national, religious, or ethnic lines (Hume & Hardwick, 2005). Boundaries between groups become greater as unity and identity needs are served by increased numbers of specific tribal or national groups. This phenomenon might occur on a smaller level as well. For example, if a community of Somali refugees is small yet ethnically diverse, they may band together under the shared Somali identity; as the community grows with new arrivals, however, ethnic divisions might once again become more prominent.

Most diaspora communities remain deeply connected to others in the diaspora and in the homeland. Group members are connected to their own history and memories of place, to others who have migrated to different parts of the world, to friends and relatives whom they have left behind, to ongoing social and political events back home, and to the possibility that they might someday return. During our dialogue processes, one thing that became particularly clear was the power of this connectivity. In some of our sessions, group members worked together to develop a concept of how they saw their experience in the dialogue groups and in the diaspora experience itself. They created the Model of Diaspora Interconnectivity, which informed much of our thinking and work within ADDP. The dialogue circles, from the smallest to the largest, are Inner Experience of Each Individual, Portland Dialogue Groups, Portland Diaspora Communities, U.S. Diaspora, International Diaspora, Home Region in Africa, and International Community.

The model is bi-directional in influence, as community members felt that what was happening inside their own dialogue circles would inform the wider diaspora communities, circumstances back home, and the wider international community. Similarly, they believed that global events and relationships from the home context continued to inform diaspora populations worldwide, their dialogue groups, and their own internal experiences. This Model of Diaspora Interconnectivity reflects the communal nature of the African diaspora, as well as the power of diaspora communities in impacting others across a wide range of circumstances. It also reflects the hope and possibility that reconciliation processes in diaspora communities have the potential to impact wider circles in the diaspora and in the home context.

Conflict in the Great Lakes

> He who knows only one side of a thing, knows little of that. — African proverb

The conflict in the Great Lakes (Burundi, DRC, and Rwanda) is complex and difficult to comprehend without a deeper understanding of its history. As with other regions in Africa, the Great Lakes region has experienced a deeply devastating and protracted conflict, the root causes of which are broad and multifaceted. In the macro view, it includes the legacy of European colonialism, competition for power and resources, and identity issues. Within the region, ethnic conflict contributed to the 1994 genocide in Rwanda, human slaughtering in the DRC, and communal wars in Burundi. These conflicts have created massive internal displacement of people into neighboring countries and other parts of the world. Along with these devastating histories, most people in the Great Lakes region also share common experiences such as the connection to the land and its natural recourses, the length of traumatic encounter, the impact of colonialism, and the phenomenon of forced migration.

The 1994 genocide in Rwanda was the result of a long-standing ethnic conflict between the majority Hutus and minority Tutsis. The struggle for power and the right to return home for many Tutsis exiled in Uganda ignited a war in 1991. For the next three years, the rebels, mostly Tutsis, gained ground, which influenced former President Habyarimana, a Hutu, to negotiate peace. His plane was shot down on April 12, 1994, when returning from a peace summit in Tanzania. Many believe that his killing fueled extremist Hutus to start the campaign of extermination of Tutsis and moderate Hutus, which killed over 500,000 people in 100 days.

In Burundi, the Tutsi minority clung to power since its independence from Belgium in 1962. An attempt to democratize the country in 1993 failed after the Hutu elected president, Melchior Ndadaye, was killed by the predominantly Tutsi army after only three months in office. His assassination sparked an array of violence and massacres between the Tutsi and Hutu ethnic groups, and ultimately fueled a decade-long conflict. Burundi's subsequent president, Cyprian Ntayamira, also a Hutu, was killed in the plane crash alongside President Habyarimana of Rwanda on their way back from the peace summit in Tanzania.

In the DRC, the conflict is based partially on ethnic differences, but largely on the invasion of Congo by external armies of Rwanda, Uganda, and Burundi. After the 1994 genocide in Rwanda, many Rwandans, including genocide perpetrators, sought and found refuge in neighboring Congo. In 1998, the Rwandan army invaded Eastern Congo claiming to hunt genocide perpetrators. The invasion of the Rwandan, Ugandan, and Burundian armies has resulted in more than 5 million Congolese killed and considerable mineral resources stolen from Congo. Therefore, while the DRC was not directly involved in the ethnic issues contributing to the genocide and ethnic conflict, it has been deeply impacted by events in the surrounding countries.

The events of these conflicts have had a devastating effect on the people from the region. The ethnic conflict between Tutsis and Hutus in both Rwanda and Burundi intensified to the extent that millions of people fled to the neighboring countries of Tanzania, Congo, Zambia, and Uganda. Further migration has taken place overseas, contributing to one of the largest African diaspora populations in the world. In the DRC, millions have died from poor living conditions, preventable diseases, hunger, and displacement. Many Congolese believe that they were victims of an exported ethnic conflict between Rwandan Hutus and Tutsis. To that end, many feel enmity toward the Rwandans whom they blame for their misery. Some dimensions of these conflicts continue to this day and lead to ongoing divisions in refugee communities around the world.

African Diaspora Dialogue Project (ADDP)

Great fires erupt from tiny sparks.—Libyan proverb

In an attempt to support people in addressing these historical conflicts, the ADDP team developed a dialogue and training process to strengthen internal capacity for reconciliation. Key stakeholders were identified and invited to participate in a 10-week dialogue series. Dialogue was structured in weekly, four-hour sessions and focused on topics such as: diaspora experiences, community strengths, community challenges, transition experiences, identity, history, community goals, and action plans. Facilitators for this round of dialogue were from the United States and Chad and did not carry historical issues related to the communities in dialogue. Processes were developed blending U.S. Western approaches to reconciliation (dialogue circles; invitation to confidentiality; combination of structured and unstructured sessions; external, impartial facilitators; direct approach to certain content) and traditional African approaches to reconciliation (ritual, prayer, storytelling, shared food, focus on ubuntu—a philosophy of shared humanity and collective orientation).

Toward the end of the dialogue series, participants developed a plan to take their experience into their wider community. Drawing on the Model of Diaspora Interconnectivity, participants believed in the importance of the work they were doing and its impact on wider circles. Participants felt that going out to their respective national communities was the best place to start for deepening the possibilities for reconciliation. Therefore, mixed participant teams including citizens of Burundi, DRC, and Rwanda went to community gatherings for each of the respective countries and led a series of community conversations about their dialogue experience and the hope of bringing the wider communities together in similar ways. From there, recruiting for another round of dialogue sessions began.

Simultaneous to the community conversations and recruitment process for a second round of dialogue sessions, training began with dialogue participants who were motivated to become facilitators. In the next round of dialogue, all dialogue groups were conducted by internal community members who were previous participants. In the Great Lakes group, there was one facilitator each from Rwanda, Burundi, and DRC — a vital step toward the goal of community capacity building.

Capacity building in dialogue

> If people come together, they can even mend a crack in the sky.—
> Somali proverb

The importance of the deep skill required for dialogue facilitation is addressed by many (Bohm, Nichol, & Senge, 2004; Ellinor and Gerard, 1998; Saunders, 2001; Tint, 2009). Saunders (2001) asserts that dialogue's power lies in its ability to engage groups with each other to listen deeply enough to be changed by what they hear. The holding of safe space where this interaction can occur is an art and requires skills that might not necessarily be present among dialogue participants. Thus, if intergroup dialogue is to be taken on by community members themselves, then training and capacity building with community members are essential to effectively and sustainably hand over these processes to internal actors.

If one were to consider the four interrelated qualities that Ellinor and Gerard (1998) call essential to dialogue work — suspension of judgment, suspension of assumption, listening and inquiry, and reflection—as cultivated qualities not easily attainable in conflicted societies, then the need for training in order to further cultivate these qualities is crucial in capacity building efforts for communities in conflict. ADDP facilitator training focused on dialogic skills such as listening, suspension, framing questions, attending to process dynamics, issues of reconciliation, transitions and change, and the holding of multiple perspectives around challenging topics. The development of these skills allows community members involved in dialogue processes to achieve a level of mastery where they can foster this in other member of their communities. Modeling is a key element in capacity building efforts where internal processes allow new understandings of the "other" to emerge. In-group facilitators have to have had their own experience of transformation around internal community dynamics before they are able to effectively facilitate other community groups in a reconciliation process.

In-group facilitators of dialogue may unwittingly add to the challenges that participants face in processes such as these. Limited skill in facilitation can contribute to confusing and potentially detrimental outcomes. Glyn (2009) outlines three common problems that occur in groups and that may be associated with ineffective facilitation: unclear purposes and misaligned activities, defensive and over-reactive communication, and abuses of power. Compounded by the sensitivities inherent in historical conflict, these problems can be exacerbated and include the potential for facilitators to be easily triggered by dialogue dynamics, have significant bias around process and content, and have difficulties in seeing and honoring multiple perspectives.

In spite of these potential challenges, capacity building holds a philosophy of valuing internal community wisdom and empowerment. Strengthening the cultural knowledge and voice from within is key in mobilizing conflicted communities toward their own vision of reconciliation (Freire, 2006; Lederach, 1995). It was with this philosophy and value in mind that the ADDP team moved in this direction. Below we explore the benefits and challenges of these efforts. Throughout some of the following sections are reflections from Vincent, a participant-turned-facilitator from the DRC; Marie, a participant-turned-facilitator from Rwanda; and Djimet, the director of Africa House from Chad, who was the non-community co-facilitator in the first round of dialogue with the Great Lakes group. Our facilitator from Burundi was not available for this discussion.

Benefits of internal capacity building efforts

Given that one of our primary goals in ADDP was to increase community capacity, we anticipated benefits from these efforts. We were not disappointed. Some of the specific benefits included:

Increased facilitator credibility

The newly trained facilitators were seen by the community as people who were connected to a reputable institution and thus were given more trust by all parties as insider facilitators. Training and credibility were key elements for community buy-in. Djimet talks about the benefit of starting with outsiders and then training insiders to be dialogue facilitators. He suggests that the project's connection to an outside institution played a key role in lending legitimacy to the training that the participants received:

> We provided enough skill to the insider to be able to resist some of the temptation that may trigger something, because those insiders we used are equipped with training, with tools, how to approach people, how to talk with people — coming there, not as an insider trying to bring people together, but they are coming there as people from the project. So those people are going into the community with a badge. It's not just that they work out in the community; now they are going with a name tag as somebody that got skill, got training, and who wants other people to benefit, too. So we prepared them. We prepared the ground for them. Also, combining them with outsider, it helps a lot, too. So at the same time, they have a kind of credibility. It helps a lot. Had we started the project directly using an insider, I don't think it would have worked.

Learning to listen and develop empathy

Facilitator training not only allowed community members to develop skills in this area, but it also added to their own internal shifts regarding the conflict. Vincent and Marie suggest that, through training, they actually learned how to listen in ways to enhance the potential for gaining empathy. This proved invaluable not only in becoming dialogue facilitators but also in increasing their own capacity for understanding and transformation. Marie stated:

> I learned a lot, but the first part was listening ... not to interrupt because he say what I don't want to hear. Just give him a time to finish and just listen ... how I can give the empathy to someone when he is saying what is happening to his or her family. So when I get that part I say now I can move on ... because when we try now to trust and share the story, is the moment now we start to say no, this person has the same problem, like me. Even he's Congolese, I'm Rwandese, we all have the same problem. We find out that, let's just leave the politics aside and talk about our problems now.

Vincent reflected that the dialogue project made him question the appropriateness and effectiveness of his culturally constructed expectations and modes about listening. The cultural listening practices he had internalized saw silence as disrespectful. However, through training, silence was seen as a way of deep listening and receptivity to others.

> Honestly, I think the great experience in that dialogue was to change my perception first to be able to listen to someone. In the beginning people

maybe shared those stories but I wasn't able to listen to it, because I know where it was coming from ... mine is the best, yours is not. Sometimes in our cultures also ... we talk over each other ... to show we are paying attention because if you stay quiet like this.... Did the French bring that? The French say "you respond to an imbecile by being quiet." So to show you are listening, *uh-huh*, make some noise, responding. You can't just let someone talk for five minutes and you are just quiet. Remember there is no eye contact. So how do you tell me you are listening if I can't even hear a voice from you [laugh]? So the listening capacity was also maybe a new concept for some of us. But when we opened up with the trust, we start to listen to one another; it doesn't matter how we did it.... We started getting the same experiences ... those are the ones I call transformation. That was a great experience.

Demonstrating understanding about historic relationships

Marie felt that being an insider facilitator was key because of accumulated historical knowledge. Outsiders could not carry the same level of background or information into the dialogue process. Through the process of building an increased understanding of historic relationships and connections beyond the conflicts back home, participants were able to let go of feelings of enmity. As Marie stated:

> It was beneficial to have community members facilitating because they know already what they were talking about. Because we know that now what we are talking about is not between the countries, but we are going to talk about what is happening in our communities.

Increased community comfort, ownership, and empowerment

As feelings of enmity decreased, and the project moved deeper into the communities, those involved in the project witnessed an increased sense of ownership and empowerment in these refugee groups. Djimet, who has been working with disempowered refugee communities here in the U.S. for the past decade, witnessed a sense of pride develop. He saw that this understanding, rooted in the ADDP dialogue process, could be used to empower community members to make sense of the processes that they were going through and to take their reconciliation efforts into the direction of advocacy. As community members entered the role of facilitator, the comfort and safety with the project increased.

Developing community leadership

Vincent and Marie reflect on the change in roles they have experienced since becoming dialogue facilitators. They have grown into community advocates for conflict transformation and understanding. Vincent also enrolled in the conflict resolution program at PSU to get a master's degree.

> Honestly, when I hear someone saying bad things about the Rwandese now I stand up as an advocate and try to tell that person, here is a story I heard from the Rwandese, because I don't necessarily have the capacity to bring them together.

Marie stated:

> I am grateful because I made my community aware of ADDP. Since the ADDP we went up together to have a 501(c)3: The Pacific Northwest Rwandese Association. I am in the executive committee. We are interested in many things; we are trying to ask for grants to see what we can do for our children. The Congolese talk about us because we invaded their country and people died. We feel sorry about what happened to the Congolese but we don't discuss about it. We feel like we have passed the ethnic divide in our community.

Djimet has witnessed several leaders come out of the ADDP process and has seen the growth of more than one community organization. Through the dialogue process and inclusion in the facilitation training, Somali and Great Lakes youth expressed their sentiments on how the dialogues had increased their role in building community cohesion. The youth who founded the Somali Youth Coalition shared with him how they had decided to start their organization to address their needs and give a platform for their voice in their community. As Djimet relayed:

> We took the skills we learned during the project to apply to our community. This is one of the reasons we were successful to come together and sit down to create a Somali Youth Coalition of Oregon. Same with the Rwandese — one Hutu man and one Tutsi woman came together to create the 501(c)3.

Language and cultural understanding

In-group facilitators allowed for an increased awareness of cultural cues present in the dialogue process along with flexibility of language. The first round of dialogue groups was conducted in English, thereby limiting the participants to English speakers. Newly trained community facilitators were able to conduct dialogue processes in native languages that not only increased the participant pool, but also increased the fluidity by which community members could communicate about challenging issues. Furthermore, many dynamics of relationships and nonverbal communication were understood by in-group facilitators in ways that would not have been possible by outsiders.

Commitment toward future generations

Reflections from dialogue facilitators and observers was that dialogue participants and those who stayed engaged as facilitators were motivated to do the hard work for the next generations — the kids and grandkids — so that their communities, now in the U.S., did not have to interact with each other in the same ways as they did back home. Djimet related:

> Even though they had hardness in their own hearts, they wanted a different life for the future generations. And it was for them that they willing to do this hard work. That it was hard work. That being in the room together was sometimes painful and sometimes scary. They didn't want to do it and we had people walk out. And yet they stayed with it because they really wanted a different life for their children — they didn't want their children and grandchildren to suffer. I think that is hope about the future and about the possibility for new beginnings.

Modeling

Balanced facilitation teams (i.e., facilitators who represent all the identity groups in conflict) were able to model cooperation, constructive dialogue, and potential for healing to other community members. Skilled in-group facilitators were able to inspire dialogue participants to develop dialogic skills and reconciliation of their own. Djimet explained:

> Before the project when people had a little problem they made it big. But through the project they learned skills in how to be calm and try to reason. In learning how to create safe space for other community members the dialogue facilitators were able to manage the kind of transformative space that they had experienced in the first dialogue. This space used the power of storytelling that has been witnessed by so many as having true transformative power.

Challenges of Internal Capacity-building Efforts

Along with the benefits that we have identified in these efforts, there were also challenges that offer insight into the balance and struggles necessary in this kind of work.

Difficulties in transitioning from participant to facilitator

Not only were the trainees required to learn new skills in order to facilitate dialogue, they also had to shift roles from community participants to community facilitators. This was a line that often felt blurry, potentially compromising the facilitators' comfort level and efficacy in the dialogue. They had to fight the urge to participate in the dialogue content. They knew from their training that they were there to create the space for the dialogue, which sometimes included pulling back from offering their own feelings or perspectives on things. As Vincent reported:

> I felt like I wanted to be a participant again so that I could say something, because as a facilitator you cannot always say something that comes to your mind.

And Marie:

> Because some time they bring up something that you think is a good subject and you want to talk about, but you can't because you are the facilitator and you have to do a better job of bringing those ideas out from others.

Community pressures and perceptions

Vincent and Marie both knew that they walked fine lines within their communities when they attended the first dialogue and then made a commitment to become trained facilitators for the second dialogue process. They both spoke to the potential that they might be viewed as traitors for participating. Vincent admitted to how he struggled with this knowledge at first. Yet their desire to participate in something transformative won over the fear of community estrangement. After the facilitation training they both felt that they could more successfully address issues of community conflict. However, there were multiple relational and communal challenges that they had to overcome in establishing their new roles. According to Vincent:

> For people just coming they will hear many things about people who were here before. This person is very bad, that person is not good for you. You remember that Marie [they laugh]? We just don't know what those guys have been told. So, how would they trust you? But I did it anyway because it was important for our communities, and even though some people didn't understand and were sometimes mad at me.

Limited training capacity

Becoming a skilled dialogue facilitator is something that takes a great deal of time, effort, and training. We were unable realistically to provide the level and depth of training necessary for these kinds of sensitive processes. This was due to limited team capacity, limited availability from community members, and differing backgrounds and skill levels of facilitator trainees.

Some of the participants that went through the facilitation training were unable to commit to the second round of dialogues due to financial and familial obligations. Without knowing the long-term structures for continuing the work and without future financial support, some community members had to withdraw their commitment. Furthermore, while there were many people who were motivated to become facilitators, candidates did not always demonstrate the maturity, skill, and potential to move into that role.

Limited ability to follow up in community planning

Vincent and Marie both felt that they left the training equipped to facilitate the dialogues, but discovered that they needed further training and capacity building in order to work with community members beyond the 10-week dialogue process. They expressed interest in seeing the work through and keeping in touch with participants after the dialogue ended to check in and see where they were in the process of conflict transformation, including Vincent:

> I don't think you just finish the dialogue and just let the people go and not keep in touch with them, and find out how they are doing. It is like seeing an ELL [English Language Learner] student in elementary school and then telling her to go into junior high and not recognizing that she missed out on advanced math while she was in ELL class. It is about checking up. Find out what they are doing right now. What is the community engaged in? We might call it peacemaking because they made peace. But, what are they doing to build the peace? To continue to be at peace? I did not see anything coming after the dialogue. What I am saying is the dialogue should be part of the community, not only something that comes and goes. Marie and I can keep it because we have been in the process and we have been facilitators. There is no way I can go back and start at the beginning and say "I hate Rwandese because I don't understand why they attacked my country." But, I would not go there because of the knowledge I have. But, I don't know if the people who participated in the 10-week dialogue they are not back there. I just don't know.

And Marie:

> We need to have some follow up and see where they are now. We had some training and some facilitation. Now the people just left and they did not hear from us anymore. Are they doing something right now? How are they engaging that outside of the dialogue? Are they coming back to the conflict phase again?

Resources for sustainability

Programs like this need funding for survival. While ADDP was fortunate to have generous support from the Andrus Family Fund, most refugee services will focus on needs other than community reconciliation. Vincent explained the challenge:

> We need resources, because when you have to call people there has to be some way to motivate them. I know some people will say, "this is your community, you have to be motivated and devote your time to your community to come." But honestly, this is a fragile community and people have to be motivated to come.

Marie further explained:

> So, you know when you provide services it is easy for the people to connect with you. If I give good services to Congolese people they are not going to be able to say I am bad. If I give them support they are going to find out that that lady from Rwanda is nice, she did that for me. They are going to find out that even if they think Rwandese are bad, that this Rwandese helped them. If you never provide anything for that person, how is that person going to know you?

Perceived need for outsider intervention

While the internal capacity-building efforts came with community empowerment and ownership, there was some perception that what gave the project legitimacy in the eyes of community members was the role of the outside organization. Sometimes, the very challenges that existed in the community were seen as barriers to internal solutions and interventions. Djimet defended the approach:

> The only option is to give up what you know. You are not losing your identity, but you come together to build your community, to have one voice in order to advocate for yourself. So those are the things that will help people to let go. And they are not going to let go on their own. You have to have a third party that is helping guide them to let go, and reassure them. So those are the things we need to help people as a third party, as an outsider, help them let go.

Challenging in-group dynamics

There were a variety of factors that made in-group facilitation difficult. Facilitators were sometimes too closely involved with some of the participants, creating blurred group boundaries and roles. This also increased the potential for facilitators to be triggered by the content, process, and relational issues that surfaced in the dialogue. Furthermore, depending on the situation, some facilitators were not always trusted because of their identity challenges that needed to be addressed.

Conclusion

A tree is known by its fruit. — Zulu proverb

While we outlined both the benefits and challenges of developing internal community capacity, we still hold firmly to the overall benefit of strengthening communities from within. Capacity building in diaspora communities achieves the multiple goals of community empowerment, reconciliation, and more successful resettlement. Ideally, however, this work continues through partnerships with other organizations (educational institutions, governmental agencies, nongovernmental organizations) that can provide resources, support, and external credibility as important dimensions to these efforts.

ADDP was a labor of love and struggle for those involved. It was not a panacea, and much has been learned through the successes and failures of this project. It has changed the lives of many, and has the potential to transform many more. Following the thread of the Model of Diaspora Interconnectivity, the community facilitators are thinking about the next level of impact. This includes connecting with other diaspora community members nationwide, training other community agencies in this work, and working to influence policy for reconciliation efforts. This will be done in conjunction with the publication of a manual for dialogue and reconciliation stemming from this project. Not only do members of the diaspora deserve to have the opportunity for healing from a traumatic past and reconciliation for a different future, they are also a population that can be a powerful resource for constructive dialogue and transformation, both for resettlement communities around the world and within the home region. One thing that all agree on: it is for the children that this work must continue.

Note

1. Our team consisted of PSU Conflict Resolution faculty and students and Africa House staff and included community members from Burundi, Chad, the Democratic Republic of the Congo, Ethiopia, The Gambia, Liberia, Rwanda, Somalia, South Africa, Sudan, and the United States.

References

Bohm, D., L. Nichol and P. Senge (2004). *On dialogue*. London: Routledge Classics.
Ellinor, L., and G. Gerard (1998). *Dialogue: Rediscovering the transforming power of conversation*. New York: John Wiley and Sons.
Freire, P. (2006). *Pedagogy of the oppressed, 30th anniversary edition*. New York: Continuum.
Glyn, T. (2009). Difficult groups or difficult facilitators? Three steps facilitators can take to make sure they are not the problem. In S. Schuman, (Ed.), *The Handbook for Working with Difficult Groups* (pp. 339–352). San Francisco: Jossey-Bass.

Hume, S. (2008). Ethnic and national identities of Africans in the United States. *Geographical review, 98*(4), 496–512.

_____, and S. Hardwick (2005). African, Russian and Ukrainian refugee resettlement in Portland, Oregon. *Geographical review, 95* (2), 189–209.

Lederach, J.P. (1995). *Preparing for peace: Conflict transformation across cultures.* Syracuse: Syracuse University Press.

Saunders, H. (2001). *A public peace process: Sustained dialogue to transform racial and ethnic conflicts.* Hampshire: Palgrave Macmillan.

Tint, B. (2009). Dialogue, forgiveness and reconciliation. In A. Kalayjian & R. Paloutzian (Eds.), *Forgiveness, reconciliation, and the pathways to peace* (pp. 269–285). New York: Springer.

Mainstreaming Feminism in Conflict Resolution

Rhea A. DuMont

In the infancy of the field of peace and conflict studies, pioneer Elise Boulding labored to make the essential connection between feminism and peace. Her 1976 work *The Underside of History: A View of Women through Time*, was critical in forging the connection between women's studies and feminism with conflict resolution or peacemaking (Morrison, 2005), and illustrated the shifting role of women through time and the relationship between women's empowerment, deconstructing patriarchy, and valuing diversity in the creation of a more peaceful society.

Feminist theory, as a central teaching of the women's studies discipline, offers conflict resolvers and peace practitioners an effective way to approach conflict which aims at arriving in a state of positive peace and advocating equal rights for everyone. This essay builds on Boulding's connection between feminism and conflict resolution, and the necessity and constructive value of rooting the peace and conflict studies discipline in feminism. Several feminist scholars since Boulding have addressed the failure of the field of conflict resolution to examine gendered dichotomies that are inherent within it. This essay draws on their important work and advocates the necessity of recognizing and embracing the marginalized voices and perspectives within the field.

Understanding Feminism and Women's Studies

A common misconception about women's studies is that it focuses solely on women's issues. Rather, the women's studies discipline examines the relationship gender has with other aspects of social location (i.e., race, class, gender, and ethnicity) to manufacture and perpetuate hierarchical power structures (Dill & Zambrana, 2009). At the core of women's studies is feminist theory, also commonly stereotyped and misunderstood. In the dominant culture, the general understanding of feminism is that it is a movement operated by angry women, stereotypically categorized as "male bashers," and interested solely in moving beyond the power of the male. This image is indeed false, and it is with urgency that we need to see feminism for what it really is—particularly within the discipline of peace and conflict studies.

Like nonviolent resistance, which has as its goal "resisting oppression, domination and any other forms of injustice" (Dudouet, 2008, p. 3), the essence of women's studies and feminism is the shared goal of rebalancing power structures and moving from *power-over* relationships to ones that are *power-with*. Feminism is associated with and advocates for, some would argue demands, nonviolence (Berg, 1994).[1] Feminist theory insists that we look at the ingrained ideas, assumptions, and values promoted and maintained through the mainstream culture, those that praise domination and control of one group over another and the environment. Though gender is often at the root of discussion in feminist theory, it is concerned with examining intersecting systems of oppression and how they relate to the creation and maintenance of those systems. Feminist theory is about social justice.

By examining gendered dichotomies present in the dominant system, feminist theory reveals how gender relationships are often a reflection of how our system operates in a way that systematically favors certain groups over others, and the ways in which such asymmetrical structures impact peace and conflict. By examining power relationships, the dominant culture, hegemonic masculinity, and gender and conflict, the relationship between feminism and peace and conflict studies becomes increasingly transparent. It is impracticable to approach conflict in the absence of feminist analysis.

Examining Power

There is a distinct relationship between feminist theory and conflict resolution discourse on power relationships. As mentioned, the root of feminist discourse is the idea that power and dominance are an integral component of society and the sources of perpetuating oppressive relationships that help maintain a hierarchical power structure (Baca Zinn & Thornton Dill, 1996; Burguieres, 1990; Caprioli & Boyer, 2001; Confortini, 2006; Francis, 2004; Hegde, 1998; Lazar, 2007; Pankhurst, 2003; Warren & Cady, 1994). As Diana Francis (2004) contends, "a thread running through almost every generalized, mainstream culture in recent millennia is the central value placed on domination: of one species over others; of one group over others; of one person over others; and of one sex over the other" (p. 3). This idea is described by Riane Eisler and several theorists as the "dominatory culture," which must be acknowledged and addressed in the context of conflict resolution applications (as cited in Francis, 2004, p. 3).

Power relationships are an integral component to conflict on micro-, meso-, and macro- levels. To neglect the realities of structural violence,[2] oppression, marginalization, and power asymmetry within conflict is to disregard the marginalized ethno-political groups that are often most impacted by conflict (Francis, 2004). Failing to acknowledge power imbalances or work to level them in conflict ignores the needs of the marginalized group and the effects that any peace settlement might have on their well-being. When we fail to acknowledge power asymmetry, the voices of the marginalized group remain silenced. As John Paul Lederach (1995) asserts, "negotiation is only possible when the needs and interests of all those affected by the conflict are legitimated and articulated" (p. 14).

Louis Kreisberg (2007) examined the role of dominance and asymmetrical relationships in affecting the likelihood of conflict, the ways in which it escalates, and the methods in which it is actualized once it erupts. He contends that there is a distinct connection between asymmetric relationships and conflict escalation, and that evidence continuously reveals that dominatory relationships have a "natural affect" on the materialization of conflict: "Great power differences permit great abuses of power. When a conflict erupts, the power concentration contributes greatly to the kind of escalation that follows. Thus, genocides tend to occur when the target group is isolated and vulnerable" (p. 378). Conversely, relationships that are generally symmetric are more likely to involve a constructive approach to conflict, namely, nonviolent approach. In symmetric relationships, parties are not concerned with their position as oppressed or trying to maintain their dominance, and therefore are generally confident in their ability to take action within their set of circumstances without resorting to violence.

The Dominant Culture of Violence and Hegemonic Masculinity

Feminist theory explains the dominant culture as those in power in society—and whom societal systems are set up to serve. There are unquestioned assumptions about cultural values, ideas, beliefs, and symbols that function as mechanisms to maintain and perpetuate asymmetrical power relationships.

The dominant culture is patriarchal in nature, as it is indeed a patriarchal social order that systematically privileges men over women. bell hooks (2004) describes the dominant culture as "imperialist white supremacist capitalist patriarchy" (p. 17). In other words, through intersecting forms of social, economic, and political oppression and hierarchy, power-over relationships are maintained and perpetuated.

Ultimately, both the make-up and operation of the dominant culture play an inherent role in perpetuating structural violence, what conflict resolution theorists acknowledge intrinsically correlates to direct violence (Jeong, 2000). As Galtung (1990) explains, "With the violent structure institutionalized and the violent culture internalized, direct violence also tends to become institutionalized, repetitive, ritualistic, like a vendetta" (p. 302). Though he briefly gives attention to the fact that the implications of gender are implicit in cultural, structural, and direct violence, Galtung's argument lacks an in-depth analysis of the essential nature of including gender in the discussion of these typologies of violence (Confortini, 2006). What he contends about a culture of violence directly correlates to hegemonic masculinity and its role in perpetuating and maintaining both asymmetrical power relationships and a culture of violence.

Hegemony is power that gains potency through the invisible ways in which it is acquired and maintained. Hegemonic forces rely on their subordinates, who often see societal structures as "natural" and so consent to and further perpetuate the very hierarchical and oppressive relationship that they are disadvantaged by (Connell, 2002). As Michael Lazar (2007) states, "The taken-for-grantedness and normalcy of such knowledge is what mystifies or obscures the power differential and inequality at work" (p. 147). The state is involved in the coercion of the population through media representation and manipulation and the ways it organizes social institutions to give the impression that such composition is the norm (Donaldson, 1993).

Hegemonic masculinity is a core component of the dominant culture and is problematic, as it socializes boys and men to be violent, creates and perpetuates a culture of hierarchy and exclusion, privileges certain characteristics over others, and normalizes violent behavior and stark injustices. The dominant culture perpetuates the belief that to be masculine, and to become "real men," men must be strong, aggressive, dominant, controlling, and powerful — and through this legitimizes violence. When feminists refer to hegemonic masculinity, they are talking about the core of the dominant culture that, for the most part, remains unchanged.

As Stephen Whitehead (2001) remarks in *The Masculinities Reader*, "All societies have cultural accounts of gender, but not all have the concept of 'masculinity.' In its modern usage the term assumes that one's behavior results from the type of person one is. That is to say, an unmasculine person would behave differently: being peaceable rather than violent, conciliatory rather than dominating, hardly able to kick a football, uninterested in sexual conquest, and so forth" (p. 30). Here, Whitehead is referring to hegemonic masculinity versus the mainstream conception of femininity. This validates the idea that the violence we so often witness is not just glorified but also endorsed by the dominant culture. The result of this is violence as a norm, a means by which men who feel as though they cannot accurately meet the expectations of the modern idea of masculinity do whatever they can to gain control or power. As Connell (2002) explains, "Violence often arises in the construction of masculinities, as part of the practice by which particular men or groups of men claim respect, intimidate rivals, or try to gain material advantage" (p. 95). This is reflected in the continued silencing and legitimization of sexual violence, domestic abuse, and hate crimes against queer-identified persons, as well as the increasing suicide rate of gay teens. As the dominant culture operates within the context of hegemonic masculinity, it is fundamental that the conflict resolution discipline recognize the distinct relationship between hegemonic masculinity and a culture of violence, and furthermore, the necessity of addressing the structural inequities inherent within the dominant culture that maintain and perpetuate structural and direct violence.

Examining the role of gender in conflict and its resolution should naturally be an extension of addressing power asymmetry within conflict, because women continue to be oppressed across the globe and struggle to gain equal rights on different fronts in both the East and West. It is evident that in order to function effectively, the dominant culture is dependent on gender differences and discrimination. Around the world, men's domination over women is one of the most extensive and primary forces of power asymmetry (Francis, 2004). As introduced, within the dominant culture we learn to adopt unquestioned masculinities and femininities that perpetuate the gender order and cultivate a culture of violence. Not only do these masculinities and femininities shape the ways in which we interact as ideological male and female identities, they inform other ways of knowing, through perpetuating gendered thinking that exceeds biological sex. This is a direct product of the dominant culture and hegemonic masculinity. As Confortini (2006) states "feminists think about gender as a symbolic process or system, one that makes other processes or systems possible" (p. 339). Gender informs other ways of knowing and social practices by functioning as an interpretive mechanism that permeates the ways in which community members structure and acknowledge particular social customs, thereby informing asymmetrical relationships that are inherent in gendered thinking (Lazar, 2007).

As gendered thinking is an unquestioned mechanism that confirms and perpetuates a system of binary dichotomies — one greater than, one lesser than the other — it perpetuates hierarchical relations and ways of interpreting the world, essentially making power-with relationships nearly impossible (Ayele, 2010). As Muthien (2010) states, "existing ways of thinking within the prevailing patriarchies are too often premised on polarity, the kind of thinking and activism that engenders conflict rather than cooperation, and which prohibits or inhibits efforts to seek true transformative solutions for social change" (p. 78). Such gendered thinking can be seen in the dominant perspectives regarding war and peace, peace being feminine and therefore weak and negative, war being masculine and therefore strong and positive.

A gendered approach to conflict, then, is one that takes into account issues of power, thereby fostering a successful transition to a sustainable peace that will prevent the eruption of renewed conflict. Such an approach moves relationships from asymmetry to symmetry, thus eradicating hierarchical gendered structures, ways of thinking, and ways of interacting.

Existing research gives testimony to the importance of acknowledging gender in conflict, and the impact that working to deconstruct patriarchal concepts of gender can have on moving toward an increasingly tolerant and peaceful state. As Berg (1994) explains, "Feminists from the nineteenth century forward have asserted that when women attain full and equal participation in society they will make a distinctive and vital contribution to conflict resolution and a peaceful social order" (p. 326). Caprioli's (2000) research demonstrates that gender equality directly correlates with the likelihood that a state will be more peaceful, both domestically and internationally.[3] She explains:

> The inclusion of women as equal members of society will effect [sic] foreign policy, in that their domestic equality correlates with lower levels of international militarism. This analysis lends credence to the domestic-international violence theory in that domestic inequality represents a certain level of intolerance and a hierarchical organization, both of which translate into a world-view that necessarily places some people or states as superior to others [p. 63].

Caprioli and Boyer (2001) expand on Caprioli's (2000) initial work by using the International Crisis Behavior dataset, which covers 882 conflicts between 1918 and 2001, to examine the behavior of states with various levels of domestic gender equality during crisis. Their work confirms Caprioli's (2000) original findings that states with greater domestic gender equality behave more peacefully in the global arena when confronted with crisis and conflict.

Ultimately, linking feminism and conflict resolution is fundamental in addressing power asymmetry and reconstructing our ideas and understanding of how gender socialization can affect conflict. Including these perspectives in the discourse of peace and conflict studies will deepen our understanding of the roots of social conflict and provide a framework to more effectively approach conflict resolution in a way that redresses asymmetric power relationships and works to unlearn and deconstruct oppression.

Conclusion: Feminism as Conflict Resolution

It is clear how feminist theory plays an integral role in sustainable conflict transformation. If, as conflict resolution theorists and practitioners, we abide by Galtung's theory of structural violence, then we must take into consideration hegemonic structures and relationships, the impact they have on perpetuating and maintaining gendered thinking, and how this translates into power relationships and a continued hierarchically structured society. We must acknowledge how these structures effectively foment power asymmetries that, in varying contexts, have the potential to ripen into conditions of direct violence.

To approach conflict resolution through a feminist lens, or to merge conflict resolution theories and practices with concepts of the women's studies discipline, would be a positive step forward in the field of peace and conflict studies, and would make conflict transformation increasingly effective and sustainable. Including such a lens would work to address and balance asymmetrical relationships, would respect and value cultural diversity and promote tolerance, would address intersecting forms of oppression, would work to eradicate structural violence thereby decreasing direct violence, and would strengthen the discipline's commitment to achieving social justice.

NOTES

1. Notions of feminism are indeed diverse, and may vary according to culture, geographical location, and time period.
2. Structural violence is a concept developed by peace scholar Johan Galtung (1969), who considered it a form of systemic violence embedded in societal structures through unequal power systems. The result is relationships of domination that affect access to opportunities and resources. Structural violence is an indirect form of violence that is invisible, in the sense that it is a built-in mechanism of cultural and social institutions; its effects impact human values over time, as well as the human life span.
3. Caprioli's research findings were based on measuring the relationship between high levels of gender equality within a state and low levels of state militarism, and used the Militarized Interstate Dispute Dataset to measure military action between 1960 and 1992.

REFERENCES

Ayele, M.G. (2010). Challenging the patriarchal national security paradigm: The role of Ethiopian women in peace and security. In B.A. Reardon and A. Hans (Eds.), *The gender imperative: Human security vs. state security* (pp. 87–109).

Baca Zinn, M., and B. Thornton Dill (1996). Theorizing difference from multiracial feminism. *Feminist Studies, 22*(2), 321–331.
Berg, E. (1994). Gendering conflict resolution. *Peace and Change, 19*(4), 325–348.
Boulding, E. (1976). *The underside of history: A view of women through time*. Boulder, CO: Westview.
Burguieres, M. (1990). Feminist approaches to peace: Another step for peace studies. *Millennium: Journal of International Studies, 19*(1), 1–18.
Caprioli, M. (2000). Gendered conflict. *Journal of Peace Research, 37*(1), 51–68.
_____, and M.A. Boyer (2001). Gender, violence, and international crisis. *The Journal of Conflict Resolution, 15*(4), 503–518.
Confortini, C. (2006). Galtung, violence, and gender: The case for a peace studies/feminism Alliance. *Peace and Change, 31*(3), 333–365.
Connell, R.W. (2002). On hegemonic masculinity and violence: Response to Jefferson and Hall. *Theoretical Criminology, 6*(89), 89–98.
Dill, B., and R. Zambrana (Eds.). (2009). *Emerging intersections: Race, class, and gender in theory, policy and practice*. New Brunswick, NJ: Rutgers University Press.
Donaldson, M. (1993). What is hegemonic masculinity? *Theory and society, 22*(5), 643–657.
Dudouet, V. (2008). Nonviolent resistance and conflict transformation in power asymmetries. Retrieved from http:www.berghof-handbook.net.
Francis, D. (2004). Culture, power asymmetries, and gender in conflict transformation. Retrieved from http:www.berghof-handbook.net.
Galtung, J. (1969). Violence, peace, and peace research. *Journal of peace research, 6*(3), 167–191.
_____ (1990). Cultural violence. *Journal of peace research, 27*(3), 291–305.
Hegde, R. (1998). A view from elsewhere: Locating difference and the politics of representation from a transnational feminist perspective. *Communication theory, 83,* 271–297.
hooks, b. (2004). *The will to change: Men, masculinity, and love*. New York: Washington Square.
Jeong, H. (2000). *Peace and conflict studies: An introduction*. Aldershot: Ashgate.
Kriesberg, L. (2007). *Constructive conflicts: From escalation to resolution*. Lanham, MD: Rowman & Littlefield.
Lazar, M. (2007). Feminist critical discourse analysis: Articulating a feminist discourse praxis. *Critical discourse studies, 4*(2), 141–164.
Lederach, J.P. (1994). *Preparing for peace: Conflict transformation across cultures*. Syracuse: Syracuse University Press.
Morrison, M. L. (2005). *Elise Boulding: A life in the cause of peace*. Jefferson, NC: McFarland.
Muthien, B. (2010). Human security and layers of oppression: Women in South Africa. In B.A. Reardon and A. Hans (Eds.), *The gender imperative: Human security vs. state security* (62–84).
Pankhurst, D. (2003). The "sex war" and other wars: Towards a feminist approach to peace building. *Development in practice, 12*(2), 154–177.
Warren, K., and D. Cady (1994). Feminism and peace: Seeing connections. *Hypatia, 9*(2), 4–20.
Whitehead, S. (2001). *The masculinities reader*. Oxford: Blackwell.

CHamoru Values Guiding Nonviolence

LisaLinda Natividad

CHamorus (also known as Chamorros), the indigenous people of the Mariana Islands, have maintained traditional values that guide conflict prevention. This essay will first discuss the history of colonization of the CHamoru people on the island of Guahan, or Guam, and then the denial of their human rights as an unincorporated territory of the United States. It will then explore the values of *inafa 'maolek*, *fina 'taotao*, and *minaggem*, which have steered the CHamoru people toward the creation of a peaceful society in which the best interest of the people, land, and sea are at the forefront of decision-making and interactions with others.

Colonization of the CHamoru People of Guahan

Guahan is the southernmost island of the Marianas archipelago in the Micronesian region of Oceania. The island's native population, the CHamorus, migrated to the region as early as 4,500 years ago, but their first contact with the West was not until 1521, with the arrival of Ferdinand Magellan. Spain claimed the island for its own in 1565, and later established a Catholic mission. Though there were numerous battles between the Spanish colonizers and the CHamorus, the island remained under Spanish control until the end of the Spanish-American War and the U.S. purchase of Guahan in the Treaty of Paris. Between 1898 and 1941, the U.S. Department of Navy governed the island, and in 1941, the Japanese Imperial Army invaded — opening up a time of extreme hardship for the island's people. Natives suffered atrocities such as massacres, rapes, work encampments, and the enslavement of "comfort women" who were forcibly raped by Japanese soldiers. CHamorus remained under Japanese occupation until July 21, 1944, when the United States resumed control and re-zoned Guahan, occupying a majority of the island. In order to secure land for a naval base, the United States relocated the coastal village of Sumay and its inhabitants to the hills of Santa Rita in the southern part of the island. In 1950, the U.S. Congress passed the Organic Act of Guam, declaring the island an unincorporated territory of the United States, granting Guahan residents U.S. citizenship, establishing a local tax structure, and legally acquiring local lands with the power of eminent domain. Advocacy efforts on the part of CHamorus and the island's government leaders have resulted in the reduction of U.S. land possession to roughly one-third of the island's 212 square miles.

As an unincorporated territory of the United States, the island's residents, while U.S. citizens, do not have full citizenship rights. They do not have the right to vote in U.S. presidential elections, and their only congressional representative may vote only on the committee level, yet that vote is voided if it is the determining one. Structural violence can be seen in the numerous federal-territorial policies that inhibit the development of a viable local economy, and in caps on federal funding to territories (as opposed to the allocations given to full-fledged states).

The United Nations lists Guahan as one of the last 16 non-self-governing territories in the world, thus essentially acknowledging the island's colonial status — but moreover, the list acknowledges the right of the CHamorus to self-determination under international law and the principles of the UN Charter (United Nations, 2009).

Planned Guam Military Build-Up

As a colonial possession, Guahan has no ultimate authority in matters of political affairs. Perhaps the most significant community concern on the island in the first two decades of the new millennium has been the proposed Department of Defense (DoD) military build-up for Guahan and other islands in the Marianas. In 2006, the governments of the United States and Japan entered into an accord indicating that over 8,000 U.S. Marines and their families would be transferred from Okinawa to Guahan by 2014. This accord was signed with no consultation of the local government or people of Guahan. Consistent with the U.S. National Environmental Policy Act, DoD completed an environmental impact assessment on the planned military build-up for the island. It included either definite or provisional plans for, among others, the construction of facilities and infrastructure to support the full spectrum of warfare training, including a deep-draft wharf in Apra Harbor to accommodate nuclear-powered aircraft carriers; the increase of the U.S. military's landholding to roughly 40 percent of the island; and the use of Pågat — one of Guahan's oldest villages, dating back to 2,000 B.C., and listed by the U.S. National Trust for Historical Preservation as one of America's 11 Most Endangered Historic Places — as a live firing range (Natividad & Leon-Guerrero, 2010).

The release of the environmental impact assessment resulted in a groundswell of community concern for the island and its protection for future generations (We Are Guahan, 2009–11). As activist Melvin Won Pat-Borja explained, "The U.S. EPA [Environmental Protection Agency] just reviewed the DEIS [draft environmental impact assessment], and they gave it the lowest possible rating that a DEIS can receive. They labeled it 'environmentally unsatisfactory'" (Democracy Now!, 2010). Continued opposition led to the signing of a Record of Decision, modifying the DoD plans in several ways, including pacing and sequencing the construction of facilities and the arrival of Marines within the limitations of the island's current infrastructure, and deferring the placement of training ranges pending completion of the consultation process under the National Historic Preservation Act. But CHamorus deem this still inadequate, and protest continues.

As the island stands at the precipice of change in which the political structure does not support the concerns or needs of the people, the CHamorus have not resorted to acts of violence in their resistance to the U.S. military build-up. They instead have been raising their voices and mobilizing nonviolently, drawing on their traditional values to create a peaceful social movement for justice.

Traditional CHamoru Cultural Values

Ancient CHamorus have been described as kind and peaceful people (Russell, 1998) who strove to live in harmony with the land, air, sea, and one another. CHamoru villages were comprised of the family unit, and sustained their livelihood through fishing, hunting, and trading with their neighbors. Modern-day CHamorus continue to have a deep sense of spirituality in which ancestral spirits, or *taotao mo'na*, are venerated and elders, or the *manamko'*, are held in high regard for their wisdom, life experience, and age. Modern-day CHamoru norms and values are referred to as *kustumbren CHamoru*.

The three elements of *kustombren CHamoru* that guide conflict prevention are *inafa'maolek*, *fataotao*, and *minaggem*.

Inafa'maolek, central to the CHamoru worldview and experience, has been defined as "to be fair with each other, to help each other, to love and be kind to each other" and as "a set of ideas or a way of thinking and living that each member of the island community should follow so that all will be well in the community" (Inafa'maolek Chamorro tradition and values, 1996). It prescribes the way in which to behave in society, encompassing the principles of fairness, justice, mutual aid, and love for humanity. In communal agrarian societies such as the CHamorus, cultural values such as inafa'maolek play a critical role in ensuring peaceful co-existence among its members and collectively meeting the needs of the community. Pereda (2009) quotes a proverb from *kantan Chamorita*, in which verses of a song are sung back and forth between different parties:

An numa' piniti hao taotao,
Nangga ma na' piniti-mu;
Maseha apmamam na tiempo
Un apasi sa' dibi-mu.
When you hurt somebody,
Expect to be in pain;
For even if it takes time,
Surely you'll pay for the pain you caused.

This verse exemplifies the circular thinking pattern in the CHamoru worldview, and the belief in a kind of karma, that causing another pain results in self-pain, reinforcing the value of inafa'maolek and the consequences of not prescribing to the CHamoru more.

The second traditional CHamoru value, similar to the first, that guides conflict prevention among its community members is fataotao, which means "to respect and treat others as a person; to treat someone with consideration and respect" (Official Chamorro-English dictionary, 2009). It refers to a deep level of respect that should be afforded fellow members of humanity by virtue of their membership in the human race. This word comes from the root word *taotao*, "person" or "man." The prefix *fa* refers to the action of "making" or "becoming." In ancient times, CHamorus would greet each other saying "'*ati adengmo*,' which translates to 'let me kiss your feet'" (Russell, 1998), exemplifying an action based on fataotao. The term is often used to guide the appropriate and dignified way of treating others after having hurt them or being hurt by them. In addition, the practice of fataotao is often employed as a proactive measure when there is the potential to hurt others. Affording the potential victims the dignity and respect of discussing the situation — even with the offense impending — is encouraged. Thus, the use of silence in this case is perceived as a sign of disrespect.

While inafa'maolek and fataotao provide guidelines for the flow of interactions with others, the third traditional CHamoru value, minaggem, refers to an inner state of being and may be defined as peace or peaceful. Minaggem is an integral component of being able to maintain peace in interpersonal relationships.

These traditional CHamoru values of inafa'maolek, fataotao, and minaggem contribute to the nonviolent social justice movement on Guahan, providing tools for conflict prevention and imparting indigenous wisdom as they seek out social justice in the resolution of their political status, as well as in their resistance to the planned U.S. military build-up on the island.

CHamoru Social Justice Efforts

CHamorus have been seeking political decolonization for centuries and still, the question of their right to self-determination remains unresolved. The remainder of the essay explores how modern-day CHamorus are attempting to achieve social justice through political and legal means.

CHamorus have used various political and legal mechanisms to exercise their indigenous rights. In the 1970s, the twelfth and thirteenth Guam Legislatures created Political Status Commissions to carry out local political status education campaigns, which explained the various options available. In 1980, the Commission on Self-Determination was created, which moved the conversation beyond status options and defined the concept of self-determination and determined who was eligible to vote in a referendum. A number of referenda were held between 1976 and 1982, the last of these on January 12, 1982. In that plebiscite, 49 percent of islanders voted for the alternate political status of a commonwealth; 26 percent voted for U.S. statehood. A runoff vote was subsequently held in which 73 percent voted for commonwealth and 27 percent for statehood.

In an effort to move toward establishing a commonwealth, the Commission on Self-Determination drafted a proposed act for Congressional approval that was locally ratified in 1987, but proved controversial in Congress. While the proposed commonwealth act was introduced to Congress on four occasions, it never passed. The Commission on Decolonization (another creation of the Guam Legislature to address CHamoru self-determination) is taking an alternate route with the establishment of a Chamorro Registry.

While CHamorus were pursuing federal channels for establishing political autonomy from the United States, they concurrently established recognition from the United Nations, as mentioned previously in its inclusion in the list of 16 non-self governing territories of the world. Since the announcement of the U.S. military build-up in 2006, CHamorus have sent a delegation to the

United Nations every year, testifying before the Special Committee on Decolonization and its Permanent Forum on Indigenous Issues, an advisory body to the Economic and Social Council. Nonetheless, CHamorus stand at the present moment in a continued state of colonization, with no resolution to their disputed political status.

What is next for the social justice movement on Guahan? By participating in the established protocols for working within the framework of the United States and United Nations, CHamorus have utilized each of their core values over the past century. They simply ask for reciprocation.

References

Democracy Now! (2010, May 25). From Japan, Guam and Hawai'i, activists resist expansion of US military presence in the Pacific.

Inafa'maolek Chamorro tradition and values (1996). Guam: Political Status Education Coordinating Commission.

Natividad, L., and V. Leon Guerrero (2010). The explosive growth of U.S. military power on Guam confronts people power. *The Asia-Pacific Journal*. Retrieved from: http://japanfocus.org/-Victoria_Lola_Leon-Guerrero/3454.

Official Chamorro-English dictionary: Ufisiat na diksionarion Chamorro-Engles (2009). Hagatna, Guam: Department of Chamorro Affairs, Division of Research, Publication, and Training.

Pereda, N.N. (2009). Chamorro proverbs. *Guampedia*. http://guampedia.com/chamorro-proverbs/.

Russell, S. (1998). *Tiempon I Manmofo'na: Ancient Chamorro culture and history of the Northern Mariana Islands*. Saipan: Division of Historic Preservation.

United Nations (2009, October 5). Remaining 16 non-self-governing territories on United Nations list are "16 too many" fourth committee told, as it takes up cluster of decolonization issues. Press Release. http://www.un.org/News/Press/docs/2009/gaspd422.doc.htm.

SECTION III — EXPANDING IDENTITY: THE NEW CONFLICT WORKER

A Paradoxical Identity: From Conflicted to Hybrid

Robert J. Gould

> You are a longitude and a latitude, a set of speeds and slownesses between unformed particles, a set of nonsubjectified affects. You have the individuality of a day, a season, a year, a life (regardless of its duration) — a climate, a wind, a fog, a swarm, a pack (regardless of its singularity). Or at least you can have it, you can reach it [Deleuze & Guattari, 1988, p. 162].

The tension between singular and multiple identities is tragically dramatized by the recent mass killing in Norway by someone who believed in preserving a Norwegian ethnic purity at the expense of a vicious ethnic cleansing.[1] This kind of tension happens, usually much less tragically, throughout the globe and in each of our daily lives, by the way we manage difference and diversity. In this context, the field of conflict resolution can proceed in three ways. First, a conflict resolver can perform the techniques of conflict resolution, while keeping the conflict at a safe distance, never internalizing the identities of the disputants, and never changing one's professional identity as a conflict resolver. In this mode, the conflict resolver does not ask the disputants to walk in the other's shoes and internalize each other's identities. In other words, the conflict resolution process is not an experience of transformative empathy; it is merely the crafting of a win-win settlement of a conflict. Second, the conflict resolver might adopt a Buddhist perspective, embodying love and compassion in the hopes of being a role model for the disputants. Third, the conflict resolver might consciously seek to internalize the identities of the disputants (be hybridized by them), and seek to be a role model for internalized transformation. I am interested in this third mode of conflict resolution because I find it to be the most powerfully empathetic.

The distinction between the second and third approaches to conflict resolution is a subtle one, deserving more clarification. If I practice love and compassion for another, I might do so in an I-It, rather than an I-Thou relationship (Buber, 1970). In the I-It relationship, I may be loving and compassionate, but I won't fully connect to another person because I am not identifying with her or him. In the I-Thou relationship, one's personal identity melts into the other and is internalized as part of a newly hybridized identity.

To state this simply, one is what one identifies with. At the very least, I am a professor, activist, husband, and outdoorsman. I identify with other professors, activists, husbands, and outdoorsmen. I socialize with them, I read what they write, and I imagine myself being like them. It doesn't matter which is the cause and which is the effect, there is a crucial, cyclical reinforcement process that consolidates my hybridized identity. Understood this way, we are all hybridized. However, I'm suggesting that conflict resolvers need *continually* to embrace this process with every conflict that they encounter, thus maximizing their hybridization, their connected empathy, and their success resolving conflict. The concern of this paper is to wonder whether this process creates a conflict regarding the *stability* of identity; does it make answering the question "Who am I?" unbearably difficult?

Who am I? is a timeless question that haunts us in more complex ways as we are exposed to increasingly diverse global philosophies and cultures, because "who I am" is overshadowed by seemingly millions of other identities that I am not. The quest to understand identity started long ago within many different traditions.

In at least the Western philosophical tradition, "identity" categorizes things that are the same, and also shows how they are different from other categories of things. Europeans are the same as each other, in the sense that they are in the same category, and they are distinct from Africans. Additionally, European/Africans are a category that is different from Canadian/Africans. In these examples, identity is established by an external relationship. However, identity gets more complicated when it is internalized into a self-concept. In our self-concepts, we might find our inner identity changing over time, or we might struggle to keep it the same in the face of our inner identity conflicts. We can be torn between having to re-categorize our identities and maintaining a singular category of identity.

Plato thought that the fundamental identity of different things resided in the realm of the Forms (Plato, 1966) — stable universals or categories with continuity over time. This view denies that basic categories might evolve and change, and assumes that the world fits into tidy categories, rather than being mobile across a wide range of continua. However, what we think is heroic might be different today than in Plato's time. Even our notion of what it is to be human can evolve and change. On this view, our inner identities can switch categories, and the categories themselves can change. Nationalists might suppose that ethnic and national identity is eternal, but this is rejected by the observation that ethnic and national identities are constantly changing because of changing circumstances and interests (Said, 1995, p. 332).

We say that someone's identity can change over time, like when someone changes occupations, religion, nationality, etc.; but does that mean that her fundamental identity has changed? Is there something about a person that never changes when physical and psychological states are constantly subject to change? We say that it's the same person who changes, but what makes her the same person? The history of a person may remain the same, but histories are subject to revision and reinterpretation using different categories of description, and depending on who tells the history. Surely, one's identity is projected into the future as one makes plans and engages challenges. But how do we know that the future won't dramatically change a person? We certainly cannot rely on the person's *name* making her the same person over time because names change. So, where are we to turn to find a person's fundamental identity?

We could say that the soul remains the same, even as the person changes; but where are we to find this soul? There is no empirical basis for it, so it has to be an object of belief. David Hume (1888) claimed that personal identity is "nothing but a bundle or collection of different perceptions, which succeed each other with an inconceivable rapidity, and are in a perpetual flux and movement" (p. 252). I am happy to allow that some people presuppose the existence of the soul to reassure themselves that we have an identity that does not change. However, there may be a better solution.

We might wonder if we *need* an essential something to justify that someone is the same person over time. Perhaps all we need are grounds to support the continuity of the person: I recognize her, or she reminds us that I know her. But this requires that she and I to have the capacity to remember this continuity. Amnesia or dementia may diminish this capacity, so how is she the same person? Another alternative is to argue that she is the same person because persons are such beings that have lifetimes and we understand a person as being the same person over his or her lifetime. A lifetime of person-singularity is what it is to be a person. So, we can establish what it is to be the same person over a lifetime, but this is from an external perspective. What is it like to be the same person in one's inner experience?

Our inner experience of identity emerges as we refer to ourselves as a "me" or "I" and reflect on what makes *me* me. Though we don't stop referring to ourselves as "me" or "I" during our lives, our experience of being "me" or "I" certainly can change over a lifetime. Furthermore, psychological theory suggests that, although we might refer to ourselves as "me" or "I," we do not have a unified self, but rather a framework of multiple selves.

For Baldwin (1897), there are two aspects of the self: the *ego* and the *alter*. The *ego* represents the way one thinks about oneself, and the *alter* represents the way one thinks of others. The various roles that one plays in life, and the various roles that others play in one's life, are internalized into a framework of multiple *egos* and *alters*. Ogilvy (1977) says that our multiplicity of selves functions with a decentralized organization. Each self interprets personal experience differently, based on different forms of interpretation. These different intrapersonal selves have different personalities, and our central sense of self is merely a mediator of a vast collection of relatively autonomous selves. Ouspensky (1949) suggests that one self becomes a temporary master over the other selves, but this mastery only lasts for less than 30 minutes until a new master takes over, while denying the existence of other selves. Clearly, a hybridized self is a potential product of Ogilvy's mediation, and the multiplicity-denying, singular self, falls in line with Ouspensky's dominance-shifting self. In other words, both descriptions appear to describe different populations accurately. It seems that identity hybridization may happen quite naturally for people in diverse societies, and perhaps in monocultural societies as well. However, people may be in deep denial of their own hybridization. I am suggesting that conflict resolvers may need to assert and embrace their hybridization, and affirm it as a powerful element of professional empathy, as well as their personal navigation across a culturally diverse world.

One of the reasons that people have difficulty acknowledging and embracing hybridization is that we often think of ourselves in terms of a unitary self-concept. This self-concept is a person's self-perception, which is formed by one's experiences and interpretations. However, the unity of this self-concept is challenged because other people play a strong role in the formation, change, and maintenance of one's self-concept (Shavelson, Hubner, & Stanton, 1976). Consequently, our self-concept is "multifaceted in that people categorize the vast amount of information they have about themselves and relate these categories to one another (Marsh & Shavelson, 1985). "Self-concept becomes increasingly multi-faceted as the individual moves from infancy to adulthood" (ibid). Sometimes those changes in self-concept can happen quite quickly.

Witnessing the rapid transformation of one's own identity is one of the most dramatically interesting events of one's life, as when one grows up, marries, ages, or is changed by a powerful experience. Resolution of a conflict is just such a place where people can be transformed by the powerful experience of identity hybridization. For conflict resolvers, there are two potential identity hybridizations: the disputants, and the conflict resolver herself. The identity hybridization of conflict resolvers can be an important aid to the conflict resolution process, and a role model for disputant transformation.

Buddhists are particularly interested in transformation as they seek enlightenment, but they tend to believe that selfhood is an impediment to enlightenment. They tend to believe that in the face of universal change, one cannot find peace and stability in one's self. One must reject the permanence of the self in favor of the permanence of background truths that seem to function like Plato's forms, providing stability and balance in the face of the instability and imbalance in our daily experience. In Buddhism, one's identity can be thought of as merely the instantiation of the principles of love and compassion. One takes refuge in the Buddha by embodying the principles that express his enlightenment. To the question of "who am I?" Buddhists can reply that "I" am not anything other than these eternal principles, infinite and everlasting.

However, Buddhists identify themselves as Buddhists and do not call themselves non–Buddhists. In their encounters with non–Buddhists, they do not internalize the other such that they become hybridized Buddhists and non–Buddhists. Rather, the Buddhist strives to become more perfectly or purely Buddhist, especially the devout monk. Even as Buddhists may reject the self, they do not reject their "higher" principled identification, or their identification as a particular kind of Buddhist.

From this, Buddhist compassion is hampered by the fact that a Buddhist necessarily identifies as a Buddhist, resisting the transformation to a non–Buddhist identity. One might object that one's identification as a conflict resolver similarly prompts one to resist being identified as a non-conflict resolver. My reply to this objection is that a Buddhist usually maintains an identity within a specific discipline of Buddhism, whereas a constantly hybridizing conflict resolver changes her identity with each conflict she facilitates, or participates in as a disputant. Whether the conflict is resolved or exacerbated — or even in non-professional occasions — she encounters another in an identity-transforming way. By doing this, conflict resolvers can indeed hybridize with the non-conflict resolvers that they are engaged with in disputes, by becoming hybridized along with them. Conflict resolvers can be both conflict resolvers and non-conflict resolvers without their identity being undermined. As an example, I am a professional conflict resolver, but my wife is not; when we have conflicts, I identify with her to the degree that my identity as a conflict resolver dissolves into our shared identity as spouses working through a dispute.

This brings us back to the underlying question of this paper: If the reader agrees with me that it is desirable to cultivate identity hybridization to facilitate deep empathy, how does one make sense of one's identity as having some kind of unity or singularity? Indeed, in the face of constant hybridization, who am I? When I become someone who has elements of identities that used to *not be me*, I face the paradox of being both myself, and not myself.

This dilemma is heightened by the observation that otherness or *alterity* may have a stronger role in identity formation than ego (Therborn, 1995, p. 229). The force of others' identities may be stronger than the force of "me," because we define ourselves in terms of other people's identities more than any created category of our own. This explains two phenomena: First, we can rather easily lose a unique sense of ourselves and be absorbed into the identities of others through imitation and role internalization. Second, we may feel that we have to fight to maintain a unique sense of self. As Connolly (2002) explains, "Identity requires difference in order to be, and it converts difference into otherness in order to secure its own self-certainty" (p. 64). We may need to construct difference and otherness in order to have any kind of identity. From this, the question, "Who am I?" in the face of hybridization becomes even more problematic for conflict resolvers. We do not want to lose ourselves into the identities of the disputants, nor do we want to fight to maintain a fixed sense of our own uniqueness against the identity of others. Conflict resolvers should not answer the question "Who am I?" by simply asserting one of the following: "I am one of them" or "I am *not* one of them."

The provisional answer to this dilemma is to return to the singular identity of my past. If I need to have some comfort in knowing who I am, I might simply find that comfort in the singular conception of my past identity, combined with the satisfying achievement of adding new elements to my past identity through the ongoing hybridization process. However, there is a problem with this formulation where I have supposed that I had a singular identity in the past. Does one ever have a singular identity, when we both consciously and unconsciously internalize others into who we are — and we have ongoing inner conflicts between these internalized identities?

One might argue that we are cultural hybridizations, whether we intend to be so or not. We might embrace and cherish these hybridizations, or we might reject and hate them. We might love being a hybrid of our role models, loyal friends, and supportive family, and hate being hybridized by our detractors and tormentors. The drama of this love and hate becomes the stuff of our dreams and nightmares. If one subscribes to the constant hybridization thesis, the question of "Who am I?" becomes: "How do I resolve these inner conflicts?" and "How can I find comfort and pride in who I have become?"

One approach to this problem is to assert that I have no particular need to specify my identity in singular, non-paradoxical, or even non-hypocritical terms. However, I do have a need to have a baseline of comfort and pride in who I have become. Otherwise, I have an identity crisis, where I am uncomfortable and ashamed about whom I have become. I am glad to have that comfort and pride challenged because that is the basis of the identity hybridization process, but I do not wish to be disrespected (by self or other) for the long process of my becoming.

Key to this position is the problem of internalized disrespect. Long-term or traumatic disrespect can easily be internalized and undermine one's positive identity, or prevent a positive identity from ever emerging. With this analysis, I am suggesting that the problem of "Who am I?" does not seem to emerge, unless one's identity is either already conceived as empty or negative: I am nothing, or I am inferior, a failure, and a fraud. On the other hand, if one's identity is thought to be positive, then its singularity, multiplicity, or even description, does not need to come up as a driving question in one's life. In the former case, inner conflicts can be threatening and confusing. In the latter case, the hybridization process can be comforting and validating.

Over my lifetime, I have had numerous identities both positive and negative, but the positive have outweighed the negative, except for a few times of crisis. During those times, as the hybridization process turned from positive to negative, I would ask myself: "Who am I?" or "What have I become?" Only when I was able to reconstruct a positive identity, with the help of family and friends, could I appreciate the positivity of the ongoing hybridization process. The help of family and friends facilitated a deeper hybridization with them. But most importantly, the key was the internalization of their positive regard for me. Unfortunately, not everyone is so lucky.

With these insights, how should we think of the need for a singular identity? I suggest that, in addition to resisting negative hybridization (as explained above); people's need for a singular identity may be generated by their fear of death. First, an eternal soul seems like the kind of singular identity that survives death; this view is common to the Christian and Muslim religions. Buddhists believe that if they identify with the eternal principle of a "ceaseless becoming of the universe," they also survive death, but not as a "soul" or "self." Other religions seem to address the fear of death in ways that require some version of a singular identity. The shared view of these religions seems to be that without a singular identity, it is hard to conceive of what might survive death. On their view, hybridizations, like compound molecules, seem to be destined toward decomposition, just like our bodies. On the other hand, a singularity seems more likely to survive death because it is elemental — and elements, by definition, seem to be eternal, just like the fundamental laws of nature. However, similar to Anselm of Canterbury's ontological argument for the existence of God, definitions do not guarantee existence. Just because we define a soul as a singularity does not contribute to the actual existence of a soul. Rather, definitions tell us about the curious structures of language, not the reality that is sometimes being expressed. In other words, humans' conceptions of reality seem to be more tied to linguistic forms, such as singularity and multiplicity, than direct unmediated experience. Unmediated mystical experience, on the other hand, defies language almost completely, making it virtually ineffable. If mystical experience is where the answer to our fear of death dwells, then no amount of worries about singularities and multiplicities directly address the reality that these concepts are employed to explain.

Singular identities are also culturally generated to secure group bonding and loyalty in families, peer groups, professional groups, communities, ethnicities, sexual orientations, religious groups, and nations, to name a few common categories. Indeed, singular identities are encouraged practically everywhere. On the other hand, hybridized identities seem to be the result of the internalization process that sometimes occurs in diverse societies; however, such hybridizations are also commonly resisted in those same societies. Curiously, cultures push identities in two directions: toward singularity and toward multiplicity — singular by the need to place people into categories, and multiple by the internalization of diverse identities.

What are we to make of the conflict between hybridization resistance and hybridization advocacy? On one hand, hybridization seems to be an observable and measurable empirical phenomenon that plays a powerful role in deepening one's empathy and promoting transformative conflict resolution. On the other hand, people have numerous reasons to resist conceiving of themselves as hybrids in favor of simple, pure, and singular identities.

My recommended way of resolving this conflict is for each of us to be happy with just being a "me" — pure, simple, and singular — along with an impure, complex multiplicity that is in a continuous hybridizing/synthesizing process. Along these lines, we need to find comfort with what each of us has become, comfortable with both our simplicity and multiplicity. We have no need for a singular identity that explains "me" any better or further than "I am just me." We can be happy to recount our influences, role models, and the diverse social roles that we embody, without further stating the nature of "me." In this way, we don't need to commit ourselves to an identity any more categorical than "me."

Disappointingly, my resolution to this conflict is not as tidy as it seems because we might still have worries about death. Secondly, how can our friends, family, colleagues, and neighbors trust us when we are contradictory and paradoxical hybrids? Don't they need to place us in a comfortable category, so they can know who we are and rely on that identity over time?

First, let us return to the death problem. What happens to "me" when I die? What happens to the unique being that I have been? What happens to all of my unfulfilled aspirations? What happens to my connections with loved ones? Does all of that disappear when I die? Sure, some people might remember and miss me, but that is not as powerful a loss as my death means to me. I believe, as Buddhists, in identifying with the "ceaseless becoming of the universe," but that doesn't help me with the losses that occur at my particular life's end. Maybe I have a problem letting go, but I can't help feeling sentimental about my life and my loved ones. I would expect my dog be just as sentimental, so does my dog have a problem letting go? Of course, I feel worse for people younger than I, especially children who die, losing the opportunity to realize many of the ambitions that I have realized as an older adult. To be honest, all of this loss is crushingly depressing. Why do we live only to experience the seemingly complete loss of others, as well as ourselves?

From this grief, I wonder if the "ceaseless becoming of the universe" needs to be so abstract and impersonal. Perhaps we can be part of it while retaining, in some mystical way, a personal "path" where we reside in a kindred network of beloved others' "paths." Does such a ceaseless network of kindred paths commit me to a singular identity? Not necessarily; I think it only commits us to similar paths with similar trajectories.

Second, can my friends, family, colleagues, and neighbors trust me when I am such a paradoxical hybrid? If I represent so many viewpoints, might those close to me wonder what I really think? I have had this problem in more ways than I am probably aware. Colleagues in the philosophy department, where I used to work, openly worried about what I *really* thought when I went into conflict resolution mode. Other people in my life are probably not so confrontational.

My response to this worry is to say that identity hybridization is not merely a collection of conflicting positions. Identity hybridization means resolving different perspectives in a reasonably coherent way. As an example, my appreciating how conservatives honor tradition, family, loyalty, and industry does not undermine my commitment to strong public institutions, social equity, full employment, nonviolence, and sustainability. My appreciation of heavy metal and rap music is not undermined by my love of jazz and classical music. There is agony in being a collection of unresolved and conflicting personality fragments; however there is an enriched comfort in being a synthesized hybrid of myriad influences. The former should be viewed as a lack of individuation; the latter should be embraced as the best identity for an empathetic conflict resolver.

Returning to the problem of other's need to place us within specific categories, we might wonder why they have this need. Such rejection of people with hybridized identities might stem from the insecurity of those with an obsession about maintaining their own singular identities. Fighting off the influences that threaten to give us conflicted identities is certainly understandable, so I sympathize with those who have this struggle, and the insecurity that it entails. It seems that only when one is able to resolve one's inner conflicts through hybridization, can one feel comfortable with multiplicity.

Given the difficulties that prevent the social validation of those of us who have become cheerfully hybridized as conflict resolvers in every aspect of our lives, I suggest that we seek validation from each other. I am a faculty member of a conflict resolution department, and I have observed that alumni of our graduate program seem to stick with the friends they made while studying with us. My friendship pool is also populated with kindred faculty and alumni. We understand and support each other's hybridization process, even as others often look at us tentatively and skeptically. Logan (1981) and Romanyshyn (1982) assert that one's identity reflects the worldviews that emerge in one's era. As hybridization, through inner transformation, emerges as a worldview in the current era, then more and more identities may be shaped by it. I hope that conflict resolvers can lead the way internally, as they resolve conflicts in the world around us.

Notes

1. In July 2011, Anders Behrin Breivik bombed a government building in Oslo, which killed 8 people, and opened fire on a youth camp of a liberal Norwegian political party, killing an additional 69 people.

References

Baldwin, J.M. (1897). *Social and ethical interpretations in mental development.* New York: Macmillan.
Buber, M. (1970). *I and Thou.* (W. Kaufman, Trans.). New York: Charles Scribner's Sons.
Connolly, W. (2002). *Identity/difference: Democratic negotiations of political paradox.* Minneapolis: University of Minnesota Press.
Deleuze, G., and F. Guattari (1988). *A thousand plateaus.* (B. Massumi, Trans.). London: Athlone.
Hume, D. (1888). *A Treatise of Human Nature.* London: Oxford University Press.
Logan, R. (1981). *An Eriksonian model for the development of the self through history.* New York: International Psychohistorical Association.
Marsh, H.W., and R.J. Shavelson (1985). Self-concept: Its multifaceted, hierarchical structure. *Educational Psychologist, 20*(3), 107–123.
Ogilvy, J. (1977). *Many dimensional man.* New York: Oxford University Press.
Ouspensky, P.D. (1949). *In search of the miraculous.* New York: Harcourt, Brace and World.
Plato (1966). *Phaedo.* (H.N. Fowler, Trans.). Cambridge: Harvard University Press.
Romanyshyn, R. (1982). *Psychological life: From science to metaphor.* Milton Keynes: Open University Press.

Said, E.W. (1995). *Orientalism: Western conceptions of the Orient*. London: Penguin.
Shavelson, R.J., J.J. Hubner, and G.C. Stanton (1976). Validation of construct interpretations. *Review of Educational Research*, 46, 407–441.
Therborn, G. (1995). *European modernity and beyond: The trajectory of European societies 1945–2000*. London: Sage.

The Journey to Conflict Resolver: Peace-Scapes

Patrick T. Hiller and *Paloma Ayala Vela*

In a biographical research study, one of this article's authors set out to explore how a select group of nonviolent peace and social justice activists in the United States construct and negotiate their identities (Hiller, 2010). Among other discoveries, the study found that their identities were consciously constructed in a stage-like process. Activists followed similar paths during their lifetimes, leading them through defined stages during which they developed a set of dynamic, integrative worldviews. The term "peace-scapes" was introduced to describe their remarkable life journeys, culminating in the adoption of an activist identity. What can be learned from these nonviolent activists that might contribute to a critical discussion of contemporary approaches to conflict resolution? This essay explores how integrative worldviews help develop a set of underlying principles that guide conflict resolution professionals in their respective approaches to resolving conflict.

In this essay, we assume that the majority of social conflicts can be directly traced back to structural inequalities, and so we are specifically concerned with the role of structural violence and the interplay of power and knowledge with respect to conflict resolution. We examine the existing body of knowledge in the field, the social environment where the field emerged, and our own role in it, in order to obtain a better understanding of our role in upholding or abolishing structural violence. We then discuss what we have learned from the life stories of nonviolent peace and social justice activists in the United States and, in particular, how we can incorporate integrative worldviews into resolving conflict.

An Inward Look at the Field

There is a vast body of literature specific to the discipline of conflict resolution, and methods such as mediation, negotiation, and facilitation provide an important foundation. As Salem (2001) argues, however, the theorists and practitioners often operate out of a macro-political context with predetermined Western attitudes and values. Due to the neglect of indigenous voices and people from the Global South, the field's scholarship, practice, and pedagogy is strongly Western-centric (Matyók, Senehi, & Byrne, 2011) and can be described as "a Euro-centric model in all aspects of its functions (e.g., degree curriculum, theoretical frame, research orientation, and practice)" (Tuso, 2011). Here, we aim, like Ramsbotham, Woodhouse, and Miall (2011), to find ways to enrich any conflict resolution tradition — Western or non–Western — by adapting integrative perspectives emphasizing common humanity.

Compared to the well-established disciplines, conflict resolution is a young field, and as Louis Kriesberg, a key thinker in the discipline, notes: "as the world changes, so does the field of conflict resolution" (2007, p. 25). Major works such as *The Sage Handbook of Conflict Resolution* (Bercovitch, Kremeniuk, & Zartman, 2008), *The Handbook of Conflict Resolution* (Deutsch, Coleman, & Marcus, 2006) or *Peacemaking in International Conflict: Methods & Techniques* (Zartman, 2007) provide an overview of dominant methods of conflict resolution such as mediation, negotiation, and facilitation. Other works that examine topics such as power (Coleman, 2006), communication (Krauss & Morsella, 2006), or broad notions of culture (Augsberger, 1992; Faure, 2008; Kimmel, 2006; Pederson, 2006) provide us with tools through which conflict can be examined.

Prominent approaches in mediation include linear and goal-oriented problem-solving mediation (Moore, 2003; Phillips, 2001), narrative mediation with a focus on relational strengths (Winslade & Monk, 2001), and transformative mediation which focuses on the parties' relations through empowerment and recognition (Bush & Folger, 2005). Some of the major difficulties of the Western mediation concept are outlined by Brand-Jacobsen and Jacobsen's (2002) essay "Beyond Mediation." The authors highlight the pitfalls of a Western mediation approach, pointing out how it revolves around a set of "how-to approaches" led by process experts (the mediators), who put forth "a universal toolkit for resolving conflicts" (p. 51). In essence, they argue that problem-solving mediation is a top-down approach. If held in cross-cultural conflict environments, mediation is "*conflict-provoking*, leading to a reduction in options, locking in the conflict and blocking the room for alternatives generated from a variety of actors" (p. 74). Lederach (1995) also criticizes these approaches as prescriptive and an "unintended residue of imperialism" (p. 38).

Brand-Jacobsen and Jacobsen (2002) do not promote another recipe for successful conflict resolution, but instead suggest alternative approaches that are based on "the empowerment of civil society, of groups, organizations and individuals at every level of society, and of the traditional networks and social structures of cultures around the world so often excluded from most modern approaches to conflict resolution" (p. 73).

Examining the method of negotiation in the literature, the approach relies almost entirely on a set of accepted presuppositions of formal written or oral exchanges; homogenous, unchanging entities; unchanging issues; and a fixed, seemingly neutral negotiation environment.[1] *Getting to Yes* (Fisher, Ury, & Patton, 1997), a best-selling negotiation guide, can be found in the libraries of all conflict resolution professionals. However, what if getting to yes is not the *non plus ultra* in negotiation? What if changing the structure within which negotiation operates is more important for a sustainable resolution of a conflict? Similarly, the well-known systems approach of multi-track diplomacy (Diamond & McDonald, 1996) is initially appealing, but closer scrutiny reveals some weaknesses. Whereas the authors correctly argue that the different parts of a conflict transformation system (government, non-government/professional, business, private citizen, research/training/education, activism, religion, funding, and communication/media) are interrelated, it is clear that the system operates within a Western paradigm and that the tracks — if they exist equally in cross-cultural contexts — do not necessarily lead synergistically toward the resolution of any conflict. What if actors are suffering from structural violence *because* of the tracks? The tracks are part of the dominant societal structure and therefore would reinforce the structure instead of resolving the underlying aspects of the conflict.

Lewicki et al. (2004) have indicated that the negotiators' social environment is probably the most poorly understood yet influential factor during a negotiation. Hopmann (1996) argues that the social conditions often assumed by mediators and negotiators "seldom pertain in the real world of international negotiations" (p. 99). Kremenyuk (2002) likewise argues that the process of international negotiation needs to adapt to the changes of the social world, which we emphasize must include an examination of power dynamics and structural violence.

To summarize, as Hughes argued, the Western worldview is, "linear, reductionist, objectivist, determinist, predictive, and rational" (Hughes, 2005, p. 681), and as Lederach (1995) asserts, Western conflict resolution models are homogenizing. Rigid models of conflict resolution developed in a Western paradigm often lack acknowledgment of the larger social environment.

Alternatives to the Dominant Approaches

A more integrative understanding of social conflict is necessary, because conflict is not linear and human behavior is complex. As Brand-Jacobsen and Jacobsen (2002) state, conflict as a social phenomenon can best be understood by discussing the contributions of different approaches and perspectives to make our understanding more complete. Therefore, it is important to "listen to the people of the non–West speaking for themselves" (p. 82). We can learn a great deal from indigenous systems of conflict resolution and applications in cross-cultural contexts, but to do so we must have the real desire to understand the system from an inside perspective, rather than approach it as an alien system.

Galtung and his colleagues (2002), in referring to third-generation peace approaches, write that "there is a reaction against simplistic peace approaches, realizing how deep-rooted — and linked to development = satisfaction of basic needs — these problems are" (p. xvi). The comprehensive *Contemporary Conflict Resolution* (Ramsbotham, Woodhouse, & Miall, 2011) surveys the theory and practice of the field while addressing the context of rapid global change. Importantly, the authors clarify the role of conflict resolution and redefine its cosmopolitan values. This overall approach merits close attention, since the authors aim to bridge the gap between the overly structured conflict resolution approaches and the pursuit of cosmopolitan conflict resolution promoting the interests of humanity. Lederach's (1995) elicitive approach to conflict resolution is another example of a much more integrative perspective than the models previously discussed. He asserts that personal and systemic transformations are fundamental to justice and equality.

Based on the conflict triangle of attitude, behavior, and contradiction, Brand-Jacobsen and Jacobsen (2002) provide another positive integrative perspective on conflict resolution. Empathy, nonviolence/peace struggle, and creativity are identified as the basic formula for achieving peace by peaceful means. These non-prescriptive principles allow for a wide range of approaches toward resolving social conflict, and involve conscientization, organization, mobilization, and empowerment of individuals and groups on all societal levels. This approach, which shows similarities to Freire's (1970) notion of critical consciousness, addresses structural violence at its roots.

What we have observed so far is the field's tendency to fit conflict into manageable models, but there are also attempts by scholars and practitioners to step out of those narrow approaches. Next, we will examine how the context surrounding our knowledge is created and how we knowingly or unknowingly contribute to structural violence.

Power and Structural Violence

Power is exercised in everyday situations and human interactions. It is a central concept in conflict analysis, and conflict resolution scholars and practitioners themselves hold power. Specifically, through the knowledge that we have obtained through our education and training, we have the power not only to exert influence over the conflicting parties, but even to determine who the parties are — and who they are not.

A myriad of academic perspectives address power as a theoretical concept. In Max Weber's (1920/1978) well-known definition, power is defined as "the chance of a man or a number of men to realize their own will in a social action even against the resistance of others who are participating in the action" (p. 926). Power is connected to class, status, and domination. In negotiation literature, power is sometimes looked at as a strategic approach to coerce the other party into making concessions (Lewicki et al., 2004). Morton Deutsch (1973) holds that people have power in certain situations through which they can satisfy their goals, desires, or wants. Kenneth Boulding's (1990) influential *Three Faces of Power* presents a much debated conceptualization of power. He distinguishes three main categories: threat power (the power to destroy), economic power (the power to produce and exchange), and integrative power (the power to integrate). Although the manifestation of these can readily be identified in given social environments, Boulding fails to consider how power comes into existence and how it is related to knowledge in this context.

Rather than looking at manifest forms of power, we wish to propose a postmodern interpretation of power, along the lines of Foucault. The French philosopher described power as an exceedingly pervasive mechanism which "reaches into the very grain of individuals, touches their bodies and inserts itself into their actions and attitudes, their discourses, learning processes and everyday lives" (Foucault & Gordon, 1980, p. 39). Foucault also maintained that "the exercise of power perpetually creates knowledge and, conversely, knowledge constantly induces effects of power" (Foucault & Faubion, 2000, p. xvi). In other words, power is a socially constructed concept; power and the social structure determine what knowledge is, how it is used, and what is conveyed, while at the same time knowledge itself is a basis of power.

An example of a contemporary social conflict illustrates how power concepts differ and how Foucaultian power/knowledge dynamics can help us better understand the conflict environment. In 1994 the indigenous Zapatistas — *los indios invisibles* — in southern Mexico started an armed rebellion against the government. According to knowledge-power-structures — the government — their actions were illegal. Yet as presented by the Zapatista movement, the actions of the government in response represented an "an undeclared genocidal war" (EZLN, 1994a), so the Zapatistas were waging their own war to acquire the basic human necessities of work, land, housing, food, health care, education, independence, freedom, democracy, justice, and peace (EZLN, 1994b). Following a very brief period of fighting, this struggle for physical survival and recognition as indigenous peoples within the Mexican nation has involved more or less formal negotiations and mediation.

On the surface we see coercive power or threat power being exercised on both sides, whereas economic and legitimate power is held exclusively by the government. Such categorization, however, only allows an analysis of power structures from a consequential viewpoint. We must also be aware that the illegality of the Zapatistas' initial actions is derived from a power context embedded in the social structure of society, framed by the rhetoric of the government and the media.[2] In his work Foucault discusses how notions like "legality" and "illegality" are derived from the interrelation of power and knowledge in a given society (Foucault & Faubion, 2000). When we start to question the truth of this knowledge and verify its legitimacy in the Mexican context, we can begin to understand the meaning behind Foucault's conceptualization of power.

In sum, ways of thinking and uses of knowledge are results of the social structure, which again is the result of an interplay with power; in other words, knowledge derived from human sciences is closely related to and "enmeshed in the problems and practices of power, the social government and management of individuals" (Foucault & Faubion 2000, p. xvi). Knowledge is not developed in a social vacuum, rather, it is a "form of subjectivity which Foucault presents as invented or instilled by the modern social disciplines of individualized surveillance and normalization" (Foucault & Faubion, 2000, p. xxxv). Foucault's discourse on power and knowledge invites conflict resolution professionals to think critically about accepted scholarship and ideas of power, as well as to look inward at their own role in power structures.

The original idea of structural violence is commonly associated with the Norwegian sociologist Johan Galtung (1969) and has been a formative influence on the field of conflict resolution. According to him, structural violence is the ongoing and institutionalized harm done to individuals by preventing them from meeting their basic needs for survival, well-being, identity, and freedom. Structural violence is embedded in the structures of social order and the institutional arrangements of power on a constant basis (Barak, 2003). As aptly defined by Bornstein (2002), "structural violence is built into everyday life, into the economy, a political system, and into the landscape" (p. 6).

Despite globalization, Western industrialized core nations, which are geographically located in the northern hemisphere, remain in a dominant position with respect to the so-called underdeveloped, periphery countries

(Galtung, 1971). A notable example of how industrial nations exercise their power can be illustrated by the contemporary HIV/AIDS pandemic in many regions of Africa. The manner in which medical aid is being distributed is completely dominated by the political and economic structure of the core nations. In her book *The Crisis Caravan: What's Wrong with Humanitarian Aid* (2010), journalist Linda Polman argues that Western humanitarian aid not only contributes to structural violence, but also to a macabre industry of aid organizations, the media, and warmongers. This industry, states Polman, leads to direct physical violence for the sake of maintaining the humanitarian aid system — a cruel manifestation of structural violence.

Structural violence is not only based on spatial separations, but can be found within societies. A common challenge to any society is its treatment of ethnic minorities. Many self-perceived "forward societies"— most notably the United States — have officially eliminated institutional racial or ethnic discrimination, a powerful form of structural violence. Yet a closer look at the American distribution of wealth, educational opportunities, and the prison system sheds light on the actual state of affairs with regard to racial discrimination.

A specific example of structural violence can be observed in the treatment of individuals in the lesbian, gay, bisexual, and transgender (LGBT) community in the United States, who suffer in a similar manner as ethnic and racial minorities. In public discourse it seems that the rights of the LGBT community have come a long way. While progress has been made, hidden and dangerous forms of homophobia remain. LGBT couples, for example, who are not allowed to marry in most states, are denied a vast number of rights that heterosexual married couples inherit with their legal marital status. The fact that such injustices are hidden behind "progress" merely nurtures and upholds structural violence caused by prevailing social ideals and institutions.

We argue that Galtung's (1969) typology of structural violence — despite its fundamental importance in the field of conflict resolution — is not enough. While it is suitable to describe a variety of social phenomena, it provides more of a societal snapshot than an in-depth understanding that includes the conflict actors' and resolvers' personal perspectives. We now move on to discuss a theory of integrative worldviews as it emerged out of the analysis of nonviolent activists' biographies.

Integrative Conflict Resolution through the Creation of "Peace-Scapes"

Our philosophy of integrative conflict resolution will be developed using the metaphor of peace-scapes. The theory emerged from a biographical study

(Hiller, 2010) of a selected group of nonviolent activists in the United States, which explored how these individuals construct and negotiate their identities. The major themes from the study suggest that throughout their lives, the participants generally developed integrative worldviews which gave meaning not only to their everyday lives, but also to their commitment as nonviolent peace and social justice activists. Integrative worldviews are understood as dynamic and emergent cognitive processes that lead to all-encompassing, conscious, human interpretations and constructions of scripts to live meaningfully. Integrative worldviews help the activists understand experiences on a personal, familial, social, political, moral, and sometimes spiritual level. They are constructs in the mind as well as guides for action.

The concept of peace-scapes as elucidated by the research study was used to describe these integrative worldviews, which were based on a sense of community; a fluid sense of organizational belonging; a broad spatial realm; the creation of a shared context; the interconnection of personal, social, and environmental issues; a long-term commitment to peace and social justice; and a positive sense of self. Just like landscapes are made up of interrelated, dynamic natural elements (water, air, vegetation, wildlife, etc.) and human elements (cultivated fields, roads, towns, power lines, etc.), peace-scapes are made up of a diversity of interconnected factors creating an organic whole. Inspired by these findings, we wish to apply the metaphor of peace-scapes to create integrative perspectives for dealing with conflict.[3] In doing so, we hope to provide a dynamic, non-hierarchical script of principles for meaningful action in the realm of conflict resolution.

Embracing the notion of "otherness"

A main concern when analyzing social conflict is how conflict is constructed through stories and where people place themselves within these stories. Along the path leading to formation of their identities as peace and social justice activists, the individuals in the study came to realize that they shared an interconnected world with those who might be considered "enemies." In the concept of peace-scapes, we suggest creating a sense of community where "otherness" is not only intellectually acknowledged, but also embraced as a more complete experience of humanity.

Looking at a social conflict with an inclusive, humanizing sense of community allows for better communication, deeper understanding, and the ability to de-construct presumptions, biases, and stereotypes. In other words, peace-scapes help to create a shared context with all individuals and groups where otherness is not reified as a threat. By doing this, the nonviolent philosophies — like moral confrontation, participation of all, and reconciliation and tolerance embraced by such influential figures as Gandhi, King, the Dalai Lama, or Mandela — are reflected. Those principles are as much about our own biases and preconceptions as about identifying them within the conflicting parties.

Interrelation of the personal, social, and professional

As in any profession, individuals tend to separate their role as professionals from the personal as well as the larger social environment. For the peace and social activists in the study, issues of personal, social, and environmental concern were interrelated. This could be seen by the issues they were engaged in as well as in the way they lived their everyday lives. Peace-scapes in conflict resolution allow for an expansion of views outside of immediate, visible, and tangible issues in social conflict. They allow individuals to consider their personal, social, and professional worlds as an organic system guided by a set of human values.

We suggest that the nature of social conflict does not allow for professionals to be entirely disconnected. Neither the conflict nor the professionals dealing with it are situated in a social vacuum. Therefore, it is crucial to look at the conflict environment from an integrative perspective — as an organic whole that includes one's own role and dispositions.

Rather than making conscious efforts to be a so-called rational decision maker in a bureaucratic understanding, the integration of the professional with the personal and social allows for a more genuine approach in conflict resolution. Our contention goes back to the earlier discussion of structural violence, where we need to realize our own role within a social structure. Thus the personal disposition toward abolishing structural violence should in all cases be part of any form of conflict intervention. To do so, there must be a willingness to interrelate personal values, social concerns, and the conflict scenario.

Being a conflict resolution professional is as much about a set of intervention tools as it is about being committed to social justice. Consequently, when we set about to intervene in a conflict, we do not have to set aside our overall concern for positive peace. In this regard, conflict resolution does not end merely with the absence of manifest conflict, but with the establishment of sustainable mechanisms leading to structural nonviolence. When we identify social structures that harm individuals or groups, we are obliged not only to address overt issues indicating acts of oppression or injustice, but, even more so, to deal with those forms of structural violence that are hidden from the everyday observer.

Identifying one's own role in structural violence

Peace-scapes help us understand how knowingly or unknowingly conflict resolution professionals contribute to structural and cultural violence, and how those forms of violence may even be reinforced by the approaches pertinent to the field. In our society, the privileged position of individuals holding a certificate or degree in conflict resolution grants them the authority to analyze social conflict and provides the tools for a successful resolution. But as discussed previously, Western notions of conflict resolution are applied within the parameters created and accepted by Western society. Consequently, we should be conscious about the power we hold through our education and training. By realizing our own role when analyzing and attempting to contribute to the resolution of conflict, we can avoid falling into "imagined entrapments" of abstract Western theorizing. Anthropologist Linstroth (2007) points out:

> Peacebuilders and peacemakers assume too much by reifying colonial discourses of patriarchy upon the people they wish to help.... [T]he most prevalent approaches to peace are limited to Western perspectives and self-interests and do not go very far in getting us closer to how non–Western and established forms of informal justice systems operate and what we can learn from non–Western others rather than vice versa. It is altogether overwhelmingly apparent how those writing about peacebuilding and peacemaking are obsessed with placing such studies in the scientific realm, which is ironic because they study "human" conflict [p. 111].

Keeping Linstroth's point in mind, the determination of a conflict's sources, parties, issues, tactics, changes, escalation, roles of other parties, outcome, and possible winners is informed by the lens through which it is viewed. The activists in the study, however, realized their own privileges, especially when they chose to acknowledge the "social facts" surrounding them.[4]

Positive peace above neutrality

Peace-scapes allow us to advocate for positive peace rather than remain in a self-imposed, professional, neutral position. From the peace activists in the study we learned that neutrality is not acceptable when advocacy is necessary to address social injustice. Do we as conflict resolution professionals jeopardize our approaches by stepping outside the paradigm of neutrality? According to many prescriptive Western theories we probably do. But what does neutrality imply? If remaining neutral means to act within a framework of structural and cultural violence or if it means to uphold hegemonic domination, then conflict resolution professionals have indeed chosen the wrong side.

Conflict resolution, as practiced by the West, is a privileged field which comes with the moral obligation not to hide behind the curtain of neutrality but to confront invisible forms of violence: structural, cultural, soft, or symbolic. To do so, challenging the dominant social discourse is sometimes necessary. As Christie et al. (2001) state, "our roles as scientists do not require us to remain politically neutral. Science itself is value laden; feigning neutrality is intellectually dishonest and socially irresponsible" (p. 366).

Long-term vision for positive peace

In his constructs of negative and positive peace, Galtung (1969) describes negative peace as the absence of personal violence, whereas in positive peace structural violence is also eliminated. Since the social structure in many societies is constructed on the basis of a negative peace — the unjust and unequal treatment of certain members to the benefit of others — any attempt to create positive peace must focus on long-term changes.

Peace-scapes create these long-term visions for change. From the peace and social activists in the study, we have learned that their dedication is not about short-term triumphs. It is an ongoing process of committing to achieve just social structures. In following an overly structured, goal-oriented approach, Western conflict resolution lacks such an in-depth commitment. Addressing a conflict only as it is manifested immediately does a disservice not only to that manifestation, but more importantly, to the underlying conflict environment. Peace-scapes, in contrast, provide both Band-Aid resolutions and well-conceived approaches to creating cultures of positive peace.

We suggest creating an integrative vision of the future based on all-encompassing efforts to create a better future for everyone. "Long term solutions require that we illuminate the systemic connections between direct and indirect levels of violence as well as between individuals and their communities" (Christie et al., 2001). Or as Ramsbotham, Woodhouse, and Miall (2011) argue, "conflict resolution is an integral part of work for development, social justice and transformation that aims to tackle the problems of which mercenaries and child soldiers are symptoms" (p. 7). Ultimately, if positive peace — regardless of whether we are talking about interpersonal, intergroup, or international conflicts — is not the ultimate goal of intervention, why bother? In this regard, individuals in the field of conflict resolution can serve as agents for social change.

Proactive form of conflict resolution

Peace-scapes include proactive forms of violence prevention and conflict resolution. Latent conflict fueled by structural violence is addressed and efforts for correcting social injustice are made. From the activists in the study we learned that they did not react only to violence and manifest conflict. Their interpretation and response to perceived injustices in society is a proactive form of violence prevention correcting these injustices before they escalate.

Conclusion

In this essay we discussed how the field of conflict resolution in theory and practice is often guided by a body of prescriptive approaches. Alternative approaches have found their way into the field, yet the dominant theories for the practice of conflict resolution are embedded in a Western paradigm. What might work in one specific social setting may be useless in another. Special concern was given to the question of how conflict resolution knowledge is created and how it is informed by Foucaultian power/knowledge relations. We contended that by more or less blindly following the structured conflict resolution approaches, we knowingly or unknowingly contribute to hidden, indirect forms of structural violence and reinforce them by acting within the accepted approaches.

In addressing our concerns with the status quo of conflict resolution, we do not call for a rejection of the existing literary and practical canon of conflict resolution. We are not trying to reinvent — or break — the wheel, but seek to provide a set of dynamic principles which can be merged with existing knowledge. Taking an integrative perspective of conflict resolution then requires us to challenge what Hastings (2006) refers to as the "master narrative"— basic, conventional, and unquestioned knowledge. We need to examine critically the accepted truisms of our own societal backgrounds.

Our idea of peace-scapes is not another model for conflict resolution, but rather a general philosophy through which we can approach conflict resolution and through which we can also look at the existing body of knowledge, approaches, and specific models relevant to this area. Peace-scapes allow us to embrace the "moral imagination" that Lederach (2005) envisions for conflict professionals. He suggests four joint capacities that help to transcend violence: (1) the imagination of people in a web of relationships including their enemies; (2) maintaining paradoxical curiosity without dualistic polarity; (3) the belief in and the pursuit of creative actions; and (4) the risk of stepping into the unknown landscape beyond violence. Moral imaginations strongly reflect perspectives taken by nonviolent activists.

From our conception of peace-scapes, we propose the following for conflict resolvers as they strive to realize positive and sustainable peace:

- Develop a genuine concept of equality of all humans;
- Develop a realization that we share an interconnected social and natural world;
- Be humble in understanding our role as conflict resolution professionals;
- Be aware and honest about our cultural biases;
- Be listeners not preachers;
- Let processes develop from the bottom-up, not top-down.

In sum, just as the dynamic qualities of landscapes are affected by such factors as natural erosion or human intervention, the contexts and dynamics of peace-scapes also change over time. Peace-scapes challenge our understanding of and approach to resolving social conflict, and should be guiding principles. Our suggestion is to merge our integrative understanding of conflict resolution with the existing knowledge and improve or even change it when it upholds structural violence.

Notes

1. We acknowledge the contribution of Essoh J.M.C. Essis in a joint, unpublished manuscript, *Rethinking International Negotiations*.
2. See Hiller (2009) for a discussion on contesting historiography through interpretations of Mexican national symbols by the Zapatista movement and the government.
3. In her ethnographic work *A Different Kind of War Story*, Nordstrom (1997) perceives the perpetrators and victims of violence in her notion of "war-scapes" as sharing the same context, i.e., not isolated from each other. We are translating her term for a shared context of peacemaking.
4. The notion of "social facts" originated with the French sociologist Émile Durkheim, and refers to generally accepted ways a social group thinks, feels, and acts, that are experienced externally and are constraining to individuals (Durkheim, 1895/2003).

References

Augsburger, D.W. (1992). *Conflict mediation across cultures: Pathways and patterns* (1st ed.). Louisville, KY: Westminster/John Knox.
Barak, G. (2003). *Violence and nonviolence: Pathways to understanding*. Thousand Oaks, CA: Sage.
Bercovitch, J., V.A. Kremeniuk and I.W. Zartman (2008). *The Sage handbook of conflict resolution*. Thousand Oaks, CA: Sage.
Bornstein, A.S. (2002). *Crossing the green line between the West Bank and Israel*. Philadelphia: University of Pennsylvania Press.
Boulding, K.E. (1990). *Three faces of power*. Newbury Park, CA: Sage.
Brand-Jacobsen, K.F., and C.G. Jacobsen (2002). Beyond mediation: Towards more holistic approaches to peace-building and peace-actor empowerment. In J. Galtung, C.G. Jacobsen and K.F. Brand-Jacobsen (Eds.), *Searching for peace: The road to Transcend* (2d ed., pp. 49–86). London: Pluto.
Bush, R.A.B., and J.P. Folger (2005). *The promise of mediation: The transformative approach to conflict* (Rev. ed.). San Francisco: Jossey-Bass.

Christie, D.J., R.V. Wagner, and D.D.N. Winter (2001). *Peace, conflict, and violence: Peace psychology for the 21st century.* Upper Saddle River, NJ: Prentice Hall.
Coleman, P.T. (2006). Power and conflict. In M. Deutsch, P.T. Coleman and E.C. Marcus (Eds.), *The handbook of conflict resolution: Theory and practice* (2d ed., pp. 120–143). San Francisco: Jossey-Bass.
Deutsch, M. (1973). *The resolution of conflict: constructive and destructive processes.* New Haven: Yale University Press.
_____, P.T. Coleman, and E.C. Marcus (2006). *The handbook of conflict resolution: Theory and practice* (2d ed.). San Francisco: Jossey-Bass.
Diamond, L., and J.W. McDonald (1996). *Multi-track diplomacy: A systems approach to peace* (3d ed.). West Hartford, CT: Kumarian.
Durkheim, E. (1895/2003). What is a social fact? In G. Delanty and P. Strydom (Eds.), *Philosophies of social science: The classic and contemporary readings* (pp. 26–30). Phildelphia: Open University.
EZLN. (1994a). First ceclaration of the Lacandon Jungle. Retrieved Febuary 19, 2011, from http://www.ezln.org.
_____. (1994b). Second ceclaration of the Lacandon Jungle. Retrieved February 19, 2011, from http://www.ezln.org.
Faure, G.O. (2008). Culture and conflict resolution. In J. Bercovitch, V.A. Kremeniuk and I.W. Zartman (Eds.), *The Sage handbook of conflict resolution* (pp. 506–524). Thousand Oaks, CA: Sage.
Fisher, R., W. Ury, and B. Patton (1997). *Getting to yes: Negotiating an agreement without giving in* (2d ed.). London: Arrow Business.
Foucault, M., and J.D. Faubion (2000). *Power.* New York: New Press.
_____, and C. Gordon (1980). *Power/knowledge: Selected interviews and other writings, 1972–1977* (1st American ed.). New York: Pantheon.
Freire, P. (1970). *Pedagogy of the oppressed.* New York: Herder and Herder.
Galtung, J. (1969). Violence, peace, and peace research. *Journal of Peace Research,* 6(3), 167–191.
_____ (1971). A structural theory of imperialism. *Journal of Peace Research,* 8(2), 81–117.
_____, C.G. Jacobsen, and K.F. Brand-Jacobsen (2002). *Searching for peace: The road to Transcend* (2nd ed.). London: Pluto.
Hastings, T.H. (2006). *The lessons of nonviolence: Theory and practice in a world of conflict.* Jefferson, NC: McFarland.
Hiller, P.T. (2009). Contesting Zapata: Differing meanings of the Mexican national idea. *Journal of Alternative Perspectives in the Social Sciences,* 1(2), 258–280.
_____ (2010). *Trajectories toward nonviolent identities: Development, negotiation and maintenance of integrative worldviews of a selected group of peace and social justice activists in the United States.* Ph.D. Dissertation, Nova Southeastern University, Fort Lauderdale, FL.
Hopmann, P.T. (1996). *The negotiation process and the resolution of international conflicts.* Columbia: University of South Carolina Press.
Hughes, C. (2005). Understanding a conflict in a postmodern world. *Marquette Law Review,* 87, 681.
Kimmel, P.R. (2006). Culture and conflict. In M. Deutsch, P.T. Coleman and E.C. Marcus (Eds.), *The handbook of conflict resolution: Theory and practice* (2d ed., pp. 625–648). San Francisco: Jossey-Bass.
Krauss, R.M., and E. Morsella (2006). Communication and conflict. In M. Deutsch, P.T. Coleman and E.C. Marcus (Eds.), *The handbook of conflict resolution: Theory and practice* (2d ed., pp. 144–157). San Francisco: Jossey-Bass.
Kremenyuk, V.A. (2002). *International negotiation: Analysis, approaches, issues* (2d ed.). San Francisco: Jossey-Bass.

Kriesberg, L. (2007). The conflict resolution field: Origins, growth, and differentiation. In I.W. Zartman (Ed.), *Peacemaking in international conflict: Methods and techniques* (Rev. ed., pp. 25–60). Washington, DC: United States Institute of Peace.

Lederach, J. P. (1995). *Preparing for peace: conflict transformation across cultures.* Syracuse: Syracuse University Press.

_____. (2005). *The moral imagination: The art and soul of building peace.* London: Oxford University Press.

Lewicki, R.J., D.M. Saunders, B. Barry, and J.W. Minton (2004). *Essentials of negotiation* (3d ed.). Boston: McGraw-Hill/Irwin.

Linstroth, J.P. (2007). Conflicts as traps and conflicting entrapments: Human rights, intractable conflicts, and pitfalls of peace negotiations. In Eusko Jaurlaritzaren Argitalpen Zerbitu Nagusia (Ed.), *2nd international conference of human rights: Conflict resolution* (pp. 81–117). Bilbao, Spain: Basque Country Administration.

Matyók, T., J. Senehi, and S. Byrne (2011). *Critical issues in peace and conflict studies: Theory, practice, and pedagogy.* Lanham, MD: Lexington.

Moore, C.W. (2003). *The mediation process: Practical strategies for resolving conflict* (3d ed.). San Francisco: Jossey-Bass.

Nordstrom, C. (1997). *A different kind of war story.* Philadelphia: University of Pennsylvania Press.

Pederson, P. (2006). Multicultural conflict resolution. In M. Deutsch, P.T. Coleman and E.C. Marcus (Eds.), *The handbook of conflict resolution: Theory and practice* (2d ed., pp. 649–670). San Francisco: Jossey-Bass.

Phillips, B.A. (2001). *The mediation field guide: Transcending litigation and resolving conflicts in your business or organization* (1st ed.). San Francisco: Jossey-Bass.

Polman, L. (2010). *The crisis caravan: What's wrong with humanitarian aid?* (1st U.S. ed.). New York: Metropolitan.

Ramsbotham, O., H. Miall, and T. Woodhouse (2011). *Contemporary conflict resolution: The prevention, management and transformation of deadly conflicts* (3d ed.). Cambridge, UK: Polity.

Salem, P.E. (2001). A Critique of Western Conflict Resolution from a Non-Western Perspective. In P.K. Chew (Ed.), *The conflict and culture reader* (pp. 220–229). New York: New York University Press.

Tuso, H. (2011). Indigenous processes of conflict resolution: Neglected methods of peacemaking by the new field of conflict resolution. In T. Matyók, J. Senehi and S. Byrne (Eds.), *Critical issues in peace and conflict studies: Theory, practice, and pedagogy* (pp. 245–270). Lanham, MD: Lexington.

Weber, M., G. Roth, and C. Wittich (1978). *Economy and society: An outline of interpretive sociology* (Vol. 2). Berkeley: University of California Press.

Winslade, J., & Monk, G. (2001). *Narrative mediation: A new approach to conflict resolution* (1st ed.). San Francisco: Jossey-Bass.

Zartman, W. I. (2007). *Peacemaking in international conflict: Methods and techniques* (Rev. ed.). Washington, DC: United States Institute of Peace.

Listening as a Practice of Conflict Transformation: Learnings from a Death Penalty Compassionate Listening Project

Rachel H. Cunliffe

> When we come together to talk ... can each of us be aware of the subtle fear and pleasure sensations that "block" his ability to listen freely? Without this awareness, the injunction to listen to the whole of what is said will have little meaning. But if each one of us can give full attention to what is actually "blocking" communication while he is also attending properly to the content of what is communicated, then we may be able to create something new between us, something of very great significance for bringing to an end the at present insoluble problems of the individual and of society [Bohm, 1996, p. 5].

Listening is not simply synonymous with the biological and neural function of hearing, but refers to the intentional selection of, and attention to, aural and visual stimuli as well as inner promptings and responses in order to construct knowledge about the other(s) in an encounter and about the world.[1] Listening is not passive, nor is it accidental. The importance of listening strategies has long been recognized in the field of human communication and conflict resolution, and whole texts are devoted to the enumeration and learning of listening skills (Purdy & Borisoff, 1997; Wolvin & Coakley, 1996). According to these texts there is a taxonomy of listening, including varieties such as self listening (Purdy, 1997), intercultural listening (Thomlison, 1997), discriminative, comprehensive, and therapeutic listening (Wolvin & Coakley,

1996). Implicit in these classifications is the orientation of the one listening to the quality of what is heard. Since what is heard is intimately connected to what is understood — and therefore to what is believed and becomes the epistemological foundation for action — consideration of the objectives and outcomes of listening is merited in the field of conflict resolution and transformation.

As Hoffman (2002) wrote, "I believe that our work as peacemakers is not to take sides but to seek truth, that there will never be peace unless both sides are listened to. We must ... listen with respect to those who disagree with or oppose us" (p.281). A peaceful and harmonious society requires listening and a search for truth and recognition through empathy. Pepinsky (2006) suggests that the practice of empathy is central to the art of peacemaking, defining empathy as "trying to put oneself in another's place, so as to imagine that in the other person or group's place I would feel and act as they do" (p. 188).

Compassionate listening is a method of conflict transformation which inserts a curious and open-minded listener into entrenched conflict and conflicting parties. Without an agenda beyond promoting respect and recognition, the listener engages with stakeholders, conveying these relational qualities through focused attention and contingent communication. These activities are suspended in, and motivated by, the belief that when people are fully actualized in the breadth and depth of their humanity, they will recognize each other's humanity and seek collaborative and harmonious ways to coexist. Hoffman (1997) describes compassionate listening as "a process in which people open up to new thoughts and ideas when they are carefully listened to" (p. 302). Manousos (2003) adds, "Compassionate listening does not try to force people to change, but it assumes that people are changeable and that listening to their concerns can facilitate transformation.... the cycle of violence can be broken only when the victims (and perpetrators) of violence learn to listen to each other" (pp. 264–5).

The death penalty controversy in the United States is often framed in adversarial terms as a debate, which is built on judgment and dismissal. My own compassionate listening project with the death penalty started unintentionally with conversations with cab drivers, colleagues, and family members who disagreed with me. I found that at least some of those "barbarians" were intelligent people for whom I had great respect in other spheres of life. I was curious how people who looked so like me and shared such similar opinions about so many other aspects of life, could so fundamentally differ from me on this issue. Not motivated by debate but rather understanding, curiosity continues to be a primary motivation in my work, and the centrality of coming to know myself as I come to know others. An ongoing differentiation of self from others at the same time as I identify with them is now attended with a certain spiritual awe as I realize each human being's unique transaction with personal history, environment, and experience. The more differentiated I become, the more differentiated my view of others, the deeper my reverence for the infinite variety of human experience and praxis — and the greater my opposition to the death penalty because of its wanton destructiveness.

I have been involved for 20 years in a compassionate listening practice with those in some way associated with the death penalty in the United States. This work has been tempered and informed by reading, reflection on my observations and impressions, as well as personal correspondence with a man on death row for more than 17 years. His execution during the writing of this essay has given me experience with some of the trauma I have been listening to during this project.

My overarching interest in the project was to understand the tenacity of retentionism in U.S. culture, especially when so many of its foreign allies have abolished the death penalty. But here, I focus on listening as a transformative approach to conflict, both for the speaker and the listener. I begin by discussing the importance of moving public discourse about controversial issues from debate to dialogue, and then briefly explore the relationship of listening to attachment. I go on to describe the listening methodology and practice which emerges from these theoretical underpinnings, with examples from my death penalty compassionate listening project.

Moving Discourse from Debate to Dialogue

Lederach (1997) proposes that the foundational framework for promoting peacebuilding must include relationship building among all the parties to the conflict. Enduring relationships accommodate the nuanced and changing natures of those with whom we relate. Our images of each other are sustained through dialogue and interactions which repeatedly challenge stereotypes and force rigid categories to flex and transform. In contrast, according to Lederach, divided societies are characterized by the narrowing and deepening of identity groups with stricter terms for inclusion and exclusion, and widely divergent views of self and other, both by the perceiver and the perceived. Kelman (1999) affirms Lederach in examining the Palestine-Israel conflict, where not only does belonging to one group necessitate the negation of essential elements of the other's identity, but each sees the other as the cause of some of its own negative identity elements. For example, Palestinians see Israelis as responsible for their landlessness, and Israelis see Palestinians as responsible for their physical insecurity. A second characteristic of divided societies is the fragmentation of power through factionalization. Combined with the deepening of identity fissures and the intensifying of faulty perceptions of each other, this characteristic militates against collaborative decision-making. Finally, the conflicts become protracted and intractable due to the ongoing evolution of these differences and the entrenchment of prejudices and stereotypes of the other which subsume notions of common citizenship.

Political controversies such as the death penalty may serve to create many of these same characteristics in microcosm. The result is the same kind of intractability and prolonged and unproductive struggle, and the same need for peacebuilding strategies. Bohm's (1996) notion of the possibilities of dialogue in this essay's epigram acknowledges the importance of collaboration:

> [I]n a dialogue, each person does not attempt to *make common* certain ideas of items or information that are already known to him. Rather it maybe said that two people are making something *in common*, i.e., creating something new together. But of course such communication can lead to the creation of something new only if people are able freely to listen to each other, without prejudice, and without trying to influence each other. Each has to be interested primarily in truth and coherence, so that he is ready to drop his old ideas and intentions, and be ready to go onto something different, when this is called for. If, however, two people merely want to convey certain ideas or points of view to each other, as if these were items of information, then they must inevitably fail to meet [p. 3, italics in the original].

Literature abounds on the importance of listening for building bridges in times of stress and hardship (Beeler, 2006; Coulehan, 2009). In the name of efficiency, contemporary political discourse as well as more intimate discourses have adopted interactional styles which are detached and impersonal, such as debate. Compassionate listening practices, in contrast, seek to build authentic intimacy and human contact through contingent dialogue in which the parties positively attach to one another and themselves.

Listening and Attachment

Attachment theory, initially proposed by John Bowlby (1982) and then elaborated by Mary Ainsworth (1979) and Mary Main (1995), suggests that there are distinct levels or schemata of attachment along a continuum of security and insecurity. Secure attachment schemata promote openness, curiosity, and confidence in an individual's approach state to new situations. In contrast, insecure attachment schemata — which are of various types (ambivalent, avoidant, or disorganized) — are associated with a variety of mildly to severely asocial behaviors and attitudes. These schemata emerge as a function of relatedness and develop initially in the carer/cared-for relationship of childhood. As the individual matures, subsequent relationships and practices can override negative attributes of attachment, thus allowing adults to operate independently of early attachment schema. However, this malleability can also operate in the other direction. For example, should a person become immersed in conflict, abuse, or violence, his or her secure attachment schema may become disorganized. Attachment schema are worldviews which allow us to proceed with some degree of certainty in our social lives and our assumptive worlds (the predictable world in which we mostly live) (Kauffman, 2006).

In my compassionate listening project, I have frequently heard family members of murder victims talk about the first days after hearing of the murder of their loved one. Even the most mundane activities which typically structure our existences and are cornerstones of our assumptive worlds, such as cleaning our teeth and showering, become almost impossible obstacles to functioning while enduring the fragmentation of all we held as true and real. Time and support might do much to reinstate a sense of predictability, but it is likely that the old assumptive world has been permanently ripped away and a "new normal" must be constructed painstakingly piece by piece.

Thinking about this profound change in terms of attachment, two interrelated components to attachment are important. The first is the attachment an individual feels to others — those who are significant and known, as well as to strangers. The second is the attachment the person feels to herself. Because a sense of self is differentiated from a sense of place indissoluble from a sense of other relatively late in human development (about 5 years of age) (Hartzell & Siegel, 2003), early caregivers' demeanors are a critical mirror of the emerging sense of self, and vice versa. Chaotic attachments to others tend to lead to chaotic attachments to self. Likewise, secure attachments to others tend to lead to secure attachments to self. Furthermore, just as we may shift along the attachment continuum within single interactions with others, our perceptions of ourselves may also undergo dramatic shifts. These shifts are compounded when they have to be sustained in the presence of stressful or traumatic events in the social and physical environment.

My listening work is primarily with people whose assumptive worlds have been shattered by violence and therefore are left adrift in an unfamiliar landscape of disrupted attachments both to self and other. It is the individual's perception which is important here, not the gravity of the events in question. As conflict transformation practitioners, it is important to look to the individual's own stories rather than to the "facts."

Briefly exploring the mechanisms fostering secure attachment is relevant here to see how these might be disrupted in cases of conflict, and how practitioners could leverage them in order to shift a person from one attachment state to a more optimal one for healing interrelatedness. Since this shift is transformational, the conflict may be more than simply resolved, changing shape and emphasis, perhaps even dissipating in the face of new understandings which promote recognition, resonance, and forms of reconciliation.

An essential condition for forming secure attachments is a curious, open, accepting, alert brain (Siegel, 2007), functioning optimally. It is not drug dependent. It is not exhausted. It is not damaged. And it is not activated by fear. While the human organism is amazingly resilient and can tolerate wide ranges and intensities of influence and still function, optimal functioning depends on adequate sleep, nutrition, stimulation, exercise, appropriate temperature levels, and relatedness with others (security). The effect of suboptimal levels is felt in different functions and regions of the brain. In extreme cases of deprivation, whole regions of the brain may essentially be "offline" and other regions, more concerned with primary survival tasks, may be supreme (Siegel, 2007). These survivalist tasks are generally based in more primitive emotions which resist inhibition or negotiation, and may promote impulsivity and rapid judgments, which are unresponsive to the moderating effects of higher executive intervention (Cozolino, 2010). Designed to protect us from physical danger in chaotic environments, these responses may become overgeneralized, crippling us in important but stressful social interactions (Siegel, 2007).

Times of intense conflict are a case in point. We may have a similar physical reaction, such as cold sweating, tunnel vision, hypersensitivity to physical stimuli, and shaking, when we are in a verbal argument as when we have been badly frightened in a car accident. It is perception that is crucial here, not some external evaluation of actual risk. In these moments, stepping back and reflecting while one is acting is extremely difficult and may be impossible without considerable deliberate practice (Schon, 1987). Therefore, most individuals will make their way through such experiences — a car accident or an intense conflict — without the use of their higher functions such as impulse inhibition, judgment, weighing of pros and cons, evaluation of perceptions, and openness to the possibility of being in error.

As mentioned previously, attachment (and disruption of attachment through conflict) has two components: relationship with other and relationship with self. The disruption of relationship to self in inner conflict may have serious repercussions. At its most intense it may result in post-traumatic stress disorder, which I believe to be strongly related to a disconnection from, and betrayal of, one's moral self (Shay, 1995; 2002). Using conflict with another as metaphor, we might say that we operate on two levels: as the person who interacts with the world and the person we believe we are. This self we believe we are may be thought of as the inhabitant of our assumptive worlds, and is identified by some scholars as the interpreter (Cozolino, 2006). We constantly have to reassess the person we believe we are in light of how we perceive ourselves behaving. Those who operate from a place of secure attachment generally think of themselves as "good." Ideally, this is not a difficult task as they find consistency between their inner and outer presentations of self (Goffman, 1959). Their self-esteem is high and they have high self-acceptance. Therefore, in situations and relationships where we feel accepting of ourselves and have high self-esteem, we might assume that we are securely attached.

However, some situations and relationships provoke very different experiences of self, including shame, self-disgust, feelings of bafflement and bewilderment, frustration, despair, and the inability to recognize the self who acts. Literature detailing the experiences of soldiers who commit atrocity reflect this (Grossman, 1996). I would argue that this is because the self one believes one is (basically moral) cannot justify the actions taken by the self that acted. Whether these actions are completed with full consideration or in the heat of the moment, if, when the higher executive regions of the brain come back online, they cannot help the individual process and integrate the self she believes she is and the self that acted, there may be a damaging disconnect. In this case, the individual may find that he is insecurely attached to himself and inhabiting a disorganized attachment schema and worldview. Effects on behavior and demeanor have already been described, and we may expect a person to exhibit emotional volatility, impulsive outbursts, and a lack of consistency and persistence when circumstances become too discomfiting.

Through a developmental understanding of attachment, we can also find a model for facilitation of peace with oneself in the example of adequate caregiving for the young child. The more consistent the child's experience of being comforted in ways that meet her needs, the more she is able to persist with discomfort before becoming overwhelmed and distressed (Hartzell & Siegel, 2003). Stephen Porges (2011) suggests this is indicative of the "toning" of interlocking systems in the brain which comprise the social engagement system. He proposes that higher tone is correlated with greater persistence of higher executive functioning in times of stress. Since the direction of cause and effect are not known, but the toning of the social engagement system is nevertheless possible, conflict resolvers could integrate toning strategies in their practice with those whose capacity to override impulsivity during stress is limited. Toning practices include encouraging a person to wait a little longer before having his needs met; this can be done through contingent communication. Eventually, this kind, attentive attention is replicated in the inner self talk between the self believed to be and the self who acts, thus fostering secure attachment at the same time as enhancing effectiveness and self-control.

Contingent Communication

Contingent communication is characterized by interested, caring attention and calm, experimental responding — confident that, even if the first trials at understanding fail, subsequent trials will bring conflicting parties closer together. Contingent communication focuses on identifying needs and intentions, and is facilitative of them being satisfied by the one caring for the one cared for (Noddings, 2003). In other words, contingent communication acknowledges imbalance and seeks to reach equilibrium both in attachment to self and attachment to other. In fact, the perfection of equilibrium in attachment to self may come about through the attachment to other.

In the ninth year of the compassionate listening project on the death penalty, I met someone who had been on an execution team. He expressed reservations about the death penalty, and so I asked to meet with him more often to explore his impressions and experiences. He agreed. Over the next four years, we met several times each month for sessions in which he told me stories about his experiences and shared his reflections and analysis about a range of facets of the death penalty, including relationships among members of the execution team, the procedures and preparations required to put someone to death legally, ironies that had come to his attention, frustrations he had. It was clear that at the core of these conversations was his desire to create a coherent narrative which encompassed all the paradoxes and contradictions inherent in any human activity, and particularly one as fraught with moral controversy as an execution.

I noticed that, as our work together continued, phrases that were used repeatedly and inflexibly in early iterations of the story began to break apart, leaving just remnants or even disappearing altogether. As they did so, new iterations of the story became less formulaic and more flexible, allowing elements that had not fit together well before to become part of a seamless story. He seemed to remember more as different aspects surfaced for emphasis and attention, and elements ebbed and flowed across the story landscape. It was as if he was trying out ways of telling the story to see which one "fit" best. I wondered what this shaping force might be, and began to realize that his struggle was this: trying to accept the self that acted during the execution as more than a professional persona he had adopted for the purpose. He was seeking a recognizable version of his moral self, the self he believed he was. Through contingent listening this coherent narrative emerged. The person I listened to had the opportunity to articulate and put his experiences to words.

I met several others on the execution team over this period. The shortest meeting was an hour on the phone, which was less than satisfactory. I felt out of sync and gravely disadvantaged in that I had to communicate all my attentiveness in sound and tone. While I believe that important qualities of listening can be replicated online and on the phone, and so we should not dismiss such modalities out of hand, as human beings we are built to convey information about our intentions and feelings with our whole bodies. Not being able to sense each other in the same physical space affects levels of trust, responsiveness, and therefore contingency. We must be even more thoughtful and intentional about signaling our attention and caring acceptance if we are forced to work remotely or virtually.

Most meetings, fortunately, were face to face and lasted several hours, allowing for a number of retellings of what I came to think of as the person's "execution story." It was notable that each of the members' first iterations were remarkably similar to each other, with the same phrases standing immutable like stones on a moor. In each case, subsequent retellings seemed aimed at retrieving the unique moral self from this barren and bleak landscape, sometimes occasioning a joyful reunion — marked by laughter and other times by tears — between the self that acted and the self he believed himself to be. One person, with what appeared to be such profound relief, fell asleep at the end of a sentence.

There are two parties to a listening event, the one speaking or telling and the one hearing and listening. During the project, what were the important aspects of listening which supported what I came to see as transformation in attachment to self, experienced by the one speaking and telling?

Hoffman (2002) says this about the listening process and the listener:

> Listeners must be trained to be non-adversarial and sensitive, to listen without judgment or rancor, and, above all, to not talk too much! After listening to one side, they must go to the other and tell of the suffering of the first. Then they repeat this with the second side. Eventually, it is hoped that through this delicate process each side will be able to listen to the other.... Listeners must be trusted by both sides, able to see the human face of the "enemy" so that the message can be carried over the battle lines. Listeners must also be convinced that *there are always new possibilities....*
> Unhealed wounds leave us with a legacy of violence, and telling our stories of suffering helps heal these terrible wounds [p. 299, italics in the original].

My own interest as listener had to be explained in a credible story in order to create a foundation on which the speaker or teller could set aside concerns about boring me or "rambling on." This invitation had to reassure the person that I would not reject him, that I would believe him, and that I would not need his protection — i.e., that he could tell me the worst details and I would not collapse under the strain, back away, or reject him. What is found to be credible will vary with different speakers, so my story also had to be flexible — and above all authentic, genuine, and true. At the heart of this credibility was the requirement that my focus was on him and that I respected him, found him interesting and unique, and that I cared for him. This was foundational.

A second facet of listening was the appearance of innocence. People from each of the stakeholder groups in the listening project knew that I have spoken to others. I needed to be very careful not to give the impression that I have heard it all before. This is not dishonest or a subterfuge, because I have not heard it before *from them*, and therefore I have in no sense heard it all before. Despite the similar turns of phrase, each man had a different perspective on the events. I was not there to build a single "true" account of the execution. Rather, I was there to acknowledge and value the multiple truths which make up the reality of human encounters. In that sense, each person was relating something that I had never heard before. While there are moments when the facts of executions are important, I cannot approach a new person thinking that any element included in her story is wrong or inaccurate, but rather must remain interested in why she remembers it that way; what role does the element characterized in that particular way have in the total coherence of her narrative? The only times I challenged those characterizations was when they appeared to amplify or intensify the intrapersonal conflict the person was experiencing.

A third important facet of listening is sustained attention; of course, this is easier said than done. I have learned to be very careful of my own physical needs so that I have eaten enough, drank enough, and have adequate sleep so that my attention does not wander or become distracted. I have a low point during the middle of the afternoon almost every day, when I am very tired. I know my limitations, and ensure that all my appointments are in the morning or evening.

Physical needs turn out to be easier to manage than emotional and mental ones, which sometimes crop up and can be very hard to set aside. The most challenging times come when a judgment is triggered in me by someone — either what he says or the way he says it. Fear is also powerfully distracting yet rare, and is usually provoked when I feel an absolute absence of resonance or goodwill emanating from the other person, as betrayed by dismissive gestures or aggressive verbal sparring. In a couple of interviews with attorneys — one a defense attorney and another a prosecutor — I felt alternately put on the spot and invisible while the person judged me as a member of a despised group ("death row whores" in one case, and "abolition activists" in the other). It was difficult not to react with offense and frustration, and not to let residual resentment distract me during the rest of our conversation. Early in this more intense phase of the listening project, I unguardedly let a reaction show, summarily terminating the conversation; that person remains evasive about renewing our acquaintance to this day. Betrayal of that kind in this tender and fragile trust we build as compassionate listeners is not easily forgiven or repaired. I regret it deeply and have reflected at length on how that kind of reactivity might be prevented in the future. Intensified focus on the practices of mindfulness has helped me persist in the face of discomfort and manage my reactions more productively.

Conclusion

An essential component of compassionate listening and contingent communication is knowing, as the listener, that we can only accompany, we cannot fix or take on the pain of another person. By providing a compassionate, present listening ear, and by focusing on helping the person build a coherent, emotionally integrated narrative of his or her own experience, we are providing an invaluable witness to it which helps people feel less lonely and isolated — and may provide a path so they can find footholds to climb their way out.

Before the project, I was a long-time abolition activist but a new arrival to the U.S. capital punishment scene. I initially thought of death penalty implementers and supporters as "barbarians." This attitude was transformed when I became part of an activist group during the early 1990s and was introduced to listening project methodology and compassionate listening through Gene Knudsen Hoffman's writings (Manousos, 2003). Little did I realize how I would be personally transformed as well as my perception of the cultural and emotional significance of the ultimate penalty in American cultural life.

Notes

1. I am indebted to the students who have taken my death penalty classes and who have engaged me in my thinking over the past seven years, as well as to my fellow activists who have sharpened my analysis. My deepest gratitude goes to those who have confided the stories of their experiences with the death penalty, and the effect their involvement has had on them throughout lives and careers. These people include family members of murder victims, people on death row, family members of those condemned people, people who have been exonerated and released and their family members, attorneys who defend and those who prosecute along with the judges who preside over the trials and appeals, members of parole boards, prison workers, execution team members, and scholars who study and write on this subject.

References

Ainsworth, M.D.S, M.C. Blehar, E. Waters, and S. Wall (1979) *Patterns of attachment: A psychological study of the strange situation.* Hove, UK: Psychology.
Beeler, A. (2006, July). Palliative care volunteers: A program of compassion. *Corrections Today,* 38–40.
Bohm, D. (1996). *On dialogue.* Oxford: Routledge.
Bowlby, J. (1982). *Attachment and loss: Attachment.* Vol. I (2d ed.) London: Tavistock Institute (Basic).
Coulehan, J. (2009). Compassionate solidarity: Suffering, poetry and medicine. *Perspectives in Biology and Medicine, 52*(4), 585–603.
Cozolino, L. (2006). *The neuroscience of human relationships: Attachment and the developing social brain.* New York: W.W. Norton.
_____. (2010). *The neuroscience of psychotherapy: Healing the social brain.* New York: W.W. Norton.
Goffman, E. (1959). *Presentation of self in everyday life.* New York: Doubleday.
Grossman, D. (1996). *On killing: The psychological cost of learning to kill in war and society.* Boston: Back Bay.
Hartzell, M., and D.J. Siegel (2003). *Parenting from the inside out.* New York: Tarcher/Penguin.
Hoffman, G.K. (1997). An enemy is one whose story we have not heard. In A. Manousos (Ed.) (2003). *Compassionate listening and other writings by Gene Knudsen Hoffman.* Torrance, CA: Friends Bulletin.
_____. (2002). Palestinians and Israelis: Two traumatized people. In A. Manousos (Ed.) (2003), *Compassionate listening and other writings by Gene Knudsen Hoffman.* Torrance, CA: Friends Bulletin.
Kauffman, J. (2006). Restoration of the assumptive world as an act of justice. In D. Sullivan and L. Tifft (Eds.), *Handbook of restorative justice: a global perspective.* New York: Routledge.
Kelman, H.C. (1999) The interdependence of Israeli and Palestinian national identities: The role of the other in existential conflicts. *Journal of Social Issues, 55*(3) 581–600.
Lederach, J.P. (1997). *Building peace: Sustainable reconciliation in divided societies.* Washington, DC: United States Institute of Peace Press.
Main, M. (1995). Attachment: Overview, with implications for clinical work. In S. Goldberg, R. Muir and J. Kerr (Eds.), *Attachment theory: Social, developmental and clinical perspectives.* Hillsdale, NJ: Analytic.
Manousos, A. (Ed.) (2003). *Compassionate listening and other writings by Gene Knudsen Hoffman.* Torrance, CA: Friends Bulletin.
Noddings, N. (2003). *Caring: A feminine approach to ethics and moral education* (2d ed.). Berkeley: University of California Press.
Pepinsky, H. (2006) Empathy and restoration. In D. Sullivan and L. Tifft (Eds.), *Handbook of restorative justice: A global perspective.* New York: Routledge.
Porges, S.W. (2011). *The polyvagal theory: Neurophysiological foundations of emotions, attachment, communication and self-regulation.* New York: W.W. Norton.
Purdy, M. (1997). Intrapersonal and interpersonal listening: Self listening and conscious action. In M. Purdy and D. Borisoff (Eds.), *Listening in everyday life: A personal and professional approach* (2d ed.). Lanham, MD: University Press of America.
_____, and D. Borisoff (Eds.). (1997) *Listening in everyday life: A personal and professional approach* (2d ed.). Lanham, MD: University Press of America.
Schon, D.A. (1987). *Educating the reflective practitioner.* San Francisco: Jossey-Bass.
Shay, J. (1995). *Achilles in Vietnam: Combat trauma and the undoing of character.* New York: Scribner.

_____. (2002). *Odysseus in America: Combat trauma and the trials of homecoming.* New York: Scribner.
Siegel, D. J. (2007). *The mindful brain.* New York: W.W. Norton.
Thomlison, D. (1997). Intercultural listening. In M. Purdy and D. Borisoff (Eds.), *Listening in everyday life: A personal and professional approach* (2nd ed.). Lanham, MD: University Press of America.
Wolvin, A., and C.G. Coakley (1996). *Listening* (5th ed.). Boston: McGraw Hill.

Violent Worldviews and Self-Projected Use of Violence

Meredith Michaud

The examination of cultural beliefs about violence and their relationship to violence may help us better understand tendencies toward violent behavior and explore ways to decrease violence. In a 1987 study, Adams and Bosch report how beliefs about war may be connected to individuals' actions toward peace. The study looked at university students' belief that "war is an intrinsic part of human nature" and how it was related to their peace activities (p. 125). The study found that there was a negative correlation between believing that war is a part of human nature and participation in peace activities (the stronger the belief, the less the participation). The authors suggest that this "may reflect the following causal chain: (1) belief that wars are not caused by intrinsic, biological, instincts enables (2) the development of an attitude that something can be done to prevent wars, which, in turn (3) facilitates decisions to take part in activity for peace" (p. 131). Their work points to a feedback loop between beliefs about war and behavior attempting to prevent war: the belief that war is instinctual may lead to fewer activities to prevent war, which may therefore increase the prevalence of war, which may reinforce beliefs that war is instinctual. Based on this evidence, it is not a great leap to imagine a similar feedback loop between beliefs and behavior when it comes to violence in general, which will be explored later in this essay.

Biological Explanations for Violence

Our beliefs are reflected in aspects of our culture, including our academic literature. The academic literature in contemporary Western culture has a tradition of biological explanations for violence. Perhaps the most well-known scholar of this tradition is Sigmund Freud, who wrote about humans' instinct for violence. In a literary exchange with Albert Einstein on the subject of war, in 1932, Freud characterizes history as being full of violent conflict. He writes that "the slaughter of a foe gratifies an instinctive craving," which is connected to a "death instinct" that humans have in their psyche (Freud, 2000, p. 10). What keeps this violence in check is culture and societal rules and laws. Thus, the death instinct is seen by Freud as natural, and our control of it is artificially imposed, but necessary. "Here is then the biological justification for all those vile, pernicious propensities which we now are combating. We can but own that they are really more akin to nature than this our stand against them" (p. 12). While Freud himself identifies as pacifist, he sees humankind in its current evolutionary state as naturally tended toward violence. "Conflicts of interest between man and man are resolved, in principle, by the recourse to violence" (p. 9). Freud's theories regarding the nature of humans and the human psyche have had a strong influence on academic discourse on violence.

Konrad Lorenz (1966), another scholar whose writings on human behavior are foundational, makes comparisons between humans and nonhuman animals in regard to "aggressive drive" (p. 50). He points out that humans are still bound to the laws of animal behavior, and takes the view that humans, unlike some other animals, do not possess the "inhibitory mechanisms preventing sudden manslaughter" because humans, until the invention of weapons, had no way to kill one another quickly (p. 241). However, the technology of weapons was a development that caused aggression to be "bred into man" (p. 243). In his view, humans' aggressive drive needs appropriate outlets in order to deter people from directing aggression toward one another, in present times just as in prehistoric times. Major societal problems are thus the result if the innate human aggressive drive does not have a proper outlet.

In more recent work, Melvin Konner (2006) asserts that violence is innate to humans, and furthermore, that ignorance of this trait impedes our ability to address it. He says that "there is in human nature a natural tendency to violence and, additionally, to war, and that the failure to fully recognize this tendency—a common failure in academic circles—increases the risk" (p. 1). His essay examines archeological evidence, which shows signs of violence beginning with the Neanderthals, though he states that early archeological evidence is weak. "For most of protohuman history there is no evidence of violence, but that is not evidence of the absence of it" (p. 4). Like Lorenz (1966), Konner draws on similarities between human behavior and the behavior of their close relatives — chimpanzees and bonobos — to show that there is a common propensity for violence that spans these species. He also reviews relevant anthropological studies, including a study of the Semai, a peaceful society whose members were recruited to fight against communists by the British in the 1950s, and who proved to be soldiers effective at killing. Konner believes "this case undermines the belief that violence stems solely from childhood experience or that the individual tendency to participate in war can be prevented by nonviolent experience during development" (p. 7).

Ginsburg and Carter (1987) discuss their experiments with mice, and observe that both agonistic and peaceful predispositions are preserved through natural selection. They conclude that "with the exception of extreme cases, neither the genotype nor the environment necessarily produce groups or individuals that are highly aggressive" (p. 67). From their examination of mice, wolves, and other animals, they find that "most individuals within the normal range of a population are biogenetically programmed for versatility," and for humans, "as a species, we are not biogenetically programmed to gain either our individual or societal ends through interpersonal aggression, violence, and war, but have equally the biogenetic potential for peaceful interactions at the individual and social level" (p. 73). The researchers emphasize the process of socialization — learning about society's values and rules — that is necessary for violence, as opposed to aggression. "While aggression can be viewed as 'innate,' violence is taught; and since violence is taught, we must turn our attention to the social practices which 'teach' violence in order to decrease its occurrence" (p. 63).

Challenges to Scientific Explanations

In contemporary Western culture, given our strong belief in biological explanations and the tendency to accept what is scientifically presented as truth, it can be difficult to recognize that science is part of culture and therefore influenced by cultural norms and beliefs. Anthropologist Douglas Fry (2006) points this out: "Scientists and scholars, like humans everywhere, are affected by the largely invisible influences of cultural belief systems on their thinking" (p. 45). Jeffrey H. Goldstein (1987), in his essay "Notes toward a social construction of human aggression," addresses this relationship between science and culture, pointing out occasions in recent history in which science was heavily influenced by culture. He draws attention to the influence of our beliefs on our behavior. "What we believe about human behavior determines how we act, both as individuals [and] as nations. In the world of human affairs, objective truth often matters less than subjective reality. If we believe something to be true, we behave as though it were" (p. 107). Goldstein's work underlines the necessity of realizing that science is affected by culture, and vice versa.

One of the most influential refutations of theories of violence as a biological imperative came in 1986, when a group of 20 scientists from varying academic disciplines collaborated on a document, the "Seville Statement on Violence." Psychologist David Adams (1989) says:

> The statement ... specifically rejects five myths: (1) that we have inherited a tendency to make war from our animal ancestors; (2) that war is genetically programmed into our human nature; (3) that in the course of human evolution there has been a special selection for aggressive behavior; (4) that humans have a "violent brain"; and (5) that war is caused by instinct or any single motivation [p. 328].

In addition to refuting these five concepts, the Seville Statement on Violence discusses the implications of believing in them, which it refers to as "biological pessimism" (p. 336), and underlines the importance of countering these myths.

Peaceful societies

E. Richard Sorenson (1978) has observed how children are treated in the Fore culture of New Guinea, and describes how their treatment and education of children from birth onward contribute to peaceful cultural norms. He encourages a wider study of aggressive human behavior across cultures, stating, "It would be helpful to have more data on non–Western patternings of human behavior which could be related to the Western concept of aggression" (p. 29). Perspectives such as Sorenson's reframe the debate away from pinpointing to what extent violent behavior is natural or ingrained, and toward a discussion of how worldview affects behavior.

In anthropologist Bruce Bonta's 1996 article "Conflict resolution among peaceful societies: The culture of peacefulness," he provides a review of the literature regarding 24 peaceful societies and finds that a common theme is a worldview that does not accept violence as a means for resolving conflict. This is quite different from Western culture, whose worldview "boils down to an acceptance of the inevitability of conflict and violence" (p. 404).

More recently, Fry has written two comprehensive works that challenge the inevitability of war and violence: *The human potential for peace: An anthropological challenge to assumptions about war and violence* (2006), and *Beyond war: The human potential for peace* (2007). In both of these, he cites his research in different cultures and synthesizes other researchers' work in peaceful societies. He questions the myth that violence is pervasive throughout all societies, stating, "Although war and other types of violence may be very noticeable, a close examination of cross-cultural data reveals that people usually deal with conflict without violence," and emphasizes the cooperative and peaceful qualities of humans. "Humans have a solid capacity for getting along with each other peacefully, preventing physical aggression, limiting the scope and spread of violence, and restoring peace following aggression" (Fry, 2007, p. 21). In *The human potential for peace* (2006), he concludes that the existence of peaceful societies disproves the inevitability of violence, and shows humans' highly sophisticated capabilities for peacemaking and nonviolent conflict resolution: "If it were true that humans are violent by nature or possess instincts that push them to violence, then logically societies with extremely low levels of physical aggression simply should not exist. The fact that such societies *do* exist contradicts such bloodthirsty images of humanity" (p. 81).

Worldview and Violence Study

The study described below, which I conducted in the summer of 2009, built on the conclusions of Sorenson, Bonta and Fry and asked whether people's beliefs about violence affected their behavior. In order to have a clear and concrete way to see how these two variables were related, a quantitative research design was used.

The focus of the Worldview and Violence Study was the correlation between Portland State University students' beliefs regarding violence and their tendency toward violent action. The first variable was tested by asking participants about their beliefs regarding violence. The second variable was tested by asking them to choose how they would behave in a hypothetical scenario with several violent and nonviolent options. This measured their likelihood to use direct violence as a strategy in conflict situations. The final part of the survey rated participants' agreement with forms of systemic violence, or violence not directly done by them but by proxy.

Based on the work of several scholars (Adams & Bosch, 1987; Bonta, 1996; Fry, 2007; Goldstein, 1987), it seemed reasonable to predict that there would be a correlation between the two main variables in the study.

Research findings

Seven beliefs about human violent and peaceful behaviors were correlated with participants' self-projected use of violence. The variable *Self-projected*

Use of Violence (SUV) was calculated by giving participants a series of 13 hypothetical scenarios for which they had a choice of options varying in levels of peacefulness or violence. Cronbach's alpha reliability test gave this combination of questions a rating of 0.802. Table 1 compares the first five beliefs about human violence with participants' self-projected use of violence, in the survey population as a whole. All five of these beliefs have a positive correlation with *SUV*, meaning that statistically speaking, as a person's strength in each of the beliefs rises, so does the likelihood of his choice of violent responses to conflict in the hypothetical scenarios. All of the correlations in Table 1 are statistically significant at the 0.01 level, which means that there is less than 1 percent probability that these results were caused by chance.

	Self-projected Use of Violence N = 215
Belief that violence is a human instinct N=225	.397**
Belief that human violence has been common throughout history N=225	.290**
Belief that violent behavior is natural in humans N=222	.408**
Belief that violent behavior can be explained by genetics N=217	.261**
Belief that violence is inevitable N=216	.237**

**. Correlation is significant at the 0.01 level (2-tailed).
N= Number of cases

Table 1

The mean of these beliefs was then taken to form a new variable called *Violent Worldview (VW)*. The beliefs had a score of 0.839 when Cronbach's alpha reliability test was performed, showing that the beliefs have a strong relationship to one another. *VW* was then correlated with *SUV* with a statistically significant correlation of .408, as show in Table 2. This positive correlation means that the more strongly a participant agreed with the component beliefs of *VW*, the more likely she was to predict she would use violence.

In Tables 3 and 4, the population is examined separately by gender. In both males and females, a positive correlation was found between *VW* and *SUV*. The correlation is higher among males (.420) than among females (.383). This correlation denotes the strength of the possible relationship between the variables *VW* and *SUV*. The results indicate that the correlation between these two variables is higher among males than among females. A male with a high

		Violent Worldview	Self-projected Use of Violence
Violent Worldview	Pearson Correlation	1	.408**
	Sig. (2-tailed)		.000
	N	225	215
Self-projected Use of Violence	Pearson Correlation	.408**	1
	Sig. (2-tailed)	.000	
	N	215	215

**. Correlation is significant at the 0.01 level (2-tailed).

Table 2

		Violent Worldview	Self-projected Use of Violence
Violent Worldview	Pearson Correlation	1	.383**
	Sig. (2-tailed)		.000
	N	131	126
Self-projected Use of Violence	Pearson Correlation	.383**	1
	Sig. (2-tailed)	.000	
	N	126	126

**. Correlation is significant at the 0.01 level (2-tailed).

Table 3

		Violent Worldview	Self-projected Use of Violence
Violent Worldview	Pearson Correlation	1	.420**
	Sig. (2-tailed)		.000
	N	94	89
Self-projected Use of Violence	Pearson Correlation	.420**	1
	Sig. (2-tailed)	.000	
	N	89	89

**. Correlation is significant at the 0.01 level (2-tailed).

Table 4

score in *VW* is more likely to also have a high score on *SUV* than is a female with an equally high score on *VW*.

In addition to beliefs about violence, the strength in two other beliefs was tested to see how strongly participants believed in the innate peacefulness of humans. As shown in Table 5, there is a statistically significant negative correlation between the belief that peaceful behavior is natural in humans and *SUV*. This means that as strength in the belief that peaceful behavior is natural in humans rose, participants' choice of violent responses to conflict fell. The second belief, that violent behavior is caused by socialization, had a very low negative correlation to *SUV*, as shown in Table 6. This correlation was not statistically significant, meaning that there is no evidence to show that it wasn't caused by chance.

		Belief that peaceful behavior is natural in humans	Self-projected Use of Violence
Belief that peaceful behavior is natural in humans	Pearson Correlation	1	-.273**
	Sig. (2-tailed)		.000
	N	225	215
Self-projected Use of Violence	Pearson Correlation	-.273**	1
	Sig. (2-tailed)	.000	
	N	215	215

Table 5: Belief that peaceful behavior is natural in humans correlated with Self-Projected Use of Violence

Tables 7 and 8 show the belief that peaceful behavior is natural in humans correlated with self-projected use of violence separately in females and males. In both genders, there is a very similar negative correlation between these two variables. This means that as the belief that peaceful behavior is natural in humans is stronger, participants' *SUV* tends to be less strong.

In Table 9, the correlation between *VW* and *SUV* is examined separately per class level. Among freshmen, the correlation is quite high, but not statis-

		Belief that violent behavior is caused by socialization	Self-projected Use of Violence
Belief that violent behavior is caused by socialization	Pearson Correlation	1	-.097
	Sig. (2-tailed)		.156
	N	224	215
Self-projected Use of Violence	Pearson Correlation	-.097	1
	Sig. (2-tailed)	.156	
	N	215	215

**. Correlation is N

Table 6: Belief that violent behavior is caused by socialization and Self-Projected Use of Violence

		Belief that peaceful behavior is natural in humans	Self-projected Use of Violence
Belief that peaceful behavior is natural in humans	Pearson Correlation	1	-.277**
	Sig. (2-tailed)		.002
	N	131	126
Self-projected Use of Violence	Pearson Correlation	-.277**	1
	Sig. (2-tailed)	.002	
	N	126	126

**. Correlation is significant at the 0.01 level (2-tailed).

Table 7: Among females, belief that peaceful behavior is natural in humans correlated with Self-Projected Use of Violence

		Belief that peaceful behavior is natural in humans	Self-projected Use of Violence
Belief that peaceful behavior is natural in humans	Pearson Correlation	1	-.274**
	Sig. (2-tailed)		.009
	N	94	89
Self-projected Use of Violence	Pearson Correlation	-.274**	1
	Sig. (2-tailed)	.009	
	N	89	89

**. Correlation is significant at the 0.01 level (2-tailed).

Table 8: Among males, belief that peaceful behavior is natural in humans correlated with Self-Projected Use of Violence

tically significant, meaning that it could have been caused by chance. One of the reasons that the correlation among freshmen is not statistically significant is because there was a small number of cases (5). Among sophomores, juniors, seniors, and graduate students, there is a positive correlation that is statistically significant. Among post-graduate students there is very slight negative correlation which is not statistically significant. Sophomores (.585*), Juniors (.428**), and Seniors (.252*) all have a statistically significant correlation between the two variables that weakened as the grade levels increased.

Tables 10 and 11 show *VW* correlated with *SUV* in participants whose income level is $45,000 or over, and for those whose income level is $45,000 and under. In the survey, a total of 6 categories were provided regarding income level. However, the number of cases in each category was too small to obtain statistically significant results, so the categories were condensed. In both tables, there is a statistically significant correlation between the variables. In Table 11, the correlation is noticeably higher.

When examining *VW* and *SUV* separately by ethnic group, the number of cases in most of the ethnic groups was too small to obtain meaningful results. The group of participants identifying as "white" was the only group large enough to obtain statistically significant results. It is worth noting that the correlation between *VW* and *SUV* is .423 when the two variables are examined among the group of participants identifying themselves as white.

The correlation between *VW* and *SUV* was identical (.411*) among

	Self-projected Use of Violence
Violent Worldview: freshmen N=5	.896
sophomores N=16	.585*
juniors N=42	.428**
seniors N=86	.252*
post-graduate students N=21	-.038
graduate students N=53	.468**

*. Correlation is significant at the 0.05 level (2-tailed).

**. Correlation is significant at the 0.01 level (2-tailed).

Table 9: Correlation between Violent Worldview and Self-Projected Use of Violence by university class standing

		Violent Worldview	Self-projected Use of Violence
Violent Worldview	Pearson Correlation	1	.257*
	Sig. (2-tailed)		.024
	N	82	77
Self-projected Use of Violence	Pearson Correlation	.257*	1
	Sig. (2-tailed)	.024	
	N	77	77

Table 10: Correlation when income level is $45,000 or over

		Violent Worldview	Self-projected Use of Violence
Violent Worldview	Pearson Correlation	1	.473**
	Sig. (2-tailed)		.000
	N	141	136
Self-projected Use of Violence	Pearson Correlation	.473**	1
	Sig. (2-tailed)	.000	
	N	136	136

*. Correlation is significant at the 0.05 level (2-tailed).
**. Correlation is significant at the 0.01 level (2-tailed).

Table 11: Correlation when income level is less than $45,000

		Violent Worldview	Self-projected Use of Violence
Violent Worldview	Pearson Correlation	1	.423**
	Sig. (2-tailed)		.000
	N	171	164
Self-projected Use of Violence	Pearson Correlation	.423**	1
	Sig. (2-tailed)	.000	
	N	164	164

**. Correlation is significant at the 0.01 level (2-tailed).

Table 12: Correlation between Violent Worldview and Self-Projected Use of Violence among students identifying themselves as "white"

respondents who were born in the United States, and those who were born in other countries.

In Table 13, the correlation between *VW* and *SUV* is examined separately by marital status. In participants who were single, had a long-term partner, were married, or were divorced, there is a statistically significant positive correlation between the two variables.

Results regarding violence by others

At the end of the survey, the participants were asked four questions regarding their support of violence on the part of others. The strength of

	Self-projected use of violence
single N=104	0.389**
long-term partner N=42	0.467**
married N=64	0.385**
divorced N=12	0.616*
widowed N=1	—

*. Correlation is significant at the 0.05 level (2-tailed).

**. Correlation is significant at the 0.01 level (2-tailed).

— No correlation possible

Table 13: Correlation between Violent Worldview and Self-Projected Use of Violence separately by marital status

agreement with these four statements was correlated with two variables from the survey. Table 14 shows the correlation between the four questions and *SUV*. Table 15 shows the correlation between the four questions and *VW*. All correlations in both tables are positive and statistically significant. It is notable that the correlations in Table 15, between the four questions and *VW*, are higher than those in Table 15, between the four questions and *SUV*.

Among the population as a whole, the belief that violent behavior is natural in humans was the one that had the strongest association with participants' selection of violent responses to situations, with a correlation of .408. A close second was the belief that violence is a human instinct, with a correlation of .397. While it isn't possible with such a small number of cases to know if there is a causal relationship between the two variables that were compared, one possibility is that they have mutual influence on each other. Believing that violence is natural and instinctual could make participants more likely

	Self-projected Use of Violence N=215
Society should execute people who commit serious crimes, such as murder. N=215	.260**
In defense of our country, it is sometimes necessary to carry out military operations that result in human casualties. N=215	.135*
Parents must sometimes use physical force to discipline their children. N=215	.255**
The earth's natural resources should be used for the good of humans, regardless of negative effects on air, water or soil. N=213	.181**

Table 14: Correlation between support of violence by others and Self-Projected Use of Violence

to choose violence. Likewise, they might justify their violent choices by believing that violence is natural and instinctual. The same thinking may be applied to the other beliefs that had statistically significant correlations with *Self-Projected Use of Violence (SUV)*. These were: belief that human violence has been common throughout history (.290); belief that violent behavior can be explained by genetics (.261); and belief that violence is inevitable (.237). The correlations of these five beliefs with *SUV* can be found in Table 1.

When these five beliefs were combined to form a new variable called *Violent Worldview (VW)*, many more interesting correlations were made. Overall, the correlation between *VW* and *SUV* was .408 (see Table 2). We can't assume that one of these variable causes another, however, it is possible that

	Violent Worldview N=225
Society should execute people who commit serious crimes, such as murder. N=215	.388**
In defense of our country, it is sometimes necessary to carry out military operations that result in human casualties. N=215	.337**
Parents must sometimes use physical force to discipline their children. N=215	.319**
The earth's natural resources should be used for the good of humans, regardless of negative effects on air, water or soil. N=213	.330**

Table 15: Correlation between support of violence by others and Violent Worldview

(1) the more that participants conform to this worldview, the more likely they are to use violence (or the more likely they *think* they are to use violence), or (2) the more that participants think they are likely to use violence, the more they conform to the worldview or (3) these variables both have an effect on each other and mutually strengthen each other.

When the correlation between *VW* and *SUV* is examined by gender, there is a stronger association among men than among women. Possible contributing factors could be that societal norms prescribe violence more often for men than for women, or that men are more influenced by the dominant belief system, or that there are other variables that mediate the effect of *VW* on *SUV* which are stronger in one gender than in the other.

Two beliefs regarding peaceful behavior were tested. The belief that peaceful behavior is natural in humans was negatively associated with *SUV*, which is to say that overall, participants who believed more strongly in this were less likely to predict that they would use violence. The correlation was -.273 (see Table 5.) If there is a causal relationship between these two variables, it speaks to Douglas Fry (2006) and Bruce Bonta's (1996) works regarding peaceful cultures, and their idea that a peaceful ideology is instrumental in maintaining peace in such cultures. When the correlation between belief that peaceful behavior is natural in humans and *SUV* was examined separately by gender, it was found to be very close (.003 difference, see Tables 7 and 8) among women and men. This might suggest that a peaceful ideology may have an equal effect on genders.

The second belief, that violent behavior is caused by socialization, only had a slight negative correlation with *SUV* (-.097, see Table 6), which was not statistically significant. It is possible that this belief is not related to participants' use of violence. It is also possible that this part of the survey was worded in a confusing way, and that the term "socialization" was unclear to participants.

This survey was conducted among university students, so a relevant question was whether students' class standing had an effect on the results. The data regarding class level and the strength of association between *VW* and *SUV* is worth looking at (see Table 9). The level of freshmen was too small to have a statistically significant result, so the extremely high correlation among freshman of 0.896 could have been entirely by chance. There is no strong indicator that all of these cases shared a demographic quality that would cause them to answer in a particular way. Sophomores (.585*), juniors (.428**), and seniors (.252*) all had a statistically significant correlation between the two variables that weakened as the grade levels increased. Post-graduate students, which were students who had a B.A., but were attending school and not enrolled in a master's or Ph.D. program, completely broke the pattern. For them, there was a slightly negative correlation (-.038), which was not statistically significant. There was virtually no association between the variables in this group. The correlation was again higher for graduate students, at .468**. What is interesting about this pattern is that, among the meaningful correlations between *VW* and *SUV*, there is a decrease from freshman-senior years, and then a resurgence in graduate students. Assuming that there is a true relationship between the variables, this pattern could be due to the influence of Portland State University's (PSU) culture. It is possible that as students move through the university, they become less affected by this relationship between belief and behavior. Graduate students may have come from other institutions with cultures that did not have a mitigating effect on the relationship between belief and behavior equal to that of PSU; therefore they would not be as affected by this phenomenon. In a future study, it would be constructive to look at how long students had attended PSU as a category of analysis. The pattern seen among class levels also speaks to the need to repeat the survey among a more diverse population, since it is possible that the culture of PSU had a significant effect on the results.

Another factor that had an effect on the correlation between *VW* and *SUV* was income level. Among respondents who made more than $45,000, the correlation was .257 (see Table 10), while among those who made less than $45,000 it was .473 (see Table 11). More specific information regarding income level was requested from participants, but despite this, the number of respondents in each category was too small to achieve statistical significance. Results were only meaningful when the categories were separated into two large groups — over $45,000 and under $45,000 — rather than several smaller ones. Without a larger population to draw from, it is hard to explain why the difference between these two groups might exist. What is likely is that income level is a secondary attribute that is related to other factors that would help explain this difference in correlation strengths. Some of these factors could be education level, social class, age, and profession. For example, among less educated or younger respondents there might be a stronger subscription to the norms of mainstream culture, which would mean that in these groups beliefs in violence might have a stronger effect on behavior.

Regarding differences in race and ethnicity, again the number of respondents in each category was too small to have meaningful results. Only one racial group, "white," was large enough to obtain statistically significant results. What is intriguing is that the correlation between *VW* and *SUV* was stronger among students who identified as white than when it was in the population as a whole (.423 among white students as opposed to .408 among all students, see Tables 12 and 1). This difference might be explained in terms of adhesion to dominant culture. Respondents who identified as white might be more affected by the norms of dominant culture than those who identified as other race/ethnic groups.

Results also were examined by differences in marital status. In this case, a similar correlation was found between *VW* and *SUV* among participants who identified as single (0.389) and married (0.385). Among participants who said they had a long-term partner, the slightly higher correlation of 0.467 was found, and when looking at divorced participants, the correlation was much higher, at 0.616. Sociologist Melissa Thompson pointed out that this may be due to divorced participants' increased experience of conflict in their lives (personal communication, December 2, 2009). Another scholar, Thomas L. Hanson (1999), in his article "Parental conflict, divorce and child welfare," bases his research on the assumption that "parents who subsequently divorce exhibit more conflict than parents who stay together," although he acknowledges that "Perhaps because this relationship seems so self-evident, few studies have examined it" (p. 1285). Additional information regarding participants' past experience with conflict could help shed light on these results.

When looking at the correlations between the four statements regarding violence on the part of others and the variables of *VW* and *SUV* (Tables 14 and 15), what is salient is that the correlations for *VW* are high across the board. A possible interpretation for this is that participants might predict that they are less likely to use violence themselves, but more likely to support the use of violence by others.

Conclusion

As discussed above, several authors of related literature point to a possible link between belief about violence and behavior. The results of this study support the viewpoints of these scholars by demonstrating a statistically significant correlation between several beliefs about human violence and peacefulness and the choice of a violent action as a response to a conflict situation. At the very least, the results show that this line of research should be further pursued.

One important observation is that finding correlations between variables does not mean that any of them cause the others. As the scientific adage goes, "correlation is not causation" (Reaves, 1992, p. 130). There may be other variables that are affecting the ones that were studied. For example, there may be other beliefs regarding violence, peace, or human behavior that are the psychological impetuses towards violent behavior. For that matter, there may be beliefs regarding fields that seem unrelated to peace and violence that cause violent behavior. Perhaps there is a psychological characteristic or certain past experiences that cause an individual to believe a certain way about peace and violence. Political or religious beliefs might also be factors. There are numerous possibilities of other variables that should be tested for in future studies.

The study was limited by its quantitative design, which did not offer open-ended questions. In addition, it can be problematic to generalize findings from a survey taken only of university students to a larger population. Ideally, future research will study diverse populations that include participants from a range of professions, occupations, backgrounds, and life experiences. Despite the narrow focus and limitations of this study, it still provides intriguing information in the exploration of the relationship between beliefs about violence and violent behavior.

This is one of the fields which may help us understand how to prevent violence and promote peaceful interactions. The results of the *Worldview and Violence Study*, though small and limited, suggest that socialization, which includes the adoption of a belief system, plays an important part in determining whether or not a person will choose violence. If we want to reduce the amount of violence in and across societies, we have to understand why it is so common and acceptable. This necessitates looking inward and examining the personal beliefs we hold.

REFERENCES

Adams, D. (1989). The Seville statement on violence and why it is important. *Journal of Humanistic Psychology, 29*(3), 328–337.

_____, and S. Bosch (1987). The myth that war is intrinsic to human nature discourages action for peace by young people. In J.M. Ramirez, R.A. Hinde and J. Groebel (Eds.), *Essays on violence* (pp. 121–137). Sevilla: Publicaciones de la Universidad de Sevilla.

Bonta, B.D. (1996). Conflict resolution among peaceful societies: The culture of peacefulness. *Journal of Peace Research, 33*(4), 403–420.

Freud, S. (2000). Why war. In D. Barash (Ed.), *Approaches to peace: A reader in peace studies*. (pp. 9–13). New York: Oxford University Press.

Fry, D.P. (2006). *The human potential for peace: An anthropological challenge to assumptions about war and violence*. New York: Oxford University Press.

_____ (2007). *Beyond war: The human potential for peace*. New York: Oxford University Press.

Ginsburg, B.E., and B.F. Carter (1987). The behaviors and the genetics of aggression. In J.M. Ramirez, R.A. Hinde and J. Groebel (Eds.), *Essays on violence* (pp. 59–76). Sevilla: Publicaciones de la Universidad de Sevilla.

Goldstein, J.H. (1987). Notes toward a social construction of human aggression. In J.M. Ramirez, R.A. Hinde and J. Groebel (Eds.), *Essays on violence* (pp. 105–119). Sevilla: Publicaciones de la Universidad de Sevilla.

Hanson, T.L. (1999). Does parental conflict explain why divorce is negatively associated with child welfare? *Social Forces, 77*(4), 1283–1316.

Konner, M. (2006). Human nature, ethnic violence, and war. In M. Fitzduff and C.E. Stout (Eds.), *The psychology of resolving global conflicts: From war to peace, volume 1: Nature vs. Nurture* (pp. 1–40). Westport, CT: Praeger Security International.

Lorenz, K. (1966). *On aggression*. New York: Harcourt, Brace and World.

_____. (1966). *On aggression*. New York: Harcourt, Brace and World.

Reaves, C.C. (1992). *Quantitative research for the behavioral sciences*. New York: John Wiley and Sons.

Sorenson, E.R. (1978). Cooperation and freedom among the Fore. In A. Montagu (Ed.), *Learning non-aggression* (pp. 12–30). New York: Oxford University Press.

Parenting for a Better Future

Terri L. Shofner

The world today is suffering the consequences of a long, shared history of bad parenting. That may at first seem simplistic, but we must recognize that even our world leaders learned their conflict management styles by watching and interacting with their primary caregivers. With this we begin to understand the importance of parenting for a better future.

In the past 100 years or so, research has started to show how we learn and grow and understand the world around us, with some early benchmark publications, such as Piaget's *The Moral Judgment of the Child* (1932) [*Le jugement moral chez l'enfant*]. With this new understanding we have a unique opportunity to bend our future toward cooperation and peace. First we have to face our own fallibility, especially those of us who are parents, and all of us who as children idolized our parents and grandparents as being above all wrongdoing. We must recognize that we are still learning how to be in relationship with one another, our children, and the planet. This essay will explore some of that history and select relevant studies, and conclude with a look at today's families and how we might move toward a peaceful future.

The concept of good parenting is very new to our species. Our history paints a grim picture for the child, one filled with hard work, pain, mutilation, abuse, sexual exploitation, and death by neglect, exposure, or sacrifice (DeMause, 1982). Many children in the world today still face these harsh realities. But in industrialized nations, for the most part, laws are in place to protect children. Before modern methods of birth control, however, children were too often seen as expendable resources, and parents had limited capacity to concern themselves with the future of their children, especially daughters. Girls have been dealt the hardest blow in virtually every culture, and yet these are the mothers of the next generation — sometimes abusing, rejecting, and even killing their children at least in part as a result of their own painful childhoods. The field of psychohistory posits that our violence can be explained by the damage created by child abuse (DeMause, 2002). Could it be that the historical reality of child abuse is a significant factor in what has brought us to the present state of affairs on our planet and with each other?

Love in Infancy

In 1945, René Spitz explored the development of institutionalized children who had been abandoned at the doors of foundling homes. Spitz used direct observation of children, following their social development. Some were placed with foster families, while others were raised in institutions. The institutionalized babies had no regular caregiver, only nurses who did not hold or caress them during their eight-hour shifts. Those children suffered severe consequences (Blum, 2002). More than one in every three died in childhood. Some were still living in institutions after 40 years, all either physically, mentally, or socially retarded. Films of the children show them rocking themselves, hitting their heads against the railings of their beds, and later becoming completely despondent — refusing food, eye contact, or any interaction. This condition is termed "institutional autism," as it resembles the physiological condition of the same name (Lubit, 2009).

Spitz's revelations into the mother/child relationship were further supported by studies of primates. Harry Harlow conducted a series of experiments between 1953 and 1963 on rhesus monkeys. His experiments involved removing a baby monkey from its mother, placing it in isolation, and then evaluating its behavior when placed either with the mother again, a mother surrogate, or with peers. One experiment placed the baby in a cage with a terrycloth-covered surrogate mother. The infant would cling to the surrogate, and once it felt secure, would begin to explore its surroundings. When an infant was placed into a cage without a surrogate, it would whimper and cower fearfully, never attempting to explore. When an infant raised in isolation was placed with peers, its behavior would vary from avoidant or aggressive, while infants raised with their mothers would play together. The results of these studies planted the seeds that led John Bowlby to formulate attachment theory (Blum, 2002).

We often hear people derided for being "needy." And yet, as the previous two studies indicate, this is our very first experience in life: we are needy. In 1950, Bowlby began observations of children orphaned during the war. What he noted, supporting the earlier observations of Spitz and Harlow, was that our very survival depends upon the bond we make with our primary caregiver

(Blum, 2002). The more secure that bond, the more confidence we'll have to explore our world and interact with our peers.

A student of Bowlby (1988), Mary Ainsworth continued to build on his observations. She developed the "Strange Situation" study to examine attachment behavior in children. In this study she postulated three distinct attachment patterns in infants: secure attachment in which the child is confident that a parent figure will be available and responsive if a fearful situation is encountered; anxious resistant attachment, where the child is uncertain if the parent will be available when needed (these children are prone to separation anxiety, clinging to the parent, and are fearful of exploring on their own); and anxious avoidant attachment, where the child has been rebuffed or rejected when care and comfort are sought (these children attempt to be emotionally self-sufficient and may later be diagnosed as narcissistic) (Bowlby, 1988). A fourth category was later observed by Mary Main and her colleagues at the University of California, Berkeley. In studies of abused children, they noted a disorganized attachment, characterized by chaotic and disoriented behavior (Siegel, 2003).

The early studies focused on mothers, since at the time women were often the stay-at-home parent while the father had little interaction with the children. As this has changed over time, more studies have shown that the attachment pattern to the father is similar to that of the mother (Ainsworth et al., 1978). Further, it has been shown that children securely attached to both parents are the most confident and most competent, while children attached to neither are the least so (Main and Weston, 1981). These studies also show that a single father can fill the attachment role of the mother. In two-parent families of opposite gender, the roles of each parent varied, the father typically engaged in more physical play while the mother provided a nurturing presence.

The revolutionary research of Spitz, Bowlby, Ainsworth and Main changed the way children's homes and hospitals care for children. If a newborn requires an incubator, the staff will encourage a parent to hold and touch the infant as much as possible, as it has been shown to improve and speed recovery and support parent-child bonding, or attunement. Subsequent studies have begun to show the full impact of attachment.

Attachment for Security

As the studies indicate, without a secure attachment to a caregiver, a young child will cower and show fear. When that fearful and insecure child is placed in a group of its peers, studies show the child will use avoidance or aggression to cope with the stress of this social situation. Another study by George and Main (1979) looked at children in special daycare centers for families under economic stress. Some of the children had been victims of physical abuse. The results showed that the abused children approached caregivers half as often as the control group, and assaulted other children twice as often as the controls. The researchers concluded that the social behaviors of abused children "resemble that of relatively rejected children found within normal samples.... Compared with their matched controls, we found abused children aggressive, inhibited in approach, and avoidant in response to friendly overtures" (p. 316). In other words, parental rejection — whether extreme as in abuse cases, or in cases of neglect — will inhibit normal social development in a child and limit that child's ability to cope in a stressful conflict situation.

Following these early studies of parent-child relationships, researchers designed long-term studies to evaluate how the securely attached child fares later in life, including a longitudinal study designed by Alan Sroufe (1999). He and his colleagues followed children through school classrooms and summer camps, collecting data on their relationship and conflict management abilities. They discovered that securely attached babies grow to be kids with leadership ability; anxious-avoidant babies were later the outcasts; anxious-ambivalent babies later became anxious; and lastly, the disorganized attached babies had difficulty getting along with other children and regulating their emotions (Siegel & Hartzell, 2003).

Main (1970), taking a different tack, wondered how a parent's own childhood and life narrative reflect on the potential for bonding with their children. She developed a research instrument called the Adult Attachment Interview. The results of the study indicated that the parent's attachment attitudes could predict the child's attachment. This didn't necessarily mean that a parent who had been poorly attached as a child was fated to be incapable of having their own child securely attached. What was of critical importance was whether the adult had been able to make sense of his/her own childhood, a process referred to as earned secure adult attachment (Siegel & Hartzell, 2003).

Mirror, Mirror

Why is it that a child securely attached to a loving caregiver is later generally better able to cope when faced with a conflict in pre-school, grade school, or later in adult life? If it takes a securely attached parent (whether learned or earned) to nurture a securely attached child, that suggests some form of social learning. In the early 1990s, mirror neurons, a key to social learning, were discovered. Experiments, led by neuroscientist Giacomo Rizzolatti (1994), were being done on a monkey, where parts of his brain were monitored as he performed various tasks. By accident it was discovered that the area of the brain that activated when the monkey ate a peanut was equally activated when the monkey watched a researcher eat a peanut. When these same studies were done on humans, something remarkable was discovered. The human mirror neurons were far more sophisticated than those in other animals. Not only did the receptors of the human brain fire when someone performed an action in front of a subject, like drinking a glass of water, but if that action was done without the glass in hand, the receptors didn't fire. The human mirror neurons were triggered on intent, not just motion. This gives us some insight, or "mindsight" as Siegel calls it (Siegel, 2003), into the mind of another human being. We can discern someone's intent from interpreting action. In watching the action, we feel what she feels without actually going through the actions ourselves — possibly explaining the prevalence of voyeurism in our species; people-watching has always been a popular pastime.

When we watch another human go through a peak experience, like the Olympic athlete doing her final routine before winning the gold, we feel elation with her. Likewise, when your favorite football kicker misses that last-chance goal, costing the game, you feel the same disappointment you see in his face. These vicarious experiences will be further heightened if you have trained in the activity you are watching. Interestingly, if an injured athlete watches videos of other athletes, once that athlete recovers, it's as if he or she was never out of training.

Mirror neurons help us learn by watching and feeling. But what if we're watching violence and are surrounded by conflict, as so many children are today? What if children immerse themselves in first-person shooting games and violent movies? What neurons are firing and learning in these experiences? Lt. Col. Dave Grossman (2000), a former Army Ranger, West Point psychology professor, and professor of military science, has shown how violence in entertainment is teaching our children to kill. Grossman is an expert on school shootings and other violence related to our children. In his article "Teaching kids to kill," (2000) he cites study after study that supports the connection between media violence and real-world violence. When television enters a new market or region, there is an "immediate explosion of violence on the playground and within 15 years there is a doubling of the murder rate" (Centerwell, 1992). According to the *Journal of the American Medical Association*, "approximately one-half of the homicides committed in the United States, approximately 10,000," are due to long-term childhood exposure to television (Centerwell, 1992). In May 2000, in response to a presentation given by Grossman at their annual conference, the American Psychiatric Association stated, "The data is irrefutable. We have reached a point where we need to treat those who try to deny it, like we would treat Holocaust deniers" (Grossman, 2000). For many of us, the violence on the streets creates fear, and that fear of the outside world puts more and more people on their couches in front of television, which fuels the fear and the violence even further.

First we watch, then we do, and then we teach. A professor told me this years ago, but I never realized how important the watching part was until I learned about mirror neurons. "Neurons that fire together wire together," known as the Hebbian Rule (1949), explains why repetition plays such an important role in teaching (Keysers, 2004). As the neurons strengthen their connections through repetition, a sheath of material grows around the connection, wiring them together so that response will be the knee-jerk reaction. That reaction, however, can be one of compassion and empathy, just as it could be one of avoidance and aggression. By the time the securely attached child is in preschool, his ability to respond with empathy and compassion to the distress of another child is apparent. If viewed in terms of mirror neurons, the child who has been the recipient of a parent attuned to her needs will learn that this is how to treat others: be attuned to those around you rather than worried or fearful for one's own self and security (Wolf et al., 2001).

How do we begin to transform families under stress so that the children in these homes are able to develop these positive coping mechanisms and pass them along to future generations? Could mirror neurons that are so effective in teaching the child also be used to guide and re-train the parent? Bowlby (1988) discovered that parenting classes were not nearly as effective as sending a skilled mother into the home of a mother in crisis. A service program called Home-Start, begun in Leicester, England, in the 1970s, paired volunteers who were experienced parents with parents in crisis, sending them into their homes. The volunteer would help with the children, listen, and give advice to the parent in crisis. Although in subsequent interviews the visiting volunteer rarely felt the visits had made a difference, in every case the parent in crisis found the visit to be a valuable learning experience. A more experienced parent goes to help a new parent, sharing hands-on wisdom by doing the actions that will help most, while the new parent can watch and learn, letting the mirror neurons begin to retrain her for more empathy and compassion for her child. This program has since expanded internationally (Harrison, 1981).

Parenting for Peace

Mothers and fathers carry the baggage of their own childhoods into their parenting strategies. We may think "Well, I did OK," and use this justification for imposing the same types of discipline, such as spanking, that our parents used on us. Many people still believe this to be a valid form of discipline, regardless of 20 years of research results to the contrary (Durrant and Ensom, 2012). The practice of spanking children has been linked to obesity, lower IQ, mood disorders, sexual difficulties, and sexual abuse. Rather than modify an undesired behavior, studies show that it actually causes increased aggressiveness and lack of impulse control in the child (e.g., Falk & Lee, 2012). Returning to the concept of attachment, once the child associates pain with the parent, the relationship between parent-child will be interrupted and the child will exhibit avoidant behavior (Gershoff & Bitensky, 2007). At the time of this writing 32 countries have enacted laws protecting children from all forms of corporal punishment. In the United States 31 states have banned corporal punishment in schools.

Parents struggle to find the right balance between making a living and parenting, and this is especially true for single parents. It is difficult to be solely responsible for the means of survival for one's self and a dependent, while also maintaining focus and determination to raise a well-adjusted and compassionate human being. The choices are hard and often frustrating for both parent and child.

The social structure of the United States is not family friendly; children pay the price with their mental development and parents pay the price with guilt. To help define family friendly, it is necessary to compare today's typical American family to that of the past. From U.S. Census data in 1960, 45 percent of households were married couples with children. By 2000, that percentage dropped to 23. In 1998, 12.8 million households were headed by single mothers. More than half first births were to single women. Of children growing up in single-mother homes 60 percent are living in poverty as compared to 11 percent in two-parent homes (Kamerman and Kahn, 1988). Single mothers experience higher stress in their lives compared to their married counterparts, regardless of income (McLanahan, 1983). Several studies have shown that the stress related to poverty, childcare, and the task heavy burden of heading a household with small children increase the risk for anxiety, depression, and health problems for the single mother (Guttenberg, Salassin & Belle, 1980; Hall, Williams & Greenberg, 1985; McGrath, Keita, Strickland & Russo, 1990; Perlin & Johnson, 1977).

With these statistics in mind, it is easy for single parents to take as criticism any suggestion of changes in parenting—there is so little time in the day and there are seemingly few resources to facilitate change. Attachment parenting, homeschooling, taking care of the house—these all take time that single parents do not have. Meeting the needs of all families—and parent and child alike—requires a shift toward community and cooperation. In the absence of traditional family support in modern modes of living, intentional communities are springing up all over the U.S. These communities are often multi-generational, which can give the single parent an extended family to help raise their children. The website http://cohousing.org shows the diversity and scope of these communities across the United States. There are also groups that cater to single mothers, like http://coabode.org, which is a network for single mothers who have interest in doing a house share with other single mothers. There are both virtual and real support groups for all varieties of family. This is cooperation. This is how we begin our journey toward peace.

References

Ainsworth, M.D., M.C. Blehar, E. Waters, and S. Wall (1978). *Patterns of attachment: Assessed in the strange situation and at home*, Hillsdale, NJ: Lawrence Erlbaum.
Blakeslee, S. (2006, January 10). Cells that read minds. *New York Times*. Retrieved from http://www.nytimes.com/2006/01/10/science/10mirr.html.
Blum, D. (2002). *Love at Goon Park, Harry Harlow, and the science of affection*. Cambridge, MA: Perseus.
Bowlby, J. (1951). Maternal care and mental health. World Health Organization Monograph. (Aerial No. 2).
_____. (1988). *A secure base: Parent-child attachment and healthy human development*. London: Routledge.
Centerwall, B. (1992). Television and violence: The scale of the problem and where to go from here. *Journal of the American Medical Association*, 267: 3059–3061.
DeMause, L. (1982). *Foundations of psychohistory*. New York: Creative Roots.
Durrant, J., and R. Ensom (2012). Physical punishment of children: Lessons from 20 years of research. *Canadian Medical Association Journal*, 1–5.
Eisler, R. (2007). *The real wealth of nations, creating a caring economics*. San Francisco: Berret-Koehler.
George, C., and M. Main (1979). Special interactions of young abused children: Approach, avoidance, and aggression. *Child Development, 50,* 306–318.
Gershoff, E., and S. Bitensky (2007). The case against corporal punishment: Converging evidence from social science research and international human rights law and implications for U.S. public policy. *Psychology, Public Policy, and Law, 13*(4), 231–272.
Grossman, D. (2000). Teaching kids to kill. Retrieved from http://www.killology.com/article_teachkid.html.
Guttenberg, M., S. Salassin, and D. Belle (1980). *The mental health of women*. New York: Academic.
Falk, A., and S. Lee (2012). Parenting behavior and conduct problems in children with and without attention-deficit/hyperactivity disorder (ADHD): Moderation by callous-unemotional traits. *Journal of Psychopathology & Behavioral Assessment, 34*(2), 172–181. doi:10.1007/s10862-011-9268-z.
Hall, I.A., C.A. Williams, and R.S. Greenberg (1985). Supports, stressors and depressive symptoms in low-income mothers of young children. *American Journal of Public Health,* 75, 518–522.
Harrison, M. (1981). Home-start: A voluntary home-visiting scheme for young families. *Child Abuse and Neglect,* 5, 441–7.
Hebb, D.O. (1949). *The organization of behavior*. New York: Wiley.
Kamerman, S.B., and A.J. Kahn (1988). *Mothers alone: Strategies for a time of change*. Dover, MA: Auburn House.

Keysers, C., and D. Perrett (2004). Demystifiying social cognition: A Hebbian perspective. *Trends in Cognitive Sciences, 8*(11), 501–507.

Kohn, A. (2005). *Unconditional parenting: Moving from rewards and punishments to love and reason.* New York: Atria.

Korten, D.C. (2006). *The great turning: From empire to earth community.* San Francisco: Berrett-Koehler.

Lubit, R.H. (2009). Child abuse and neglect, reactive attachment disorder. Retrieved from http://emedicine.medscape.com/article/915447-overview.

Main, M., and D.R. Weston (1981). The quality of toddler's relationship to mother and to father: Related to conflict behavior and the readiness to establish new relationships. *Child Development, 52,* 932–940.

McGrath, E., G.P. Keita, B.R. Strickland, and N.F. Russo (1990). *Women and depression: Risk factors and treatment issues.* Washington, DC: American Psychological Association.

McLanahan, S. (1983). Family structure and stress: A longitudinal comparison of two-parent and female-headed families. *Journal of Marriage and the Family, 45,* 347–357.

Pearline, L., and J. Johnson (1977). Marital status, life strains, and depression. *American Sociological Review, 42,* 704–715.

Piaget, J. (1932). *The moral judgment of a child.* London: Kegan Paul, Trench, Trubner and Co. *[Le jugement moral chez l'enfant].* http://ia700407.us.archive.org/18/items/moraljudgmentoft005613mbp/moraljudgmentoft005613mbp.pdf.

Rizzolatti, G. (1994). Nonconscious motor images. *Behavioral Brain Science, 17,* 220.

Rosenberg, M. (2003). *Nonviolent communication: A way of life.* Encinitas, CA: Puddle Dancer.

Siegel, D.J., and M.M. Hartzell (2003). *Parenting from the inside out: How a deeper self understanding can help you raise children who thrive.* New York: Putnam Special Markets.

Sroufe, L.A., E.A. Carlson, A.K. Levy, and B. Egeland (1999). Implication of attachment theory for developmental psychopathology. *Development and Psychopathology, 11,* 1–13.

A violent education: Corporal punishment of children in U.S. public schools. (2008). Human Rights Watch. Retrieved from http://www.hrw.org/reports/2008/us0808/index.htm.

Wolf, N.S., M.E. Gales, E. Shane, and M. Shane (2001). The developmental trajectory from amodal perception to empathy and communication: The role of mirror neurons in this process. *Psychoanalytic Inquiry, 21*(1), 94–112.

Power in the People: Urgent Transformation Toward Integration

Stephanie Van Hook

"Changing the world is not about putting a different kind of person in power. It's awakening a different kind of power in people." — Michael N. Nagler

Mahatma Gandhi once said that he was incapable of hating anyone. Portrayed so dramatically in the Richard Attenborough film, as he fell to the ground from the bullet of a Hindu fanatic, he uttered words of forgiveness for his murderer. How did he lead one of the greatest nonviolent movements the world has seen on the basis of this love? In a world of conflict where getting what we want often means by whatever means necessary (collectively if not always individually), we must find ways of explaining a new kind of power, recognizing it when we see it, and accessing that power ourselves. As a new field based on the paradigm shift from competition to cooperation, from zero-sum to win-win, conflict resolution is in a unique position to break away from the old paradigm disciplines that express power solely as dominance, privilege, and violence.

Three Faces of Power in the Face of Our War System

According to Kenneth Boulding (1989), power has three distinct faces: threat or military; transactional or exchange; and love or integrative. Boulding associates threat power with the political arena, though clearly strategic nonviolence can also be regarded as such: *Give us what we need or we strike, and you will lose money and eventually political power.* Threat power consists of an interaction where it is assumed that if Entity X does not follow the order of Entity Y, there will be negative consequences for Entity X: Either you do what I want, or else I will do something you do not want. This kind of power draws its security from the belief that one must have power over the other. Conflict resolution, drawing from game theory developed by one of the founders of the field—peace polymath Anatol Rapaport—calls this a zero-sum interaction, where one entity must lose and give up something in order for the other to gain something.

Threat power is prevalent in our world. War is threat power institutionalized: nuclear weapon deterrence, selling weapons to insecure nations or oppressed classes. In the United States we carry out the death penalty and—as threat is hollow unless periodically exercised—have maintained control over impoverished countries through bombs, drones, and thousands of military personnel.

Threats have an implicit promise of getting respect that others will not give willingly, but the confusion swirls around the differences between respect based on fear or on admiration. Threat leads inexorably to the creation of difficulties, resentments, and enemies. Threat power escalates tensions. Therein lays its cheat.

In the new paradigm, we strive to move away from threat power to something less harmful in the long run. At the Metta Center, a civil society organization based upon the intersections of philosophical nonviolence and conflict transformation, this concept is called "work" versus work: violence sometimes "works," in that it achieves what it set out to do, but it never works—it never makes the situation better down the road.

The formula for exchange power is when X exchanges P with Y in order to obtain Q, where X and Y are entities acting as responsible agents and P and Q are goods or services, where the exchange itself helps to determine their value. This is the power of the marketplace of goods, services, and our human ability to negotiate their relative values in each of our human-to-human transactions. Sometimes the power is found in money, such as the power of banks, corporations, and the wealthy class. This formula is, *Give me something I want and I'll give you something you want.* However, when infused with threat power, it can quickly become, *Give me a lot of something I want, and I'll give you a little of something you want, or else.*

Exchange power—without any threat power—harnessed for compassionate, uplifting ends brings about closer, healthier, cooperatively self-sufficient communities. Exchange power leads to a willingness to boycott when boycott is necessary, a deeper approach to understanding the long-term harmful effects of sanctions, and a more realistic commitment to human wellbeing than a mere focus on material gain. Gandhi's constructive program during the Indian freedom struggle demonstrates the potential for people to harness exchange power: Indians actively spun cloth every day in an effort to shake themselves free of the colonial yoke brought upon them through the East Indian Trading Company. This "positive spin" was, as Gandhi called it, "the song of freedom" from the British Empire (Ackerman & Duvall, 2001).

Basic economics reveal that the value of the exchange is determined by the means of production and consumer demand. If there is a higher demand, then the person who owns the means of production will hold the power. The less desire there is for the object or service, the less desirable it is to own the means of production, and the less power one has in owning those means. This is no small discovery on the part of the powerless. Gandhi, for instance, realized that though they could not change who held the means of production in the short term, they could lessen their dependency on those products while reclaiming basic human needs through cottage industries. If leaders around the world began refusing to buy from the United States arms industries, turning to other forms of "security," the stranglehold of military power would begin to loosen and reveal itself for the absurd, counterproductive form of security it is.

A culture based on exchange power takes the human being into account. Examining the somewhat fragmentary movements for social justice in the United States, peace offers a coalescing force that draws all of the movements together. For example, a culture that values peace will not manufacture and sell weapons. A culture that values war — and profits from war — will spend inordinate amounts of money on the production and sale of armaments and defense. A culture that values health will not manufacture and sell commercial, processed tobacco, massive and cheaply made alcoholic drinks, and chemically contaminated junk food. A culture that values the wellbeing of people will spend its money on restoring public green spaces and gardens, limit advertisements of destructive products, and cultivate the arts. Martin Luther King, Jr., said in his 1967 speech, "Beyond Vietnam": "A nation that continues year after year to spend more money on military defense than on programs of social uplift is approaching spiritual death." Ending unlimited growth, production, and consumption is time-urgent; without new methods of conflict management and value shifts we can expect dire public health consequences. The nonviolent starting point of the field of conflict resolution is indispensable to survival. The watershed moments are at hand.

The third face of power identified by Boulding is integrative power, which provides legitimacy to an individual or group. For example, when a ruler loses his legitimacy — as happened to Hosni Mubarak in Egypt and Slobodan Milosevic in Serbia — he is no longer fit to rule. A general formula for integrative power is, *I will do what I believe is right, you will do what you believe is right, and we will protect each other's freedom to do so without committing harms.*

It is possible to maintain false community, or pseudo-integrative networks, within institutions that use threat power. The military is a key example: soldiers willing to kill together and military wives' and families' support of the troops. The recent rise of right-wing Tea Party politics in the United States embraces collective anger and violent rhetoric — another example of using a limited form of integrated power toward a destructive, threat power end. Looking at community as social uplift and focus on the common good, these would not be authentic communities. Rather, they are pseudo-communities, providing exclusivist identity feelings that would normally emerge inclusively in authentic community.

Gandhi saw that communities fall within a circle of service in which the individual serves the family, the family serves the community, the community serves the nation, and the nation serves the world. Human beings seek that bond, making it inherently powerful — and therefore exploitable if not aware of the risk. It is therefore necessary for the field of conflict resolution to have a sense of where the power stems from, to help us redirect the energy when it has been exploited or misled.

There are institutions meant to embody integrative power: generally, churches, charities, and non-profit organizations. In practice, it is easy to see how these institutions may at times acquiesce to the other forms of power. Nazi Germany, for instance, as we learn from the life of Dietrich Bonhoeffer and others, was in part facilitated through the cooperation of the church. In a new paradigm approach to security, however, the essential element is to access integrative power within us, recognize where we direct it (and redirect it if necessary), and institutionalize that power. Integrative power is the only one that takes the possibility of human thriving into account. Unarmed civilian peacekeeping missions show this promise; they are building greater legitimacy and cost-effective, results-based performance in lieu of military intervention. Nonviolence, integrative power, brings the active element from within a person and challenges her to be courageous — without a commitment to violence. Imagine Egypt in 2011 had the people with guns instead of peaceful protest; it would have been orders-of-magnitude worse than Libya. While the revolution in Tahrir Square ultimately may unravel into threat power, enough integrative power existed to bring down what was seen as an invincible despot. Integrative power is the new realism: pragmatic politicians and policymakers will embrace it or be left behind in a cloud of historical dust.

A complement to Boulding's faces of power has been articulated in Joanna Macy's (2006) vision for a "great turning." The three main components to her vision are to stop the worst of the damage, build new institutions, and change the culture. The cultural shift she describes must happen on both the cognitive and spiritual levels. The cognitive shift regards our attitudes and understanding of the world, and the spiritual shift involves our attitudes about ourselves. This great turning represents the generation of a movement through our power and potential as human beings, and is another entry for conflict resolution. Laws and practice follow norms in some cases, and in the research, development, and deployment of best practices of conflict transformation, those laws in need of changing will do so as new norms gain purchase in the hearts and minds of an empowered people.

To believe our conflict resolution mission is less than the embrace of integrative power and the pursuit of the "great turning" ignores a body of evidence so massive it is only dismissed by those who have no hope. And hope is our duty to the generations and our greatest implement is the integrative power seen and sought for so long by spiritual masters and people of good heart. Now it is the best road to our common prosperous future.

References

Ackerman, P., and J. DuVall (2000). A force more powerful: A century of nonviolent conflict. New York: Palgrave.
Boulding, K. (1989). The three faces of power. Newbury Park, CA: Sage.
King, M.K. (1967). Beyond Vietnam. Available at www.stanford.edu/group/King/liberation_curriculum/speeches/beyondvietnam.htm.
Macy, J. (2006). World as love, world as self. Berkeley: Parallax.

Gandhi: The Grandfather of Conflict Transformation

Gail M. Presbey

What is the relationship between Mohandas K. Gandhi's experiments with truth and nonviolence and the growing field of conflict resolution, with over 60 master's degree programs, several PhD programs, and textbooks like *The Sage Handbook of Conflict Resolution* (Bercovitch et al., 2009)?[1] Certainly Gandhi is acknowledged as a precursor to the contemporary field, and key founders of the field such as Johan Galtung attribute their inspiration and key insights to him. But Gandhi scholars like Thomas Weber (2004) suggest that the contemporary field of conflict resolution has mostly forgotten Gandhi's contributions to conflict resolution. One of the goals of this essay is to remind students and practitioners of conflict resolution that key insights of the field originate from Gandhi's early experiments — that is, theory-laden activism and his reflections upon his movement's accomplishments and shortcomings.

Weber (2004) notes that American conflict resolution studies are more influenced by Kenneth Boulding and his *Journal of Conflict Resolution*—which focused on empirical studies and hard economic realities — rather than the normative emphases of sociologist Galtung. The *Sage Handbook* covers a wide range of social science methods used in the field, including quantitative studies, game theory, problem-solving approaches, and experimental research. It also includes an article by Jack S. Levy (2009) on the use of case studies, which looks at the history of political leaders who have played important roles in conflict resolution. Not mere historical exercises, Levy (2009) explains that "theory-guided/ideographic case studies" or "analytic history" can focus on a historical situation and its actors, but uses a specific conceptual framework to focus attention on aspects of the situation that might otherwise be neglected (p. 73). Thus, a second and more humble goal of this chapter is to revisit some of the historical details of Gandhi's approach and evaluate them according to current accepted wisdom in the field of conflict resolution.

Gandhi's Historical Role as Precursor

In *Contemporary Conflict Resolution,* Miall, Ramsbotham, and Woodhouse (1999) include Gandhi as a precursor to the contemporary institutionalized field of peace research and conflict resolution, which began in 1945 as a response to the bombing of Hiroshima and Nagasaki and the onset of the Cold War between the nuclear armed superpowers. They see Gandhi's contribution, along with early pacifist groups, as having "cross-fertilized with academic enterprise to enhance understanding of violent political conflict and alternatives to it" (Miall et al., 1999, p. 41). They credit Gandhi with creating a method — satyagraha—to bring to light the injustices inherent in accepted social structures of the day, so that these could be addressed in a way that did not result in a spiral of violence. The point of engaging with opponents upholding the status quo system is not to win but to build "a healthier relationship between antagonists" (p. 41). The authors suggest that these themes addressed by Gandhi were later championed in problem-solving workshops in the 1980s (alternatives to the problem-coercion-reward models), and also in the field's literature, such as the emphasis on the "win-win" situation in the popular *Getting to Yes* by Roger Fisher and William Ury (1981), and the emphasis on nurturing human relationships found in Adam Curle's 1971 book, *Making Peace.*

In Louis Kriesberg's essay on "The Evolution of Conflict Resolution" in the *Sage Handbook* (2009), Gandhi is first mentioned as having influence in the South African context of racial discrimination in the 1890s, before the preliminary developments of the field. He notes that Gandhi's practices in South Africa later influenced the African National Congress in their decades-long struggle against apartheid, and adds that Gandhi successfully "modeled methods of constructive escalation," which were used during the U.S. civil rights struggle. Academics studied these popular movements, noting their mixed record in bringing about positive social change and hoping that the interdisciplinary use of the social sciences could avoid or reduce war and injustice in the world (p. 19).

Weber (2004), a historian of Gandhi and his movement, identifies the places in Galtung's writings where he specifically mentions Gandhi's influence. Though Galtung published articles in the 1950s, wrote a book about Gandhi in 1954, and visited India in 1969 to research Gandhi, he did not publish the bulk of his material on the Mahatma until 1992, in *The Way is the Goal: Gandhi Today*. Weber attributes to this late publication a reason that many scholars in the conflict resolution field did not realize how indebted Galtung is to Gandhi's ideas.

Galtung is well-known for his emphasis on structural violence, and notes in his 1969 writings that Gandhi saw the violence built into social structures like caste and colonialism. Gandhi's version of "hate the sin, not the sinner" was intended to point out that attacking their enemies violently was a misperception of both the cause and solution to their problems. For Galtung, Gandhi's emphasis on exonerating actors focused people's efforts on dismantling or transforming violent social structures — this being both a better solution and a way to avoid violence directed at individuals.

Galtung's (1969) emphasis on structural injustice has sometimes been criticized as widening the definition of violence beyond its usefulness. If that is a fault, then blame is to be shared by Gandhi, as Galtung credits him with the definition of violence as "anything which would impede the individual from self-realization" (Galtung, in Weber, 2004, p. 38). The theme of Galtung's 1992 book is how Gandhi consistently rejects violence in all of its forms, including repression and exploitation. While Gandhi emphasized that conflicts are to be solved, he also saw them as golden opportunities for those involved to challenge themselves to become better persons through self-transformation (Weber, 2004, p. 38).

As Galtung (1996) said, "A satyagrahi tries to fight injustice, not to sweep it under the carpet" (p. 115). Of 12 possible responses to conflict, he notes that Gandhi rejects out-of-hand all but four, because the others involved some sort of violence or coercion. He writes, "Gandhi can be said to be a puritan in his choice of approaches to conflict resolution — a vegetarian here as in the choice of food, so to speak, and largely for the same reasons" (p. 115). Yet Gandhi's is no arbitrary or scrupulous narrowing; he chooses the only four approaches that attempt to transform the conflict, not escape from it. But is it really best to limit oneself and one's community only to the most ideal means to chosen ends? Galtung again: "In modern strategic terms Gandhi seems to be an adherent of the doctrine of graded and delayed response. The other party should be given time to reflect and come to see the total situation differently, just as one's own group also needs time to have a corresponding chance to learn and transcend, to improve A and B, together with the antagonist" (p.116).

While Galtung was explicit in acknowledging Gandhi's role in the construction of his ideas on conflict resolution, a large part of the literature ignores Gandhi's contribution. Weber (2006) does an inventory of the two main journals in the field, *Journal of Conflict Resolution* and *Journal of Peace Research*, and finds few overt references to Gandhi despite the many parallels between his methods and later developments in the field.

Arne Naess's 1974 book, *Gandhi and Group Conflict*, applied Gandhi's ideas to conflict resolution. Summarized by Weber (2006), the main themes of the book are that "all human beings have long-term interests in common; violence is invited from opponents if they are humiliated or provoked; opponents are less likely to resort to violence the better they understand your position; the essential interests which opponents have in common should be clearly formulated and cooperation established on that basis; personal contact with the opponent should be sought; opponents should not be judged harder than the self; opponents should be trusted; an unwillingness to compromise on non-essentials decreases the likelihood of true resolution; and that a position of weakness in an opponent should not be exploited" (p. 148). The remainder of the essay explores many of these themes.

Gandhian Practice and the "Science" of Conflict Resolution

Contemporary conflict resolution models itself on the social sciences, and as such it often attempts to articulate a secular scientific view that does not rely upon spiritual principles. But other sciences have had founders who were steeped in a religious worldview and saw their scientific explorations as an outgrowth of their spiritual quest. By the time these insights are tried and tested and passed along to the next generation, the religious backdrop is often gone. This is the situation with Gandhi's "experiments with truth," as he called them in his autobiography. As his life spanned an age of pragmatism and inventions, he wanted to see if his moral convictions worked in the practical world. He believed spirituality was central to what he was trying to achieve. But those who came after him in the field of conflict resolution reduced his experiments to an applied method of nonviolence, jettisoning the spiritual convictions of the nonviolent actor.

While Gandhi insisted that he was engaged in experiments, he admitted he did not have the time to develop these into a strict science: "To write a treatise on the science of ahimsa is beyond my powers. I am not built for academic writings. Action is my domain.... Let anyone who can systematize ahimsa into a science do so, if indeed it lends itself to such treatment" (*Collected Works*, Vol. 90, p. 2). His experiments happened not in a lab but in the world. Most often his experiments were done either on himself or with his close followers and movement. For example, his writings are filled with his experiments with his own diet; he scrutinized the effects of it on both his health and spiritual state (*Collected Works*, Vol. 44, pp. 16–17); to see if khadi spinning and sales can eliminate poverty (*Collected Works*, Vol. 70, p. 7); and to test his vow of celibacy (*Collected Works*, Vol. 86, pp. 9–10). Conflict resolution, however, typically does not rely on lab experiments (although they are part of the field), but uses events as they unfold in the world as their case studies.

The following section examines parts of Gandhi's approach that depart from current conflict resolution practice and if they hold insights that should be revived and continued.

An alternative to "tit-for-tat": Trust

Contemporary conflict resolution depends in part on game theory. In a game like "Prisoner's Dilemma," studies suggest that the best way to respond to a situation if you are unsure if you can trust the other party is "tit-for-tat"—that is, be generous and cooperate at first, but if the other party does not reciprocate, then copy what the other did in the previous move. This solution was proposed by Anatol Rapaport and was verified by computer simulation by Axelrod in 1984 (Miall et al., 1999). Gandhi's approach, however—done years before computer simulation was possible—involved trusting opponents. As Gandhi said on several occasions: "Trust begets trust. Suspicion is fetid and only stinks. He who trusts has never yet lost in the world.... It is true that I have often been let down. Many have deceived me and many have been found wanting. But I do not repent of my association with them.... The most practical, the most dignified way of going on in the world is to take people at their word" (as cited in Weber, 1991, p. 38).

Weber (2006), however, notes that studies show that exhibiting a trusting attitude is as likely to result in exploitation as in cooperation. Indeed, Gandhi knew that trusting others did not always yield the short-term results he hoped for. But he emphasized the larger goals and gains—the satisfaction of living with integrity and according to your own principles: "...satisfaction lies in the effort, not in the attainment. Full effort is full victory" (as cited in Weber, 1991, p. 139).

Look inside: Spirituality

Gandhi saw conflict as an opportunity to practice spiritual virtues. Practitioners of satyagraha should not hate their opponents, but love them, even while they refuse to cooperate with the unjust system they are a part of (Kumarappa, 1951). As mentioned previously, Galtung upholds Gandhi's definition of violence as "anything which would impede the individual from self-realization" (as cited in Weber, 2006, p. 38). While this definition includes the violence — both daily and incremental — of unjust systems, for Gandhi it also involves the selfish actions we make almost reflexively when we regard ourselves as more important than others. Have I harbored hatred in my heart today? Did I speak harshly today? Did I save the best for myself? Did I shirk work? "All of these are forms of violence," Gandhi claims (Iyer, 1986). From this perspective, we are all perpetrators of violence, trying to wean ourselves as well as others from these continual habits stemming from our baser selves. Gandhi confessed that he often felt anger at the injustices suffered by the poor, and in this he fell short of the ideal of *ahimsa*, as the goal was to oppose injustice without any anger (Kumarappa, 1951). But he would implore today's conflict resolvers as they enter a conflict situation to do so with the humility that we are all constantly prone to violence, and that we should strive as much to help others find alternatives to violence as to reject violence in ourselves.

We could be wrong, and the charitable interpretation of the opponent's motives

Gandhi explained his method in 1921, "Satyagraha is literally holding on to Truth and it means, therefore, Truth-force.... It excludes the use of violence because man is not capable of knowing the absolute truth and, therefore, not competent to punish" (Gandhi, 1921). Likewise, "What may appear as truth to one person will often appear as untruth to another person. But that need not worry the seeker. Where there is honest effort, it will be realized that what appear to be different truths are like the countless and apparently different leaves of the same tree. Does not God Himself appear to different individuals in different aspects? Yet we know that He is one.... Hence there is nothing wrong in every man following Truth according to his lights" (Gandhi, 1930, p. 39). Meeting the opponent with humility will shape the encounter. The goal is not to convince others of the rightness of our views through argumentation. It is better to approach the other with affinity. Chakravarti Ram-Prasad (2003) explains the Jain insights upon which Gandhi drew:

> Now, in the contested encounter with the Other, disputation as well as narration of one's position is epistemic violence, since both strategies seek to conquer the Other. Non-violence does not require the final repudiation of dialogue and discussion, as already noted; but it seeks to re-interpret discussion as the exchanging of views in a climate of "goodwill." Affinity includes the exchange of views, and discussion, even debate for clarification, because, as it is directed to this end and not to triumph, it can proceed free of violence [p. 7].

Gandhi received insights on the importance of open-mindedness not only from religions like Jainism and Hinduism, the religions of his birthplace, but also from the West. In his negotiations for justice in the British colonies of South Africa and India, he encountered Lord John Morley, Secretary of State of India from 1905 to 1910. Morley had published his book, *On Compromise,* in 1886, the same year he became Secretary for Ireland and advocated Irish Home Rule. When he became Secretary of State for India in 1905, he supported increased self-government for Indians while still punishing what he considered acts of sedition. Gandhi looked for friends and allies of his movement everywhere, including among those potentially considered opponents, like Morley.

In his work, Morley (1908) notes that while a free-thinker should find satisfaction in beliefs that meet the test of truthfulness according to his or her own criteria, regardless of what others think,

> when he proceeds to apply his beliefs in the practical conduct of life, the position is different. There are now good reasons why his attitude should be in some ways less inflexible. The society in which he is placed is a very ancient and composite growth. The people from whom he dissents have not come by their opinions, customs, and institutions by a process of mere haphazard. These opinions and customs all had their origin in a certain real or supposed fitness. They have a certain depth of root in the lives of a proportion of the existing generation [p. 114].

Morley (1908) goes on to explain that each person should realize his or her own fallibility, which will increase tolerance: "Earnestness of conviction is perfectly compatible with a sense of liability to error" (p. 137). Gandhi saw a direct connection between this humility and dedication to nonviolent means in conflict, and adds the stipulation that action as an expression of our commitment to truth must be such that if we are wrong, the ill effects of our error will fall on ourselves rather than others.

What does this nonviolent exchange of views in a climate of goodwill, seeking affinity, look like in concrete terms? First, it is time-consuming and requires patience. In the Ahmedabad Labor dispute of 1918, Gandhi met with striking workers every day. As Erik Erikson (1969) explained, "Rarely, if ever, had any man reached out to them more directly and without any trace of talking down to them" (p. 331). Gandhi also met daily with the opposition — the mill owner, Ambalal. The mill owner's sister, Anasuya, who served them tea every day, was on the side of the workers. At tea, Ambalal reported on what the mill owners' committee had discussed, and the men briefed each other on current developments. Erikson (1969) adds, "Gandhi, not without a chuckle, would insist that Anasuya serve her brother" (p. 333). Here the emphasis is on reinforcing friendship and amiability among all the parties despite their differences on workers' wages. Relationship building was one element that eventually led to a compromise that ended the strike and raised wages.

Gandhi's emphasis on respectful regard for opponents and a charitable interpretation of their motivations helped to de-escalate conflict. As V.K. Kool (2008) explains in his work on the psychology of nonviolence, we generally have a self-serving bias — a theory known as attribution. We interpret others' negative actions as part of their personal traits (and failings), while attributing our own negative actions to circumstances beyond our control. Likewise, we think our own good actions are due to our positive personal traits. Furthermore, some individuals caught in conflict have "hostile attribution bias"— they assume the actions of others are intentionally meant to thwart them. Such attitudes can lead to the entrenchment of conflict. A productive approach to resolving conflict therefore involves, like Gandhi's teachings and experiments, the appreciation of multiple motivations for people's actions, the acknowledgment of a partial overlap in the goals of all parties to a conflict, and the understanding that neither side has a monopoly on the "rightness" of an action (Kool, 2008).

An example of Gandhi's openness and charitable interpretation of an opponent was the 1924–1925 Vykom Temple Road satyagraha and his controversial dealings with the Brahmins of Vykom Temple, who would not allow untouchables to use the road that passed by the temple. The local satyagraha community had begun a vigil along the road in September 1924, and the police in turn put up barricades. Gandhi first arrived in Vykom in the spring of 1925 and negotiated with the state authorities, convincing them to remove the barricade. But the satyagrahis announced they would not take advantage of the removal of the barricade; they would not proceed down the road until the Brahmins were fully persuaded that the untouchables had a right to use the road despite their caste (Bondurant, 1971).

But the Brahmins had their own truth, which Gandhi respected, noting, "They believe their religion is in danger" (p. 51). Gandhi repeatedly met with them to discuss theological issues and interpretations of Hindu scripture, which they differed greatly on. When Gandhi, out of frustration, offered the Brahmins several compromises regarding the road controversy, they rejected them (Parekh, 1999). Gandhi then made a public speech, expressing his gratitude for their discussions, saying, "I appealed to their reason. I appealed to their humanity.... I was not able to produce the impression that I had expected that I would be able to. But despair is a term which does not occur in my dictionary" (as cited in Parekh, 1999, p. 246). Gandhi and his followers continued to apply "persistent reasoning supported by prayer" (Bondurant, 1971, p. 49). In autumn of 1925, the Brahmins declared, "We cannot any longer resist the prayers that have been made to us, and we are ready to receive the untouchables" (p. 50). The conversion of this group led to a larger reform movement that spread to many Hindu temples in India. It was another example of Gandhi's insistence on respecting others' truths while encouraging and patiently anticipating transformation in his opponents.

Evaluation

Gandhi's critics

Gandhi has been criticized for not living up to his own prescriptions for handling conflict, including not being able to see the other's point of view (Jurgensmeyer, 1989). Also, a reader suggested to Gandhi that his decision to support the British against the Zulu in South Africa showed that he neglected to hear both sides of the issue (Gandhi, 1948). It is important to note that Gandhi often reflected on his life and admitted mistakes, and sometimes changed his views to rectify situations.

Some of Gandhi's contemporaries did not believe that his "soft" approach of respecting the opponent and seeing others' point of view could end up with sure and favorable results. Acharya Kripalani argued that "Gandhi could not turn the heart of even one capitalist" (as cited in Bourai, 2004, p. 118). Participants in satyagrahas interviewed by Nakhre (1982) also registered skepticism that Gandhi ever succeeded in converting the enemy. Jetha Lal Joshi from Rajkot said, "I believe conversion in a satyagraha is more an exception rather than a rule" (p. 102).

Gandhi noted in 1947 that in the eyes of his critics, 30 years was wasted — that Gandhi's nonviolent experiment delayed independence from the British, which could have been won more swiftly if the movement embraced violence against the British. One outspoken critic of Gandhi argued even more forcefully that his policy of compromise and redress made him a "half-way" leader. Himansu Roy (2001) argued that Gandhi was used as a buffer between the government and terrorists, the latter whom Roy thought could win Indian independence more quickly. But Gandhi argued that even without foreign domination, there would be no self-rule in India unless Indians stopped their mutual hatreds and learned to live with each other in harmony (Krishnadas, 1951). His way was a calculated attempt to change social structures — not just British imperialism, but Indian society as well.

Evaluation in light of contemporary conflict resolution

Certainly Gandhi is not irrelevant to the field of conflict resolution. He was a major influence on Galtung, one of the founders of the field. He popularized approaches to conflict that were instrumental in subsequent movements in the United States, South Africa and elsewhere. But more specifically, what are we to make of the aspects of his approach that do not fit comfortably into secular, more practical-oriented forms of conflict resolution?

Adherents of Gandhian nonviolence typically justify it either because it is morally coherent and spiritually based or because of its proven efficacy. At times, the approach in the conflict resolution field is so dominated by game theory which emphasizes strategic rationality, Gandhi's insights seem irrelevant or naïve. While some studies have shown that cooperative bargainers can be exploited by others, Braver and Rohrer (1975) have challenged this in their own studies, noting that while exploiters will take advantage of "martyrs," it can "evoke a high degree of cooperation from a later opponent who observes the martyrdom" (as cited in Weber, 2006, p. 163). Other studies confirm Gandhi's emphasis on trusting opponents, noting that it can become a self-fulfilling prophecy (Weber, 2006).

Michael Sonnleitner (1985) argues that there are three levels to Gandhi's idea of nonviolence: secular, religious, and mystical. On the latter, Gandhi claimed soul force is endless. This led to his great confidence: "Given a just cause, capacity for endless suffering and avoidance of violence, victory is a certainty" (as cited in Kumarappa, 1951, p. 56). He had "an implicit belief in the absolute efficacy of innocent suffering" (as cited in Kumarappa, 1951, p. 172). While Gandhi referenced the *Bhagavad-Gita* as the source of his insight, he also referred to Christian metaphors, saying to seek first the Kingdom of God, then everything will be added (as cited in Kumarappa, 1951). It is this lack of attachment to the results of actions, paired with vigorous commitment to eradicate injustice and love one's neighbor, that is one of his enduring contributions — one often overlooked by contemporary conflict resolution literature, which is largely concerned with results.

Note

1. The author acknowledges the support of the J. William Fulbright Foundation and USEFI in India for making possible the research for this essay, carried out in 2005, and the host institution, World Peace Center, Maharashtra Institute of Technology, in Pune, India.

References

Bercovitch, J., V. Kremenyuk, and W. Zartman (Eds.) (2009). *The Sage handbook of conflict resolution*. London: Sage.
Bondurant, J. (1971). *Conquest of violence: The Gandhian philosophy of conflict*. (Rev. Ed.). Berkeley: University of California Press.
Bourai, H. (2004). *Gandhi and modern Indian liberals*. Delhi: Abhijeet Publications.
Braver, S.L., and V. Rohrer (1975). When martyrdom pays: The effects of information

concerning the opponent's past game behavior. *Journal of Conflict Resolution, 19*:4, 652–62.
Curle, A. (1971). *Making peace.* London: Tavistock.
Erikson, E.H. (1969). *Gandhi's truth: On the origins of militant nonviolence.* New York: W.W. Norto.
Fisher, R., and W. Ury (1981). *Getting to yes: Negotiating agreement without giving in.* Boston: Houghton Mifflin.
Galtung, J. (1969). Violence, peace, and peace research. *Journal of Peace Research, 6*(3), 167–191.
_____. (1992). *The way is the goal: Gandhi today.* Ahmedabad: Gujurat Vidyapeeth.
_____. (1996). *Peace by peaceful means: Peace and conflict, development and civilization.* London: Sage.
Gandhi, M.K. (1921). 240. Notes. *Young India,* 23-1-1921, included in Gandhi, *Collected Works* Vol. 22, p. 451.
_____. (1930). Satyagraha Ashram Vows. In *Yeravda Mandir: Ashram observances.* Ahmedabad: Navajivan.
_____. (1948). *Nonviolence in peace and war.* Ahmedabad: Navajivan.
_____. (1988). *Collected works.* New Delhi: Government of India Ministry of Information and Broadcasting.
Iyer, R. (Ed.). (1986). *The moral and political writings of Mahatma Gandhi, truth and nonviolence.* Vol. II. Oxford: Clarendon.
Jurgensmeyer, M. (1989). Shoring up the saint: Some suggestions for improving satyagraha. In J. Hick and L. Hempel (Eds.), *Gandhi's significance for today* (pp. 36–50). London: Macmillan.
Kool, V.K. (2008). *The psychology of nonviolence and aggression.* New York: Palgrave Macmillan.
Kriesberg, L. (2009). The evolution of conflict resolution. In J. Bercovitch, V. Kremenyuk and I. Williams (Eds.), *The Sage handbook of conflict resolution* (pp. 15–32). London: Sage.
Krishnadas. (1951). *Seven months with Gandhi.* Abr. and ed. Richard B. Gregg. Ahmedabad: Navajivan.
Kumarappa, B. (Ed.). (1951). *Gandhi: Nonviolent resistance (Satyagraha).* New York: Schocken.
Levy, J.S. (2009). Case studies and conflict resolution. In J. Bercovitch, V. Kremenyuk and I. Williams (Eds.), *The Sage handbook of conflict resolution* (pp. 72–85). London: Sage.
Miall, H., O. Ramsbotham and T. Woodhouse (1999). *Contemporary conflict resolution.* Cambridge: Polity.
Morley, J. (1908). *On compromise.* 2d ed. London: Macmillan.
Naess, A. (1974). *Gandhi and group conflict: An exploration of satyagraha, theoretical background.* Oslo: Universitetsforlaget.
Nakhre, A. (1982). *Social psychology of nonviolent action: A study of three satyagrahas.* Delhi: Chankya.
Parekh, B. (1999). *Colonialism, tradition and reform: An analysis of Gandhi's political discourse.* New Delhi: Sage.
Ram-Prasad, C. (2003). Nonviolence and the other: A composite theory of multiplism, heterology and heteronomy drawn from Jainism and Gandhi. *Journal of the Theoretical Humanities 8*(3).
Roy, H. (2001). *Poverty of Gandhian philosophy.* New Delhi: Concept.
Sonnleitner, M.W. (1985). *Gandhian nonviolence: Levels of satyagraha.* New Delhi: Shakti Malik Abhinav.

Weber, T. (1991). *Conflict resolution and Gandhian ethics.* New Delhi: Gandhi Peace Foundation.
_____. (2004). The impact of Gandhi on the development of Johan Galtung's peace research. *Global Change, Peace and Security, 16*(1), 31–43.
_____. (2006). *Gandhi, Gandhism, and the Gandhians.* New Delhi: Roli.

About the Contributors

Marie **Abijuru** is a case manager for the Refugee and Immigrant Family Strengthening Program of the Immigrant and Refugee Community Organization. She was one of the first participants in the African Diaspora Dialogue Project and served as a facilitator for the second group from the Great Lakes. In 1999, she was named Person of the Year by the Pacific Northwest Rwandan Association.

Paloma **Ayala Vela** has an M.A. in conflict analysis and resolution from Nova Southeastern University. She has been an active member of Colectivo Gandhiano Pensar en Voz Alt and SERPAJ-Mexico and is involved with peace work and education in indigenous communities in Mexico. She works for PeaceVoice, a program of the Oregon Peace Institute.

Shaazka **Beyerle** is a writer and educator on people power, a senior advisor for the International Center on Nonviolent Conflict, and a visiting scholar at the Center for Transatlantic Relations, School of Advanced International Studies, Johns Hopkins University. She co-authored two essays in *Civilian Jihad: Nonviolent Struggle, Democratization and Governance in the Middle East* and has been published in several academic journals and news outlets.

Vincent **Chirimwami** has an M.A. in conflict resolution and an M.S. in special education, both from Portland State University. He is a native of the Democratic Republic of the Congo.

Rachel H. **Cunliffe** is an assistant professor in the Conflict Resolution Graduate Program at Portland State University. Her research interests are in restorative and nonviolent responses to extreme violence. She has a Ph.D. in special education and rehabilitation/language, reading and culture from the University of Arizona, and master's degrees from Cambridge University in England and the University of Minnesota.

Djimet **Dogo** is the manager of the Africa House of the Immigrant and Refugee Community Organization, a one-stop service center for African immigrants and refugees in Portland, Oregon. Before coming to the United States, Dogo was a human rights activist with Tchad-Nonviolence, in Chad, which helped to bring warring groups together in dialogue. He holds a master's degree in public administration and a bachelor's degree in communication from Portland State University.

Véronique **Dudouet** is a senior researcher and program director at the Berghof Foundation in Berlin. She has been coordinating participatory action research and training activities on resistance and liberation movements in transition since 2005. She holds an M.A. and a Ph.D. in conflict resolution from Bradford University, and an M.Phil. in international relations and security from the Institute d'Etudes Politiques in Toulouse, France.

Rhea A. **DuMont** has an M.A. in conflict resolution from Portland State University and, since 2010, has been working as a group facilitator and board member with the Insight Development Group to facilitate restorative justice in prisons. She is a board member of the Oregon Peace Institute and has worked on the African Diaspora Dialogue Project. She is also a professional coach in higher education with students working to get out of generational poverty.

Robert J. **Gould** co-founded Portland State University's Conflict Resolution Graduate Program in 1993 and is its director. In 1984, he co-founded the Oregon Peace Institute with congresswoman Elizabeth Furse, and continues to serve on the board of directors. More recently, he co-founded the Northwest Institute for Conflict Resolution, the Peace and Conflict Studies Consortium, and the Newhall Nonviolence Institute.

Tom H. **Hastings,** Ed.D., teaches in the Conflict Resolution Graduate Program at Portland State University. He is a nonviolent activist, a veteran of many peace arrests, and has spent time in many jails and three prisons. He has written a number of books and serves on several academic boards and councils, including the International Peace Research Association Governing Council, the Peace and Justice Studies Association Board of Directors, the Oregon Peace Institute, and the Academic Advisory Council of the International Center on Nonviolent Conflict.

Patrick T. **Hiller** holds a Ph.D. in conflict analysis and resolution from Nova Southeastern University and an M.A. in human geography from Ludwig-Maximilians-University in Munich. He is an adjunct professor at Portland State University and the director of the War Prevention Initiative of the Jubitz Family Foundation.

Mindy **Johnston** is the program coordinator for a victim advocacy program at Lutheran Community Services Northwest and has an M.S. in conflict resolution from Portland State University. She volunteers as a mediator in small claims court in Multnomah County and as a facilitator for the Oregon Department of Corrections Serious and Violent Crime Facilitated Dialogue Program. From 2008 to 2011, she worked with the African Diaspora Dialogue Project.

Julie **Koehler** is education officer at the Mercy Corps Action Center and is a core member of Mercy Corps' Gender Working Group, providing technical support for gender issues within the agency. She has a master's degree in conflict resolution from Portland State University and a bachelor's degree in international gender issues from the University of Oregon, and teaches a course on gender and international development through the Women's Studies Department at PSU.

Carmina Rinker **Lass** has an M.A. in conflict resolution from Portland State University and worked on the African Diaspora Dialogue Project. She helped to found Innovative Changes, a non-profit community development financial institution in Portland. She provides consulting services and curricula development for several organizations across the United States.

About the Contributors

Meredith **Michaud** has taught in Italy and Benin, where she was a Peace Corps volunteer from 2005 to 2007. She leads licensed friendship-building trips to Cuba and has an M.A. in conflict resolution from Portland State University.

Sa'eed **Mohamed Haji** is originally from Somalia. From 1996 to 1998 he lived as a refugee in Kenya, and then came to the United States without knowing English. He attended Portland Community College and then Portland State University, where he earned an undergraduate degree in political science and later a graduate degree in conflict resolution. He worked on the African Diaspora Dialogue Project and plays an integral role at Portland State's Multicultural Center.

LisaLinda **Natividad** is a native CHamoru from the island of Guahan (Guam). She is an assistant professor and chair of the Division of Social Work at the University of Guam, and president of the Guahan Coalition for Peace and Justice. She serves on the Guam Decolonization Commission and is a host on the local NPR radio show *Beyond the Fence,* which examines the impact of militarism on communities.

Emiko **Noma** is editor at the Joan B. Kroc Institute for Peace & Justice (IPJ) at the University of San Diego. She has written or edited two dozen narratives of women from conflict-affected areas who are building peace in their communities, through the IPJ's Women PeaceMakers Program. She received her master's degree in conflict resolution, with emphases in international conflict resolution and nonviolent social change, from Portland State University.

Julie M. **Norman** is an assistant professor of political science at Concordia University in Montreal. She has published two books on unarmed resistance in Israel-Palestine, and is active with Concordia's Centre for Oral History and Digital Storytelling. She has held fellowships at Dartmouth College, MIT, and the Palestinian American Research Center, and has a Ph.D. in international relations from American University in Washington, DC.

Gail M. **Presbey** is a professor of philosophy at University of Detroit Mercy. She has received Fulbright grants for research in Kenya and India. Formerly the executive director and president of Concerned Philosophers for Peace, she is the author of *Philosophical Perspectives on the "War on Terrorism"* and the co-editor of *The Philosophical Quest: A Cross-Cultural Reader.*

Terri L. **Shofner** has a master's degree in library and information science, with emphases in human-computer interaction and the use of technology to facilitate distance learning and working groups, from the University of Washington. She is on the board of the Oregon Peace Institute and the coordinating and communications committees of the U.S. Nonviolent Peaceforce Chapters Association.

Janjira **Sombatpoonsiri** received her Ph.D. from La Trobe University in Australia on the nexus of nonviolent resistance and humor in protests in Serbia in the 1990s. She previously served as a researcher at the Nonviolence International Southeast Asia and the Peace Information Centre, in Bangkok, Thailand, and lectures in international relations in the Political Science Faculty at Thammasat University in Bangkok.

Laura K. **Taylor** is a dual Ph.D. candidate in psychology and peace studies at the University of Notre Dame's Kroc Institute for International Peace Studies. Her research examines the impact of political violence on children, families, and communities in Colombia, Croatia, and Northern Ireland. She has field experience in rights-based empowerment in the Caribbean, Latin America, and Nepal.

Barbara **Tint** is an associate professor of conflict resolution at Portland State University and served as director of the African Diaspora Dialogue Project. She has a background in the psychological dynamics involved in the causes of, intervention in, and prevention of international conflict. She has worked as a dialogue facilitator and trainer in Australia, Costa Rica, East Africa, India, Israel-Palestine, and Sri Lanka, and with multicultural groups in the United States.

Stephanie Nicole **Van Hook** is executive director of the Metta Center for Nonviolence Education. She has an M.A. in conflict resolution from Portland State University and was a Peace Corps volunteer in Benin. She is on the board of the Peace and Justice Studies Association and has contributed essays to *Beyond Forgiveness: Reflections on Atonement* and *The Encyclopedia of Domestic Violence*, and *Nonkilling Korea: A Six Culture Exploration* (forthcoming in 2013).

Index

Abdulkader, Hayi Solung 53
Adams, David 183
Afghanistan 8, 71, 77–79
African National Congress 214
Aga Khan Foundation 78
Ainsworth, Mary 170, 201
Al-Hariri, Rafiq 68
Al-Qaeda 70
Alternative Information Center (AIC) 44
Anarchists Against the Wall 38, 41
Anselm of Canterbury 147
Arab Spring 7
Arafat, Yasser 42
Armenia 86
Arusha peace process 94

Bahrain Youth Society for Human Rights 68
Baldwin, J.M. 144
Barghouti, Mustafa 43
Belgium 94, 113
Berg, E. 131
Bergen, Doris 92
Berghof Foundation 7
Bhagavad-Gita 222
Bonhoeffer, Deitrich 211
Bonta, Bruce 183–84, 195
Boonratklin, Sonthi 62
Bornstein 157
Bosnia 94
Boulding, Elise 126
Boulding, Kenneth 156, 208, 210, 212–13
Bowlby, John 170, 200–1, 204
Boycott, divestment, and sanctions (BDS) 26, 39, 49
Boyer, M.A. 131
Brand-Jacobsen, Kai 153–55

Braver, S.L. 222
Buddhism 141, 145, 147, 149
Burma 1, 19, 83n3
Burrowes, R. 30n8
Burundi 109–10, 113, 114, 115

Calderon, Felipe 71
Cambodia 8, 90, 91, 92, 93, 94, 98–101, 104–6
Cameroon 70
Caprioli, M. 131, 132n3
Carter, B.F. 182
Chad 114, 116
CHamorus 134–39
Chandler, D. 93
Chenoweth, Erica 69
Child-rearing *see* Parenting
Chile 25
China 19, 23, 92
Christian Peacemaker Teams 41
Christianity, the Church 25, 147, 222
Christie, Daniel 162
Chulanon, Surayut 61, 63n10
Clark, Howard 73
Cold War 10, 214
Colombia 23, 80
Commission on Decolonization (Guam) 138
Commission on Self-Determination (Guam) 138
Commission to Investigate Cases of Injustice (Thailand) 55, 58, 60
Confortini, Catia 130
Connell, R.W. 130
Connolly, W. 146
Corrie, Rachel 30n10, 30n13
Cuba 23
Curle, Adam 214

Dalai Lama 160
Delesgues, Lorenzo 77–79
Democratic Republic of the Congo 70, 109–10, 113, 114, 115, 116, 117, 119, 123
Des Pres, Terrence 95, 103
Deutsch, Morton 156
Dudouet, Véronique 7, 8, 73
Durkheim, Emile 164n4

Egypt 1, 27, 68, 211
Egyptians Against Corruption 68
Einstein, Albert 181
Eisler, Riane 128
Ellinor, L. 115
Erickson, Erik 219
Ethiopia 110
Europe 15, 23, 30n13, 92
European Commission 69

Fateh 37, 42, 69
Fateh Youth 42
Feminism 8
Finnegan, Amy 72
First intifada 13, 16, 17, 20, 25, 29
Fisher, Roger 214
Foucault, Michel 156, 157, 163
France 93, 118
Francis, Diana 127
Free Gaza movement 27
Freire, Paulo 155
Freud, Sigmund 181
Friedrich-Ebert Stiftung 80
Fry, Douglas 182–84, 195

Galtung, Johan 24, 29n2, 129, 132, 155, 157–58, 162, 213–15, 217, 221
Gambia 70
Gandhi, Mohandas 2, 8, 14, 17–18, 21, 23, 27, 67, 69, 74, 81, 160, 208, 210–11, 213–22
Genocide 8, 86–106, 113–14
George, C. 202
Gerard, G. 115
Germany 25, 92, 211
Ghoori, Pajhwok 77
Ginsburg, B.E. 182
Glyn, T. (facilitators) 116
Goldstein, Jeffrey H. 182–83
Gourevitch, Philip 99
Grossman, Lt. Col. Dave 203
Guam (Guahan) 134–39
Guatemala 8, 71, 79–81
Guinea-Bissau 70

Gulf War 30n7
Gush Shalom 38, 41

Habyarimana, 94, 113
Hackley, Susan 72
Hamas 27, 37, 42, 69
Harlow, Harry 200
Hastings, Tom H. 163
Hatzfeld, Jean 99
Hinduism 219–21
Hitler, Adolf 92, 93
HIV/AIDS 158
Hoffman, Gene Knudsen 168, 175
Holocaust 8, 90, 91, 92, 93, 95–97, 100–1, 103–6, 204
Holy Land Trust (HTL) 40, 41, 43
hooks, bell 129
Hume, David 143
Hurndall, Tom 30n10
Hussein, Saddam 30n7

Immigrant and Refugee Community Organization 109
India 23, 219, 221
Indigenous peoples 5, 8, 134–39, 153
Integrity Watch Afghanistan 77–79
Inter-American Commission on Human Rights 80
International Center on Nonviolent Conflict 3, 8
International Commission against Impunity in Guatemala 80
International Court of Justice (ICJ) 39, 50n2
International Middle East Media Center (IMEMC) 43, 44, 50n5
International Solidarity Movement (ISM) 26–27, 38, 41, 44, 50n5
Intifada *see* First intifada; Second intifada
Intifada for Independence 68
Iran 1, 23, 74
Islam, Muslims 8, 52–63, 76, 147
Islamic Jihad (political party) 37, 42
Israel 10–11, 13–14, 16, 20, 22–27, 29, 34, 36, 38, 39, 44, 47, 49, 50n2, 68–69, 169
Israeli Committee Against Home Demolitions 41
Israeli Defense Forces 37

Jacobsen, C.G. 153–55
Jainism 218
Japan 93, 134–35, 214
Jihad 16
Judaism, Jews 92

Kelman 169
Keo, Darith 98
Khmer Rouge 90, 92, 93, 98, 104
Kiernan, Ben 98
King, Martin Luther, Jr. 9, 21, 73–74, 79, 160, 210
King, Mary 68
Konner, Melvin 181–82
Kool, V.K. 220
Kosovo 19, 24
Kremenyuk 154
Kriesberg, Louis 128, 153, 214
Kriesi, H. 43
Kripalani, Acharya 221
Kuwait 68

La Boetie, Etienne 15
Lafayette, Bernard 72
Lajee Center 45
Laue, J. 10
Lazar, Michael 129
Lebanon 68
Lederach, John Paul 128, 153–55, 163, 169
Levi, Primo 102, 104
Levy, Jack S. 213
LGBT community 158
Liberia 110
Libya 211
Linstroth, J.P. 161
Logan, R. 150
Lorenz, Konrad 181–82

Ma'an News Agency 44
Macy, Joanna 212
Magellan, Ferdinand 134
Main, Mary 170, 201–2
Malcolm X 5
Maldives 1, 2
Mandela, Nelson 160
Manousos 168
Mavi Marmara 27
Mazdoor Kisan Shakti Sangathan (Right to Information) 78
McCarthy, R.M. 15
McCormick, G. 11
Metta Center 209
Mexico 71, 80, 156, 157, 164*n*2
Miall, Hugh 153, 162, 214
Middle East 13, 66, 68
Milgram, Stanley 87
Milosevic, Slobodan 211
Morley, Lord John 219
Mouth, Sophea 98, 104
Mubadara (political party) 37, 43

Mubarak, Hosni 2, 211
Muthien, Bernedette 131

Naess, Arne 216
National Reconciliation Commission (Thailand) 53
NATO 77
Nazism 25, 91, 92, 211
Ndadaye, Melchior 113
Neve Shalom 13; *see also* Wahat el Salam
Niger Delta 70
Nigeria 70
Nol, Lon 98
Nonviolent Peaceforce 26
Norman, Julie 68
Norway 141
Ntayamira, Cyprian 113

Occupy movement 7
Ogilvy, J. 144
Okinawa 135
One Year of Peace and Resistance 45
Orange Movement 68
Oslo agreement 13, 20, 23
Ouspensky, P.D. 144

Pakistan 70
Palestine 1, 8, 10–11, 13–14, 16–18, 20, 22–29, 34–50, 68, 83*n*3, 169; East Jerusalem 42; Gaza Strip 11, 20, 22, 27, 30*n*10, 42, 44; West Bank 11, 20, 22, 29*n*1, 30*n*6 30*n*14, 34, 36, 39, 40, 41, 42, 44, 47, 48, 50*n*2, 68
Palestine News Network (PNN) 40, 43, 44; Palestinian Authority 13, 23, 43, 49
Palestinian Centre for Rapprochement between Peoples (PCR) 43, 50*n*5
Palestinian Environmental NGOs Network 40
Palestinian Liberation Organization (PLO) 13, 23, 30*n*7
Palestinian People's Party 43
Palestinian Popular Struggle Front 43
Palestinian Solidarity Project 41
Parenting 5, 8, 199–206
Pat-Borja, Melvin Won 136
Peace Brigades International 26
Peace Now 41
Philippines 23, 25
Piaget, J. 199
Pinochet, Augusto 25
Plato 142–43
Pol Pot 90, 92, 93, 98

Polman, Linda 158
Porges, Stephen 173
Portland State University 109, 119, 124, 184, 195–96

Quakers 15

Rabin, Yitzhak 13
Ram-Prasad, Chakravarti 218
Ramsbotham, O. 153, 162, 214
Rapaport, Anatol 217
Rasmussen, Anders Fogh 77
Reiling, Kirby 75
Republic of Congo 110, 114
Rigby, A. 22, 30n8
Rizzolatti, Giacomo 202–3
Rohrer, V. 222
Romanyshyn, R. 150
Roy, Himansu 221
Rusesabagina, Paul 103
Russia 23
Rwanda 8, 90, 91, 93, 99–101, 103, 109, 113–17, 119, 122–23
Rwandan Patriotic Front (RPF) 94, 103

Salem, Paul 11, 153
Samayoa, Claudia 83n7
Satha-Anand, Chaiwat 56
Satyagraha 2, 27, 215, 217–18, 220–21
Saunders, H. 115
Scharbatke-Church, Cheyanne 75
School for Peace 13
Scott, J. 89
Scott, J.C. 46
Second intifada 13, 25, 29, 34–50
Senegal 70
Serbia 1, 2, 211
Seville Statement on Violence 183
Sfard, Michael 38
Sharp, Gene 1, 7, 16, 23, 25, 52, 67, 74
Shinnawatra, Thaksin 53, 61
Siegel, D.J. 203
Social justice 9, 10, 11
Somali Youth Coalition of Oregon 119
Somalia 94, 110, 112, 119
Sonnleitner, Michael 222
Sorenson, E. Richard 183–84
South Africa 25–26, 214, 219, 221–22
Southern Border Provinces Administration Centre (SBPAC) 53, 63n9
Spanish-American War 134
Spitz, René 200
Sroufe, Alan 202

Stephan, Maria 69
Stop the Wall (Anti-Apartheid Wall Campaign) 39, 40, 50n4
Student Network to Protect the People 54
Sumoud (steadfastness) 46
Syria 68, 82

Ta'ayush 38, 41
Taliban 71
Tanzania 113, 114
Thailand 8, 52–63
Thoreau, Henry David 15
Tibet 2
Tolstoy, Leo 15
Treaty of Paris 134
Tunisia 1, 2, 68

Uganda 94, 113, 114
Ukraine 2, 23
Unified National Leadership of the Uprising 17, 22
Unit of Protection of Human Rights Defenders (UDEFEGUA) 83n7
United Kingdom 25, 204, 210, 219, 221
United Nations 135, 138–39
United Nations Development Programme 80
United Nations Office on Drugs and Crime 71
United States 8, 9, 13, 15, 20, 25, 30n13, 88, 93–94, 110, 114, 118, 120, 134–36, 138–39, 152, 158–59, 168–69, 191, 205–6, 210–11, 213; civil rights movement 25, 73, 79, 214, 222
Ury, William 74, 214

Vietnam 92, 93

Wahat el Salam 13; *see also* Neve Shalom
Weber, Max 156
Weber, Thomas 213–17
West Papua 2
Whitehead, Stephen 129–30
Wong-Araya, Aree 62
Woodhouse, T. 153, 162, 214
World War I 92

Yesh Din 38
Yugoslavia 24

Zambia 114
Zapatista movement 156, 157, 164n2
"Zones of peace" 23

www.ingramcontent.com/pod-product-compliance
Ingram Content Group UK Ltd.
Pitfield, Milton Keynes, MK11 3LW, UK
UKHW021845140426
5217IPUK00022B/1589